Date Due

MY 6 '03			
JA 03 '04			
JA 15 '04			
FE 1 '05			
FE 16 '10			
OCT 15 2012			
SEP 0 3 2013			

BRODART, CO.   Cat. No. 23-233-003   Printed in U.S.A.

Other Books of Related Interest:

Opposing Viewpoints Series

American Values
America's Children
America's Cities
America's Prisons
Chemical Dependency
Child Abuse
Crime and Criminals
Criminal Justice
The Death Penalty
Drug Abuse

Education in America
The Family in America
Gangs
The Homeless
Mental Illness
Poverty
Race Relations
Social Justice
Suicide
Work

Current Controversies Series

Alcoholism
Drug Trafficking
Ethics
Family Violence
Gun Control
Hate Crimes
Illegal Immigration
Police Brutality
Violence Against Women
Violence in the Media
Youth Violence

At Issue Series

Domestic Violence
Ethnic Conflict
Immigration Policy
Legalizing Drugs
Policing the Police
Rape on Campus

violence

OPPOSING VIEWPOINTS®

David Bender & Bruno Leone, *Series Editors*

Scott Barbour, *Book Editor*
Karin L. Swisher, *Book Editor*

OPPOSING
VIEWPOINTS®
SERIES

Greenhaven Press, Inc., San Diego, CA

Cover photo: Clement Mok Design

Greenhaven Press, Inc.
PO Box 289009
San Diego, CA 92198-9009

Library of Congress Cataloging-in-Publication Data

Violence : opposing viewpoints / Scott Barbour, book editor,
   Karin L. Swisher, book editor.
      p.   cm. — (Opposing viewpoints series)
   Includes bibliographical references (p.   ) and index.
   ISBN 1-56510-355-6 (lib. bdg. : alk. paper). —
ISBN 1-56510-354-8 (pbk. : alk. paper)
   1. Violence—United States. 2. Family violence—United
States. 3. Violence—United States—Prevention. I. Barbour,
Scott, 1963–   . II. Swisher, Karin, 1966–   . III. Series:
Opposing viewpoints series (Unnumbered)
HN90.V5V52   1996
303.6—dc20   95-35628
                                                          CIP

"Congress shall make no law . . . abridging the freedom of speech, or of the press."

First Amendment to the U.S. Constitution

The basic foundation of our democracy is the First Amendment guarantee of freedom of expression. The Opposing Viewpoints Series is dedicated to the concept of this basic freedom and the idea that it is more important to practice it than to enshrine it.

Contents

Why Consider Opposing Viewpoints?

"The only way in which a human being can make some approach to knowing the whole of a subject is by hearing what can be said about it by persons of every variety of opinion and studying all modes in which it can be looked at by every character of mind. No wise man ever acquired his wisdom in any mode but this."

John Stuart Mill

In our media-intensive culture it is not difficult to find differing opinions. Thousands of newspapers and magazines and dozens of radio and television talk shows resound with differing points of view. The difficulty lies in deciding which opinion to agree with and which "experts" seem the most credible. The more inundated we become with differing opinions and claims, the more essential it is to hone critical reading and thinking skills to evaluate these ideas. Opposing Viewpoints books address this problem directly by presenting stimulating debates that can be used to enhance and teach these skills. The varied opinions contained in each book examine many different aspects of a single issue. While examining these conveniently edited opposing views, readers can develop critical thinking skills such as the ability to compare and contrast authors' credibility, facts, argumentation styles, use of persuasive techniques, and other stylistic tools. In short, the Opposing Viewpoints Series is an ideal way to attain the higher-level thinking and reading skills so essential in a culture of diverse and contradictory opinions.

In addition to providing a tool for critical thinking, Opposing Viewpoints books challenge readers to question their own strongly held opinions and assumptions. Most people form their opinions on the basis of upbringing, peer pressure, and personal, cultural, or professional bias. By reading carefully balanced opposing views, readers must directly confront new ideas as well as the opinions of those with whom they disagree. This is not to simplistically argue that everyone who reads opposing views will—or should—change his or her opinion. Instead, the series enhances readers' depth of understanding of their own views by encouraging confrontation with opposing ideas. Careful examination of others' views can lead to the readers' understanding of the logical inconsistencies in their own opinions, perspective on why they hold an opinion, and the consideration of the possibility that their opinion requires further evaluation.

Evaluating Other Opinions

To ensure that this type of examination occurs, Opposing Viewpoints books present all types of opinions. Prominent spokespeople on different sides of each issue as well as well-known professionals from many disciplines challenge the reader. An additional goal of the series is to provide a forum for other, less known, or even unpopular viewpoints. The opinion of an ordinary person who has had to make the decision to cut off life support from a terminally ill relative, for example, may be just as valuable and provide just as much insight as a medical ethicist's professional opinion. The editors have two additional purposes in including these less known views. One, the editors encourage readers to respect others' opinions—even when not enhanced by professional credibility. It is only by reading or listening to and objectively evaluating others' ideas that one can determine whether they are worthy of consideration. Two, the inclusion of such viewpoints encourages the important critical thinking skill of objectively evaluating an author's credentials and bias. This evaluation will illuminate an author's reasons for taking a particular stance on an issue and will aid in readers' evaluation of the author's ideas.

As series editors of the Opposing Viewpoints Series, it is our hope that these books will give readers a deeper understanding of the issues debated and an appreciation of the complexity of even seemingly simple issues when good and honest people disagree. This awareness is particularly important in a democratic society such as ours in which people enter into public debate to determine the common good. Those with whom one disagrees should not be regarded as enemies but rather as people whose views deserve careful examination and may shed light on one's own.

Thomas Jefferson once said that "difference of opinion leads to inquiry, and inquiry to truth." Jefferson, a broadly educated man, argued that "if a nation expects to be ignorant and free . . . it expects what never was and never will be." As individuals and as a nation, it is imperative that we consider the opinions of others and examine them with skill and discernment. The Opposing Viewpoints Series is intended to help readers achieve this goal.

David L. Bender & Bruno Leone,
Series Editors

Introduction

"We have to start thinking about violence as a public health crisis that requires public health solutions."

Donna E. Shalala

"The very notion of violence as a public-health problem undercuts the true causes of violence in the inner city."

Peter Breggin

Statistics on the rate of violent crime in America vary, but most sources agree that levels are high and that they have been increasing or have remained consistently high for the past three decades. According to the FBI's Uniform Crime Reports (UCR), the rate of violent crime rose over 370 percent between 1960 and 1991. And while in recent years overall levels of violence appear to have stayed stable (and actually may have fallen slightly), they remain high enough that many Americans would agree with Delaware senator Joseph R. Biden's 1993 declaration that America is "the most dangerous country in the world."

Officials are particularly alarmed by reports of skyrocketing rates of violent crime among juveniles. The U.S. Department of Justice states that the number of juveniles arrested for homicide increased by 85 percent between 1987 and 1991. Along with the reported upswing in number of violent juvenile crimes, commentators also are concerned by changes in the characteristics of those perpetrating the violence. Younger and younger children—even preteens—are committing crimes such as sexual assault and murder. Moreover, Northeastern University's James Alan Fox and Glenn Pierce write that "this new generation of youngsters is more inclined to resort to violence over trivial issues—a pair of Nikes, a leather jacket, or even a challenging glance—or for no apparent reason." Indeed, some commentators argue that this generation's teens are increasingly more callous than those of prior generations. For example, in July 1993 *Newsweek* magazine reported the rape and murder of two young girls in Houston, Texas. The viciousness of the crime, according to *Newsweek*, was surpassed only by the "cavalier attitude" of the six teenage boys arrested in the case. After hearing they might be tried for murder, one of them boasted, "Hey, great! We've hit the big time."

While youth violence occurs among all segments of society, recently many commentators have focused their attention on the violence among young minority males (especially blacks) in the inner cities. John J. DiIulio Jr., a professor at Princeton University, writes that "never before has violent crime been so concentrated among teenage and young adult male inner-city blacks." DiIulio cites FBI statistics indicating that in 1991 the violent crime arrest rate for black youths was five times higher than for white youths. However, DiIulio and others point out that while arrest rates are disproportionately high for African-American youths, black youths are also more likely than white youths to be victims of violent crime. In fact, homicide is the leading cause of death for young black men.

No consensus exists on the reasons for these reported changes in the extent and nature of youth violence. Many explanations are offered, all of which are the subject of much debate. Focusing on the inner cities, some commentators maintain that the recent increase in youth violence began with the arrival of crack cocaine in the mid-1980s, which resulted in fierce competition for drug turf among rival gangs. Some people blame youth violence on a rise in single-parent, female-headed families, which these critics believe produce children who are more prone to emotional problems and violent behavior than the children of two-parent families. Others argue that the violence that pervades American popular culture—especially the mass media—contributes to youth violence in two ways: It reinforces the notion that violence is an acceptable means of resolving conflicts and it desensitizes young people to the harmful consequences of violent acts. Still others contend that the widespread presence of guns in American society and the ease with which such weapons can be obtained by young people are important factors in the rising rates of youth violence.

Responding largely to the increase in youth violence, in recent years health officials and members of the medical profession have advocated a public health approach to violence in American society. This approach is based on the idea that rather than reacting to incidents of violence after they occur, the medical community should attempt to keep violence from happening. In order to achieve this goal, they advocate treating violence as a social disease. This involves identifying where violence is most prevalent and how it occurs, then devising and implementing interventions to prevent its occurrence. Most interventions involve education designed to alter attitudes and behaviors that researchers believe contribute to violence and to encourage people—especially teenagers—to settle their conflicts without resorting to violence. Such efforts include public education campaigns, conflict resolution programs in the schools, and various programs intended to teach parenting and social skills in neighborhoods with high rates of violence.

Some commentators, however, are critical of the public health approach to youth violence. Most opposition comes from those who believe that the underlying causes of violence—especially in the inner cities—are social and economic problems such as poverty, racial discrimination, a lack of employment opportunities, and decaying social institutions. Rather than attempting to change the attitudes and behaviors of inner-city teens, these critics argue, the nation's leaders should address these structural causes of violence. To illustrate his reservations about the public health approach to violence, Nathaniel Hupert, writing in the *Pharos* magazine, examines one violence-prevention program conducted by the Centers for Disease Control (CDC). Following the Los Angeles riot of 1992, CDC doctors visited emergency rooms in L.A.'s inner-city neighborhoods and counseled individuals whom they considered to be at risk for engaging in violent activity. Hupert reports that local medical and community leaders objected to the CDC's efforts, arguing that they were "palliative remedies that avoided the type of socio-economic intervention that would begin to address issues like unemployment and economic racism," which the leaders believed were responsible for youth violence in the inner city.

The public health approach to youth violence is one of the issues addressed in *Violence: Opposing Viewpoints*, which contains the following chapters: Is Violence a Serious Problem in America? What Causes Violence? How Serious a Problem Is Domestic Violence? How Should Youth Violence Be Addressed? What Policies Would Reduce Violence? Authors in these chapters discuss violence in the American home, workplace, and society at large, and they offer their suggestions for creating a more peaceful nation.

Is Violence a Serious Problem in America?

violence

Chapter Preface

On July 19, 1995, Los Angeles city employee Willie Woods reportedly shot and killed four of his supervisors at the technical center where he worked. A number of similar incidents have occurred across the country in recent years, leading some commentators to speak of an "epidemic" of violence in the workplace. "The violence in the streets of America has opened the door and walked into the workplace," states Chris Hatcher, a clinical professor of psychology at the University of California, San Francisco.

Many analysts cite statistics to support the view that violence has invaded the American workplace. In a 1993 study, the Northwestern National Life Insurance Company estimated that 2.2 million workers had been assaulted, threatened with violence, or harassed during the previous year. According to the U.S. Bureau of Labor Statistics, 1,004 Americans were murdered on the job in 1992 (an increase of 32 percent from the annual average in the 1980s) and 1,063 were murdered at work in 1993. The bureau also reported that in both 1992 and 1993 homicide was the number two cause of death in the workplace, second only to transportation accidents.

Some critics believe that these statistics—along with dramatic media reports of rampages by disgruntled employees—exaggerate the danger of workplace violence. For example, Erik Larson, a staff reporter for the *Wall Street Journal*, argues that the risk of being murdered by a disgruntled coworker has been overstated. He notes that of 120.8 million people in the workforce in 1993, only 59 were killed by coworkers or former coworkers. "That is one in 2.1 million," he writes, adding that "the National Weather Service puts the odds of getting struck by lightning at one in 600,000."

Anxiety over violence in the workplace—and in society as a whole—is mounting. The authors of the following viewpoints debate whether such concern is justified.

=====

"Big crime stories have invaded virtually every sanctuary where Americans thought they were safe."

=====

Violent Crime Is a Serious Problem

Ted Gest

In the following viewpoint, Ted Gest reports that several instances of violent crime have raised public alarm over the severity of violence in American society. He contends that while the level of crime has not increased (it has been high for years), the nature of violent crime has changed: It is spreading to small and middle-sized towns, and more stranger-on-stranger violence is occurring. Gest is a senior editor with *U.S. News & World Report* magazine.

As you read, consider the following questions:

1. What three reasons does Gest give for the rise in anti-crime sentiment among the public?
2. According to the author, why did violent crime increase in the late 1980s?
3. What is the proportion of murders committed by strangers, according to Gest?

Excerpted from "Violence in America" by Ted Gest, *U.S. News & World Report*, January 17, 1994; ©1994 by U.S. News & World Report. Reprinted by permission.

It hardly made a ripple in the deluge of violence news gripping the nation, but it was enough to frighten relatively placid Indianapolis. Members of a drug-trafficking gang called the Getto Boys opened fire with a rifle and 9-mm handguns one evening in the fall of 1993 outside the Blackburn Terrace housing project. More than 60 shots failed to hit their intended target, a figure in a narcotics-sales dispute. Instead, they killed a 16-year-old girl visiting friends at the project and critically wounded a 7-year-old boy lying in bed watching "Monday Night Football." All Mayor Stephen Goldsmith can hope is that the shoot-'em-up in an area not usually known for blood and gore will help galvanize public opinion to expand his programs to combat gangs.

That scenario of violence against innocent bystanders has been repeated across the nation. The drumbeat of news coverage has made it seem that America is in the midst of its worst epidemic of violence ever. That sense is not supported by the numbers. The latest evidence is that crime levels actually fell [in 1993]. But that does not mean that [1993] wasn't the scariest [year] in American history. Overriding the statistics is the chilling realization that the big crime stories of recent months have invaded virtually every sanctuary where Americans thought they were safe: their cars (James Jordan's murder); their public transit (the December Long Island Rail Road murders); even their bedrooms (the December kidnap and murder of young Polly Klaas in Petaluma, California). Gangs have taken root in small towns and suburbs. In addition, a holiday-season burst of multiple killings showed how potent modern weapons are and how random the slaughter can be.

The nation has been through any number of anticrime seasons in the past generation. In many of them, the public's preoccupation with crime rose as citizens' concerns about the economy subsided—and then waned as economic issues regained center stage. Public attitudes also are driven by periodic media orgies of crime coverage. Yet, there are some who believe that the forces gathering behind this season's efforts are different because the threat seems so much graver. There is some hope, too, that a much more serious and comprehensive national attack on violence will emerge—and maybe even show real results. "This is not just a blip on the chart," says Barry Krisberg of the National Council on Crime and Delinquency, who has not seen such sustained public interest in violence since Lyndon Johnson created a crime commission in 1965. Krisberg predicts a new "barrage of punitive, get-tough measures."

New Forces

A prime element of the new anticrime upswelling is the degree to which the public is furious at the failure of previous efforts to solve the problem. Nothing has stemmed the upward

spiral of reported violent incidents: not massive spending on social programs for the poor; not a massive buildup of prison cells;
not sweeping changes to impose mandatory minimum sentences; not innovative new policing techniques. . . .

Two other new forces are at play that give the current interest
a different shape. One is the rising anger of African-American
leaders like Jesse Jackson about black-on-black crime; Jackson
complained in January 1994 that more American blacks are
killed by each other each year than died during the entire history of lynching. Then there's the heightened anticrime fervor of
many officials in middle-sized and small towns, which now are
experiencing some of the same trends in the violence contagion
that cities have faced for a generation. Typical is the view of
Claire McCaskill, chief state prosecutor in the Kansas City area,
on violent juvenile repeat offenders who have terrorized her
community: "We've got to lock them up for as long as we can."

As the debate shapes up, several points help put it in perspective:

• The startling string of heinous killings does not represent a
sudden new wave of crime. Violent crime levels have been ex-
traordinarily high for many years. The nature of some of the
crime is changing, though, making some people more vulnerable and bringing the worst kinds of problems into communities
that many thought were safe.

• Some of the most frightening trends in crime—like the increasing prevalence of stranger-on-stranger robberies and drive-
by shootings—might be susceptible to new crime-prevention
techniques, but only in the long term. "We are not going to
come up with the magic solution to a genuine national crisis,"
admits Peter Edelman, a senior official of the Department of
Health and Human Services who cochairs a Clinton antiviolence team. The group is examining nine basic elements of the
problem, including family strife, hate crimes and the role of the
media. It could lead to the creation of an unofficial "Department
of Violence" to coordinate disjointed federal aid programs.

• The most likely governmental actions against crime in the
short term—expanding police forces and prisons—tend to be
costly and yet might only reduce crime marginally. For instance,
the prison-building boom of the 1980s had little effect on violent-
crime rates.

• The most promising lines of attack start at the local level,
where authorities and residents are mounting block-by-block
campaigns to reclaim cities.

The Biggest Mystery

The true level of violence in America is a mystery. Reports to
police compiled by the Federal Bureau of Investigation steadily

increased for years after 1960 but leveled off in 1992 and actually declined in the first six months of 1993. 1993's total probably exceeded 1.9 million incidents. Yet a Justice Department survey that asks Americans if they have been victimized, thus including crimes not reported to authorities, estimates the figure at closer to 6.6 million. Even that understates the total, because some victims refuse to disclose even anonymously what happened to them. . . .

IT KEEPS GOING AND GOING AND GOING....

Engelhart/*Hartford Courant*. Used by permission.

Whatever the bottom line, the violence now is just the latest of the historic peaks the nation has experienced. America has been hit with surges of violence that begin roughly 50 years apart, in 1850, 1900 and 1960, says Ted Robert Gurr, a political scientist at the University of Maryland. Ethnic strife played a large part in all three periods, and crime totals within each era have fluctuated. After murder, robbery and assault reached record levels in 1980, for instance, rates in almost every major category dropped for half a decade. Then, fueled by the crack cocaine epidemic, violent crime climbed back up: A new murder record was set in 1992, even though the total number of youths—the cohort most associated with crime—was dropping. (The shrinking of the teen population did seem, however, to help reduce the number of property crimes.)

Among the basic crime patterns policy makers must confront:

- *Murder.* While the absolute numbers fluctuated [between 1984 and 1994], an increase in random murder was especially ominous. Decades ago, most murders were committed by relatives or acquaintances of the victim. Now, the proportion committed by strangers may have risen to one third, fueling the growing fear that there's no place where anyone is really safe. Criminologist Alfred Blumstein of Carnegie Mellon University blames a "large growth in crimes committed by young people who appear not to have absorbed much concern about the value of human life." A new book by Marc Riedel of Southern Illinois University, *Stranger Violence*, concludes that such cases are "pervasively underreported."

- *Robbery.* Stickups, from simple street muggings to heists at automated teller machines, remain the most prevalent crime that Americans should fear from strangers. The latest victimization survey estimates that robbers strike 1.2 million times each year, injuring their prey a third of the time. Unlike most other violent crimes like murder, rape and assault, in which the assailant more often than not knows the victim, an estimated 84 percent of robberies are committed by strangers. Still, the national robbery rate has declined since a peak in 1981, and most encounters do not end in violence: One in 20 cases results in both serious injury and lost property.

Shooting Sprees

- *Random crimes.* A common error of citizens and policy makers is to mistake big news stories for big trends and to demand action on a new "crime wave" that really isn't that big. For instance, contrary to conventional wisdom, random slaughters like [December 1993's] Long Island Rail Road massacre and recent shooting sprees at postal facilities are not increasing sharply. The annual count of cases in which more than four persons were killed in a single incident varied from 10 to 30 each year between 1976 and 1991, reports criminologist James Alan Fox of Northeastern University. . . . "Most mass murderers do not kill at random in public places," Fox concludes.

- *Workplace killings.* Murderous episodes at job sites are growing, and a cottage industry of high-priced consultants is arising to exploit it. But like mass killings, they are relatively rare. A Labor Department count for 1992 found 45 revenge-type murders by workers or former employees. A preliminary compilation for 1993 by the Chicago-based National Safe Workplace Institute that included killings in personal or family feuds tallied 70 cases. Although that toll is up from fewer than 20 per year during the 1980s, institute Director Joseph Kinney says it "is hardly at epidemic proportions."

- *Child snatchings.* Though the nation was sickened by the abduction and murder of 12-year-old Polly Klaas in California and the killing of two elementary school students in St. Louis, the best evidence is that between 50 and 150 such episodes have occurred each year since the late 1970s. . . . Parents need not be so frightened that they keep children indoors excessively, says Ernest Allen of the National Center for Missing and Exploited Children, but they "need to recognize that teenagers are the single most victimized segment of society."

• *Carjackings and drive-bys.* These are clearly on the rise. Each year, criminals attack nearly 30,000 drivers to rob or rape them or steal their vehicles. While the figure is alarming, it pales when compared with the 1.6 million auto thefts. As for bystander shootings, a survey of news reports by Maryland criminologist Lawrence Sherman found a fourfold increase of such cases in New York City in the late 1980s compared with a decade earlier.

• *Family strife.* This is one problem that doesn't get the attention it deserves. There are 800,000 or more violent incidents within families each year, but the terror of living in many homes is largely overlooked with the exception of sensational cases like Lorena Bobbitt's slashing of her husband John's penis.

• *Justice system.* The escalating crime numbers also have an impact on the beleaguered criminal justice system, which gets much of the blame for not controlling violence. So many violent criminals are repeat offenders—estimates range from 50 percent up—it is inevitable that many former prisoners as well as defendants awaiting trial and convicts on probation will be arrested for new crimes. Critics charge that the system remains unaccountably lax; justice professionals respond that their record of singling out career criminals for longer incarceration has improved. . . .

Grass-Roots Efforts

With resources scarce at all levels of government, the best hope for progress against violence is at the local level, where grass-roots organizations from San Antonio to Boston are rising up to mount more sophisticated campaigns against street crime. Such drives are hardly new, but anticrime activists report a new, aggressive spirit. Instead of merely reporting crimes to police, some groups, like Washington's Metro Orange Hat Coalition, videotape streetcorner drug transactions. Members of the Ivar Hawks Neighborhood Watch in Los Angeles make citizens' arrests of dealers who offer to sell them drugs.

"There is no magic trick or secret formula," says Alvin Wright of the Houston Police Department. "Crime went down here when the citizens of our town decided they were not going to just sit back and watch things." That's just the attitude that seems to be catching on elsewhere.

"Despite the impression one would get from news coverage, the incidence of crime has not risen dramatically."

The Threat of Violent Crime Is Exaggerated by the Media

Janine Jackson and Jim Naureckas

Polls indicate that Americans are concerned about violent crime. In the following viewpoint, Janine Jackson and Jim Naureckas argue that this public preoccupation with violent crime has been generated by inaccurate and sensationalistic media coverage. Focusing on a *U.S. News & World Report* article, they contend that the media have created the impression that levels of violent crime have escalated dramatically when in fact they have remained stable. Jackson is the research director and Naureckas is the editor of *EXTRA!*, a bimonthly publication of the liberal media watchdog organization Fairness and Accuracy in Reporting (FAIR).

As you read, consider the following questions:

1. According to the National Crime Victimization Survey, cited by the authors, how many violent crimes were there in 1973 as opposed to 1992?
2. According to Jackson and Naureckas, how does *U.S. News & World Report* avoid appearing overtly racist?
3. How is the text of the *U.S. News & World Report* article contradicted by the accompanying pictures and captions, according to the authors?

Janine Jackson and Jim Naureckas, "Crime Contradictions," *EXTRA!*, May/June 1994. Reprinted by permission of Fairness & Accuracy in Reporting (FAIR), New York, N.Y.

That's how *U.S. News & World Report* opened its Jan. 17, 1994 cover story on "Violence in America." It encapsulates the tone of much of the overheated and overhyped reporting on crime in 1993. Despite the impression one would get from news coverage, the incidence of crime has not risen dramatically since 1992. The most reliable research suggests, in fact, that there is no more violent crime today than there was 20 years ago.

What there is more of—much more—is crime coverage. According to *The Tyndall Report*, crime took up more than two and a half hours (157 minutes) a month on the three nightly network news shows from October 1993 until January 1994. In the three years ending with January 1992, by contrast, these network shows spent 67 minutes a month on crime stories. And the coverage has taken on a shrill tabloid tone, designed to evoke fear, as with *NBC Nightly News'* regular feature "Society Under Siege."

The coverage seems to have had an effect. In June 1993, 5 percent of those polled by a national *Washington Post*/ABC poll named crime as the most important issue facing the country. By February 1994, after months of saturation media coverage of crime, 31 percent said it was the most important problem—far outstripping any other issue. When asked in an *L.A. Times* survey where they got their information about crime, 65 percent said they learned about it from the media.

How did mass media give people the false impression that crime was climbing dramatically? How did they justify portraying steady crime rates as a "scary orgy" that demands drastic, immediate action? An examination of *U.S. News'* special report on crime is revealing, illustrating the major themes, distortions and self-contradictions of much of mainstream crime coverage in 1993 and 1994.

"Rough, Flawed Estimates"

A recurring theme in *U.S. News'* crime report, headlined "The Truth About Violent Crime" on the cover, is that crime is up. "Violence in modern America began its upward climb in 1960," we are told. "Nothing has stemmed the upward spiral of reported violent incidents." The coverage—which consists of a main article, four companion pieces and several sidebars—is sprinkled with casual references to the ongoing "wave of violence" and the "escalating crime numbers." A graph charts the crime statistics' "relentless growth."

The claim that crime in the U.S. is on the rise is based on the FBI's Uniform Crime Reports, which collect data on reported crimes from police agencies across the country. The rate of violent crime, according to FBI statistics, has risen by 81 percent since 1973 (and has more than quadrupled since 1960).

But there is another source for crime numbers, the Bureau of Justice Statistics (like the FBI, a branch of the Department of Justice). This agency conducts the annual National Crime Victimization Survey, which asks people across the country whether they or members of their household have been victims of crime in the past year—tabulating unreported as well as reported crimes. According to the NCVS, the crime rate has been basically flat since the survey began: There were 32.6 violent crimes per thousand persons (12 years old and up) in 1973, and 32.1 per thousand in 1992.

Of the two surveys, many experts consider the NCVS more reliable. The Uniform Crime Reports "are widely mistaken as indicators of the 'real' level of crime, rather than merely rough, and flawed, estimates," says Tony Pate of the Police Foundation, an independent crime research institute. There is "enormous variation in reporting procedures and policies" between the thousands of police agencies that take part in the survey, Pate says. "Not all agencies follow the reporting instructions properly."

This variation makes it extremely difficult to compare the FBI statistics from different years, since there is no way to say whether local police are classifying and reporting crimes consistently. While the NCVS is not a perfect gauge of crime rates—it is notoriously bad, for example, at counting rapes—Pate calls it the "preferable indicator," since it is "applied in a standardized fashion over time."

U.S. News reporters were well aware that an alternative measure of crime exists—they use NCVS figures more than once to show that the number of all crimes is much greater than the number of reported crimes. But the magazine never mentions that this survey contradicts its picture of "relentless growth" in crime.

"Invading Sanctuaries"

To be sure, *U.S. News* does have a disclaimer toward the front of the article, noting that "the latest evidence is that crime levels actually fell" [in 1993]—because even the FBI figures showed a drop in reported crimes. There is even an implicit criticism of "the drumbeat of news coverage [that] has made it seem that America is in the midst of its worst epidemic of violence ever. That sense is not supported by the numbers," the magazine acknowledges.

U.S. News immediately follows that, however, with an assertion that the numbers don't matter: "But that doesn't mean that [1993] wasn't the scariest [year] in American history." This appears to say that the perception of danger from crime is as important as the reality—even if the perception is in part a product of media hyperbole.

But the magazine seems to realize that media-inspired worry about crime does not justify yet another cover story on the crime threat. The article goes on to argue, "Overriding the statistics is the chilling realization that the big crime stories of recent months have invaded virtually every sanctuary where Americans thought they were safe."

Racist Notions of Crime

Who do we find portrayed as criminals in the newsweeklies [*Time*, *Newsweek*, and *U.S. News & World Report*] over the last 35 years? Well, it's changed some: first it was Negroes, then it was blacks, and now it's African-Americans. Blacks and other non-white minorities were described and pictured in the newsweeklies' crime coverage most frequently, even though these groups *do not* commit the majority of crimes (even as selectively defined). In contrast, the newsweeklies described and pictured victims mostly as white people. Consider the sensational coverage of the Carol Stuart murder case, as the media cheered on the Boston police's "search and destroy" mission to hunt down the allegedly black assailant. Never mind that she was actually murdered by her husband Charles Stuart, a far more likely suspect, who made up the story of the black assailant; never mind, too, that the real story here was yet another female victim of domestic violence.

What emerges from my study of the newsweeklies is a pattern of discrimination in which criminals are conceptualized as black people and crime as the violence they do to whites. Yet this didn't prevent *Newsweek*, for example, from running a post–L.A. riot story which claimed to discover that the public, the media, and politicians have all been engaged in a "conspiracy of silence" by *refusing* to admit they associate crime with blacks. Given the way the media have regularly contributed to and reinforced such racist notions of crime, is it any wonder there are such terrible race problems in our country?

Robert Elias, *The Humanist*, January/February 1994.

This theme of "invading sanctuaries," prominent in much current crime coverage, runs throughout *U.S. News'* report: "To many, this wave of violence is ominous because safe havens are violated," a caption declares. "The nature of some of the crime is changing," the main article states, "making some people more vulnerable and bringing the worst kinds of problems into communities that many thought were safe."

The "some people" whose communities are no longer safe are apparently supposed to be (white) suburbanites, an assertion that is usually implicit but occasionally overt: "Middle-sized and small towns . . . are now experiencing some of the same trends in the violence contagion that cities have faced for a generation," the magazine states. Writing about "coldblooded kids" from "America's mean streets," a companion piece declares that "their malign ethos has metastasized to the suburbs, where youthful murder is increasingly common."

In both these references, urban crime is compared to a disease—a "contagion" or a "metastasized" cancer—that city-dwellers carried into previously uninfected suburbia. But the reality of crime distribution is very different from this pathological imagery.

As *U.S. News* briefly notes in a sidebar, crime is not rising in suburbs, it is falling. According to the latest NCVS statistics, a suburban resident was 13 percent more likely to be a victim of violent crime in 1973. Crimes like theft and burglary have declined substantially in the suburbs, and in rural areas as well.

The magazine does note that black people are disproportionately victims of crime. But when African-Americans figure in *U.S. News'* report—as in most U.S. crime coverage—they appear as "them," not as "us."

"Random Slaughter"

U.S. News avoids appearing overtly racist by focusing not on violence against whites, but on "random" violence. The message is the same: You, our reader—whom we assume to be a white, middle-aged suburbanite—are in danger.

Thus, *U.S. News* gives us "safety tips" that begin: "No safety rules can protect the law-abiding from being hit by random fire from crazed gunmen." "Many are terrified by the random nature of current violence," a caption asserts. "A holiday-season burst of multiple killings showed . . . how random the slaughter can be," the magazine reports.

This focus on "random" violence resulted in strained logic. Under the heading of "Murder," the magazine notes, "While the absolute numbers fluctuated [between 1984 and 1994], an increase in random murder was especially ominous. Decades ago, most murders were committed by relatives or acquaintances of the victim. Now, the proportion committed by strangers may have risen to one third, fueling the growing fear that there's no place where anyone is really safe."

In other words, since the murder rate isn't really changing much—it's fluctuated between 8.3 per 100,000 people and 10.2 per 100,000 for the past 20 years—*U.S. News* is searching for another way to make the numbers seem scary. Actually, the FBI classifies 13.5 percent, not one-third, of murderers as strangers to their victims—so "most" murders are still committed by relatives and acquaintances, just as was the case "decades ago." At any rate, it's unclear how a drop in the proportion of murders committed by family and acquaintances would make people feel *less* safe in everyday places.

If that wasn't confusing enough, two paragraphs later, *U.S. News* is telling us that "contrary to conventional wisdom, random slaughters like [December 1993's] Long Island Railroad massacre and recent shooting sprees at postal facilities are not increasing sharply." The writers seem not to notice that they had been reporting on the "increase in random murder" just moments earlier.

U.S. News' report, like crime coverage in general, is filled with such contradictions. The magazine seems to be torn between the impulses to alarm and to reassure. Usually, it's the boldface assertions—particularly in captions—that end up being contradicted in the text.

Thus, the pictures that accompany the main article of *U.S. News'* report feature the December 1993 Long Island Railroad slaughter, two examples of revenge killings at workplaces, the suspect [Richard Allen Davis] in the December 1993 Polly Klaas murder, and the site of a random killing at a Dallas mall—all of which are presented as evidence of disturbing new trends ("Angry disputes often end in gunfire," "Impulsive violence is also on the rise," etc.).

In the text, however, we are told that mass murders in public places are not becoming more common, that child snatchings likewise continue to be very rare, and that workplace killings are "hardly at epidemic proportions." Although *U.S. News* says it is "a common error of citizens and policy makers . . . to mistake big news stories for big trends," the magazine's own report makes that mistake over and over again.

"Sanctioning Criminals"

Although the central article of *U.S. News'* report has little to say about the causes of crime, a companion piece on youth violence deals with the question with more seriousness than most mainstream accounts. Writer Scott Minerbrook stresses the fact that violent offenders are often victims of severe child abuse, a connection well-documented by social scientists but little noted in the media.

The attempt to find explanations for violence has its blind spots: Is it a "tragic trend," for instance, that the number of single-parent families is growing, or is it tragic that single mothers are given only the barest level of support in this country? Scandinavian countries, noted for progressive welfare systems, have high rates of out-of-wedlock births along with very low murder rates.

Listing contributing factors to crime, Minerbrook mentions

that "not least, there's the loss of millions of urban manufacturing jobs that are no longer available to kids willing to work to avoid lives of crime." If that's not the least important factor, isn't it worth more than one sentence?

While underlying issues of poverty and job loss don't figure much in *U.S. News'* explanation of the causes of crime, economic issues are entirely left out of their discussion of solutions. According to the main article, "massive spending on social programs for the poor" is just an example of a failed, outdated attempt to stem crime.

But *U.S. News'* descriptions of crime remedies are as convoluted as their discussion of the problem. For example, money for more police officers is cited as "the most important item" in new crime legislation. But in the next paragraph, *U.S. News* cites its own survey that "found that more police does not necessarily mean lower crime rates."

Similarly, the "massive buildup of prison cells" and the imposition of mandatory minimum sentences are cited as anti-crime strategies that have been tried and failed. Yet the article praises the "heightened anti-crime fervor" of local officials, as represented by one Kansas City state prosecutor, who is quoted as saying, "We've got to lock them up for as long as we can."

Ultimately, what come across as the preferred solutions to crime are not programs that would require government investment, but those of "grassroots organizations"; ie, those that residents of the poorest and most crime-ridden areas carry out themselves.

Political solutions may help in the "larger community," as Michael Barone argues in an accompanying column, but "something more is required to reduce the sickening violence in poor communities where violence and sexual predation can be overwhelming."

Barone contends that those who are most frequently the *victims* of crime are the ones ultimately responsible for it, because by allowing it to happen to them, they "sanction" it. Because they "take pains to avoid and never anger" the suspected criminals among them, Barone states, residents of poor neighborhoods tell "the criminal that his misdeeds are expected, assumed, in some sense understood and approved."

Having told readers who ought to fear crime—white suburbanites, or "us"—*U.S. News* here reminds readers who's really to blame for crime—black city dwellers, or "them." Having argued that now "crime can strike anywhere," the magazine—like much of U.S. crime coverage—still traces the roots of crime back to the same old place: poor urban neighborhoods whose residents need not more jobs, but more morals.

"Murder in the workplace is definitely on the rise."

Violence in the Workplace Is a Serious Problem

Brigitte Maxey

Reports of shooting sprees in places of employment—especially at post offices—have received much attention since the late 1980s. In the following viewpoint, Brigitte Maxey, a freelance writer who specializes in business, argues that such incidents reveal a growing problem of violence in the workplace. According to Maxey, there are two types of workplace violence: internal (in which the perpetrator is familiar with the company and workers) and external (in which the perpetrator is unfamiliar with the employer and employees). She presents a profile of a workplace killer, which includes such characteristics as paranoia, aggressiveness, and a fascination with weapons.

As you read, consider the following questions:

1. According to Joycelyn Elders, quoted by the author, why should workplace violence be approached as a public health problem?
2. What are some of the root causes of workplace violence, according to Maxey?
3. According to Daniel Hardy, quoted by the author, what should employers do to prevent workplace violence?

Brigitte Maxey, "Workplace Killers." This article appeared in the August 1994 issue and is reprinted with permission from *The World & I*, a publication of The Washington Times Corporation, ©1994.

The blur of swirling lights and the squeal of a siren signal yet another pickup of a dead body. But the sight and sound of death zoom past stereotypical locales like public housing projects and alleyways, ending up in front of a pristine glass high rise.

Murder and violence have come to a place where Americans spend the majority of their waking hours. Between 15 and 20 Americans are murdered on the job each week, triple the workplace homicides committed in the mid-1980s. Guns are the weapon of choice, accounting for about 71 percent—or 822 of the 1,034 homicides committed at the workplace in 1992.

Victims of workplace violence are overwhelmingly white, male, and between the ages of 25 and 54, according to the Bureau of Labor Statistics (BLS). However, blacks, Asians, Pacific Islanders, and Hispanics incurred a disproportionate share of workplace homicides compared with total workplace fatalities.

Workplace homicide is the leading cause of death for women who work and the third main killer of men who work, according to the BLS. In a February 1994 report, the bureau showed that while total workplace fatalities decreased over the previous decade, intentional killings increased. Homicide accounted for 1,034, or 17 percent, of the 6,083 work fatalities in 1992.

Workplace violence is mostly an urban problem. Four-fifths of workplace homicides are committed in metropolitan areas. New York City leads the nation in workplace homicides. Los Angeles, the second largest city based on population, comes in second.

The Centers for Disease Control in Atlanta has declared workplace violence an epidemic. Piggybacking on the CDC's proclamation, U.S. Surgeon General Joycelyn Elders vowed to approach workplace violence as a public health problem. Her reasoning was that "public health focuses on prevention, and violence is a problem much more easily prevented than stopped," according to an address for a U.S. Post Office symposium on workplace violence held in December 1993.

Two Kinds of Violence

Workplace violence is perpetrated on two fronts: internal and external. Internal violence comes at the hands of individuals who are familiar with supervisors and coworkers. External violence is carried out by third parties unfamiliar with the employer or the employees. The best example of external violence is random killings at fast-food restaurants. Robbery is the motive for most external acts of violence at the workplace.

Nearly half of the homicides occurring at work are in food stores, according to the BLS. Robberies frequently occur while workers lock up at night or make money drops or pickups. Attacks at fast-food establishments have increased so much that many chains have stepped up security and have ceased opening stores in areas identified as dangerous.

Internal workplace homicides most likely end in suicide—nearly one-quarter of employees who kill at the workplace take their own lives. Suicide usually results in cases where the perpetrator is either married to or is acquainted with the victim.

Confrontations with personal acquaintances resulted in at least 39 workplace homicides in 1992. Twenty-four workers were killed by relatives, 19 of them husbands or ex-husbands. Random violence, such as being caught in crossfire or being struck by a stray bullet, took the lives of at least nine workers during 1992.

An example of a workplace homicide ending in suicide is Carl Baird, a former Walpole, New Hampshire, police chief. He shot to death a local government worker who he thought orchestrated his forced resignation following allegations of misappropriations. After killing the worker, Roger Santaw, Baird turned the gun on himself. He had no history of violence and just seemed to have snapped.

Costs

The sheer fear of falling victim to violence hampers the performance of workers whose colleagues have been killed or injured. Northwestern National Life Insurance Company in Minneapolis surveyed 600 such workers and found that 126 of them, or 21 percent, suffered from mental distress, reduced productivity on the job, and missed days on the job, among other things. The respondents wanted to change jobs and the number of hours of the day they worked.

"Workplace violence and fear can translate into costs to the employer in the form of increased medical and stress-related disability claims, lower productivity, higher turnover and possibly greater legal liability," the BLS survey concluded. Employers paid $4.2 billion in medical, legal, and psychological treatment fees in 1992, and corporations paid an estimated $22 billion a year for corporate security. . . .

Increasingly, America's workers are faced with multiple life-threatening problems for which there are no easy answers. They have to consider getting killed at work by a stranger or coworker, injury (both intentional and unintentional), and someone's suicide. Many experts say that until creative approaches to the problem are found, American workers' morale and productivity will continue to decline.

Acts of Revenge

Violence against employers has increased so much that "you can't fire anyone anymore," says Rosemary Erickson, who heads Athena Research Corporation, a Seattle group that researches violence in business. This type of violence is becoming more prevalent, as evidenced by numerous news reports of disgruntled workers killing or wounding their supervisors. The most widely recognized examples of workplace violence occur at the U.S. Post Office, which has become notorious for having distraught and overworked employees killing their administrators.

A Technician Named Larry

Say the words "workplace violence," and what comes to mind first is something like what happened at a 300-employee San Diego electronics manufacturer in 1991.

In March of that year, as the recession hit, the company laid off several employees, including a technician named Larry. He visited the plant off and on over the next three months, seeking help in finding another job, and he never seemed to have less than a cordial relationship with his former employer.

But then, one morning in June, Larry came to the plant and confirmed that three of its executives—two vice presidents and his former supervisor—were on the premises. Later that day, Larry returned to the plant, this time wearing a bandolier across his chest and carrying a shotgun. He set off two radio-controlled pipe bombs, starting small fires, and shot out the receptionist's switchboard before she could call the police.

Then Larry ran upstairs to the executive offices. He killed one of the vice presidents, as well as a regional sales manager who tried to help his colleague. Another executive escaped death only by hiding under a desk. As Larry exited the building, he walked calmly past a crowd of terrified employees and then rode away on a bicycle.

Michael Barrier, *Nation's Business*, February 1995.

Frequently, companies are laying off tens of thousands of workers at a time and are hiring supervisors who lack employee management skills. Dennis Johnson, president of Behavior Analysts and Consultants in Stuart, Florida, told the attendees at the 1993 U.S. Post Office symposium on workplace violence that a toxic work environment contributes to workplace violence. "Authoritarian management styles that are overcontrolling, working environments that demand more and support less, and lack of value for the worth and dignity of employees produce these harmful working conditions."

A worker's instinct to strike back at an employer who lays off, demotes, or fires him is a question of survival. Work security has been the mainstay of the American family. Jobs generate the pay that allows people to survive. If bills cannot be paid and food cannot be purchased, the worker is left with a feeling of helplessness and is theoretically backed up against a wall. When they think they are boxed into a corner, humans, like animals, strike back.

Blame the Family?

Michael Mantell, who coauthored *Ticking Bombs: Diffusing Violence In the Workplace*, blames workplace violence on the breakdown of the American family.

"The problem is the failure of the American family to train children how to become productive human beings. Kids aren't able to cope with frustration and can turn into the adult who acts out at work," Mantell says. He suggests that the federal government create programs to help families train their children. "It will take two to three generations of government helping people to solve the problem."

Government intervention in child rearing is a highly debatable subject, however. Several professionals involved in workplace violence doubt that this approach would be taken seriously. Government involvement in such a delicate matter would almost resemble a police state, they say.

"Pointing the finger of responsibility at the family releases society from the role it plays," Erickson says. "Society's value system plays a greater role than the public is willing to admit." Root causes of workplace violence include poverty, lack of education, racial discrimination, underemployment, and lack of job training. Erickson adds, "Society teaches individuals that if they work hard, they'll be rewarded with job security, and that is no longer the case."

But when distraught workers murder coworkers or supervisors the criminal justice system should take over, Erickson says. In many cases, the justice system has failed to "carry out sentencing on these perpetrators. It's extremely frustrating to see shortened sentences because of prison overcrowding.". . .

A Chilling Profile

For the last decade or so, sociologists and psychologists have employed a general profile of a workplace killer. The profile is used for overall identification purposes and does not necessarily indicate that the person who fits the profile is a murderer in sheep's clothing. Moreover, the profile describes a person who directs violence toward his employer and has a known relationship with coworkers, supervisors, and customers.

The perpetrator is:
- a 35-year-old white male who perceives an injustice has

been done to him;

- a loner with a romantic interest in a coworker;
- in a state of despair over personal, financial, or job matters;
- usually paranoid;
- aggressive;
- grudgeful;
- threatening (verbally);
- fascinated with weapons;
- someone who has access to weapons.

Thomas Harpley, clinical director of National Trauma Services in San Diego, has worked extensively with verbally threatening employees. He recalls one case where an employee, infuriated by his job situation, was on his way to work with a gun laid across his car's passenger seat. Somehow, by the time he got to the end of the driveway, he realized that what he was about to do was wrong. He drove back up to his house and called his employee assistance representative, who sought help for him.

"Workplace violence perpetrators are crying out for help, and employers have to hear it," Harpley says. He further emphasizes: "Employers have to recognize that violence can happen anywhere, and they've got to look out for behavioral patterns."

One of the most important signs of a violent employee is a significant change in behavior. At-risk employees do not get along well with their coworkers and may display evidence of personal problems.

Employees who kill at the job are often transient. They are most likely to live in southern and western states, where the weather is warmer, says Mantell. "When a worker goes from job to job, he sometimes has to live in his car. It wouldn't be pleasant to sleep in your car where the weather is cold."

The Role of Employers

Employers can stem the tide of workplace violence by screening job applicants for previous work problems, unexplained gaps in employment history, and evidence of criminal activity, suggests Daniel Hardy, president and chief executive of Isaac Ray Center in Chicago. They have to be more responsible in securing a safe workplace for their employees, he says.

Harpley suggests that employers train supervisors to look for and recognize warning signs. Employers should set up a trauma response plan before an incident occurs. Part of that plan is to require troubled employees to undergo psychological fitness-for-duty exams. If the employee does not comply with testing, then he should be suspended.

"It has to be stressed to potential employees that the emotion of anger is fine, but the expression of it is dangerous. Employers have to tell employees to contact their supervisors if they feel threatened," Harpley says.

The Society for Human Resource Management in Alexandria, Virginia, conducted a survey of human resource managers across the country and found that 153 of the 479 respondents had experienced one or more acts of violence at their workplace since 1989, and more than 80 percent of those incidents had transpired since 1991. More than half of the incidents were committed by an employee toward another employee, followed by employee toward supervisor and customer toward employee.

Although 48 percent of the respondents have employee assistance programs, only 22 percent said they would consider a preventive program to deter violence in the workplace. The highest incidence of violence in the workplace has taken place in manufacturing organizations employing 100–499 employees, according to this report. Manufacturers in the Northeast report the highest rate of violence.

Employer Liability

Employers can be held liable for workplace violence under the Occupational Safety and Health Act. The federal government can fine a company if an employer fails to implement proper emergency plans or if violence erupts in the workplace.

States can take action against an employer who negligently hires an employee who commits an intentional act of violence in the workplace. To establish a case, it must be shown that the employer hired the violent worker, the worker was unfit for the position, the employer knew or should have known the worker was unfit, the unfit worker caused injuries, the employer's hiring of the violent worker caused injuries, and finally that someone was injured.

An employer can also be held responsible for hiring an individual after it is known that the person may have the tendency to act violently toward others. Criminal charges loom for an employer if an employer's negligence rises to a level equivalent to criminal intent. On yet another front, workers' compensation laws may offset losses incurred by an employee who is injured during the course of employment.

No matter who is held responsible, one fact remains: Murder in the workplace is definitely on the rise, and the highest price is paid by victims, no matter who is determined negligent.

> *"The fear that a co-worker could suddenly 'go postal'. . . is grossly exaggerated."*

Violence in the Workplace Is Not a Serious Problem

Erik Larson

In the following viewpoint, Erik Larson challenges the common perception that violence in the workplace is a growing crisis. He scrutinizes studies by the Bureau of Labor Statistics (BLS) and others and concludes that workplace murder is rare—especially for many white-collar professions. He also finds that, contrary to the popular conception, very few workplace murders are committed by disgruntled employees or ex-employees: three-fourths of them are committed during robberies. Larson is a staff reporter for the *Wall Street Journal*.

As you read, consider the following questions:

1. According to Larson, what are the odds of being murdered by a coworker or former coworker as opposed to being struck by lightning?
2. How many people were killed by coworkers or ex-employees in 1993, according to the August 1994 BLS study, as cited by Larson?
3. Why is the Northwestern National Life Insurance Company study unreliable, according to the author?

When callers to a Virginia Beach, Virginia, production company are put on hold, they hear this recorded promotion for a new video on workplace violence: "Homicide is the second leading cause of workplace death in the U.S."

Readers of the handbook *Breaking Point*, by North Carolina consultant Joseph A. Kinney, learn that violence by workers is "a new poison" that has "made all of our lives very fragile, giving us a vulnerability that was never felt before."

In a pitch soliciting attendance at a seminar in Detroit, the Midwest Coalition for a Safer Workplace asks, "Are you sitting on a powder keg?"

Stressed-Out Companies

Across America the message, at first glance, seems clear: Human time bombs are ticking throughout the Fortune 500. Driven by a fear of disgruntled workers that now verges on hysteria, companies are forming threat-assessment teams and violence hotlines. Security directors have dusted off Cold War jargon and now talk of "target hardening." After repeated queries from psychologists and corporate security officials, Hilson Research Inc., a Kew Gardens, New York, developer of preemployment tests, in 1994 introduced a test aimed at establishing a job candidate's propensity for violence. One indicator: Reckless driving.

Some companies are so skittish they won't discuss their antiviolence efforts. Motorola Corp. is said by managers of other companies to have developed a comprehensive antiviolence plan, but a spokeswoman declined to comment for fear of somehow making the company a target. "There are too many crazies out there," she said.

But just how violent is the American workplace? The answer depends in large part on how you define workplace, and what kinds of crime you include. One thing is certain, however: The fear that a co-worker could suddenly "go postal," as some now put it, is grossly exaggerated. A federal census of workplace homicides released in August 1994 found that 59 employees were killed by co-workers or former co-workers in 1993, out of a total national workforce of 120.8 million people. That is one in 2.1 million. The National Weather Service puts the odds of getting struck by lightning at one in 600,000.

Misplaced Fear

Herewith, the anatomy of a false crisis: How a series of horrendous mass murders, overblown news reports, widely misinterpreted research and an emerging army of consultants have driven companies to a fear of their own workers that is largely unjustified. "Executives are scared to death," says Jack Levin, a criminologist at Northeastern University in Boston, "but they're scared of the wrong thing."

Until lately, no one spent much time thinking about workplace violence. It became a distinct category of crime only after murders by disgruntled employees captured the nation's attention and caused reporters and researchers alike to hunt for evidence of a new crisis. Only as recently as 1992, for example, did federal researchers standardize criteria to be used by medical examiners for determining whether a murder occurred on the job.

Murder at Work

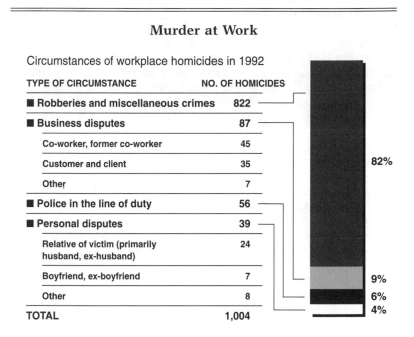

Circumstances of workplace homicides in 1992

TYPE OF CIRCUMSTANCE	NO. OF HOMICIDES	
■ Robberies and miscellaneous crimes	822	
■ Business disputes	87	82%
Co-worker, former co-worker	45	
Customer and client	35	
Other	7	
■ Police in the line of duty	56	
■ Personal disputes	39	
Relative of victim (primarily husband, ex-husband)	24	
Boyfriend, ex-boyfriend	7	9%
Other	8	6%
TOTAL	**1,004**	4%

Note: Percentages do not add to 100 due to rounding.

Source: Census of Fatal Occupational Injuries, Bureau of Labor Statistics, in cooperation with federal and state agencies.

But workplace violence is not new. By current definition, the category would include attacks on Pony Express riders, even the St. Valentine's Day Massacre of 1929, in which mobsters killed seven people at the S.M.C. Cartage Co. in Chicago. Criminologists, however, date the current preoccupation to Patrick Henry Sherrill's 1986 attack on an Edmond, Oklahoma, post office, which killed 14 people and wounded six.

Corporate fears intensified markedly in 1993, a banner year for workplace gore. In January, Paul Calden opened fire on his former colleagues at Fireman's Fund Insurance Co. in Tampa, Florida, killing three. Over the next two weeks, four more workers attacked their employers. In May, two postal workers, one in Michigan and one in California, chose the same day to launch shooting sprees. On July 1, Gian Luigi Ferri attacked a San Francisco law firm, killing eight before killing himself.

Abundance of Statistics

The year also saw the arrival of the first research on workplace violence from federal and private sources, almost all of it prone to misinterpretation.

In September, Mr. Kinney released his widely cited book, in which he presented his personal calculation that murder by employees had "doubled or tripled" since 1989. On October 1, the Bureau of Labor Statistics released its first Census of Fatal Occupational Injuries, which found that in 1992 homicide was the second leading cause of death in the workplace, after transportation-related accidents. Seventeen days later, the employee-benefits division of Northwestern National Life Insurance Co., Minneapolis, released a survey showing that 2.2 million workers had been physically attacked on the job in the 12 months ended July 1993.

In July 1994 the Justice Department published its first report devoted solely to nonfatal workplace assault, breaking out data it collected from 1987 through 1992 as part of its ongoing survey of crime victims. It reported that nearly one million workers a year fall prey to nonfatal violence on the job.

A Closer Look

The convergence of so much blood and data infused the common wisdom with the conviction not only that workplace violence was rampant, but that invariably the culprits were disgruntled workers or ex-employees. In fact, the underlying data actually *challenged* popular perceptions.

Consider, for example, the widely reported Bureau of Labor Statistics finding that homicide is the second leading cause of death in the workplace. Reporters often insert the finding when reporting the latest murder by a disgruntled worker, conveying the impression that workers are to blame for elevating homicide to the number two position. "You read the headlines," says Tom W. Smith, director of the General Social Survey at the University of Chicago's prestigious National Opinion Research Center, or NORC, "you think, 'Gee that many killed by psychos.'"

The numbers, however, depict a far more complex landscape, one most news accounts fail to describe.

In August 1994, for example, the BLS released its workplace death toll, covering deaths in 1993. Once again it ranked homicide second.

But a closer look at the study shows first of all that workplace murder is a rare event. Of 120.8 million people in the work force, 1,063—one out of 114,000—were killed while at work or on duty. However, the risk varied dramatically among occupations. Raw numbers supplied to the *Wall Street Journal* by the BLS show that the chances that an executive, manager or administrator (other than hotel or restaurant managers) would be slain on the job by anyone, disgruntled or otherwise, were one in 226,000. For secretaries, the risk fell to one in 370,000. For doctors, engineers, computer scientists and other members of the Census Bureau's "professional specialties" category, the chances were still more remote: one in 457,000.

The study, moreover, provided a resounding vindication of co-workers and ex-employees, attributing to them only 59 killings, up from 45 the year before. Says Martin Personick, a senior BLS economist, "One of the first things you see is that this co-worker stuff is not a big deal."

The study itself helped obscure this conclusion, however, by defining workplace violence so broadly as to beg the question: When is workplace violence merely ordinary violence under a new name?

The bureau, like virtually every other organization that studies workplace violence, includes violent attacks that occur on company property or while the victim was on duty, regardless of whether the killing was related to work or not. By this standard, a New York City housing inspector murdered aboard a subway while traveling between inspection sites is counted as a victim of workplace murder; if killed riding the very same subway home after work, his death is omitted. The BLS tally included the slayings of 67 police officers and 52 security guards.

The Usual Motive

The study also found that three-quarters of the year's homicides were committed during robberies where the motive was plain old greed. These 793 victims included cab drivers, convenience-store clerks, owners of inner-city bodegas and pizza delivery drivers.

"It's robberies," says Guy Toscano, program manager of the BLS survey. "That's it. But who wants to read about a robbery, when you can read all the little details of the sex between two co-workers who go and kill each other?"

The Justice Department's 1994 study, which found one million workers a year to be victims of nonfatal workplace violence, inadvertently compounded confusion about the sources of such violence. It didn't collect information specifically identifying whether the offender was a worker or an ex-worker, just whether the crime occurred at work or while on duty, and whether the victims knew their attackers. The department found no evidence that the incidence of workplace violence was on the rise, according to Ronet Bachman, the Justice statistician who commissioned the study. It did find that one-third of the crimes, which ranged from threats of assault to rape, occurred in parking lots, garages or on public property ("such as streets and parks"). Only 14% occurred in an office, factory or warehouse. Its tally also included attacks on police officers, prison guards and convenience-store clerks.

James Alan Fox, dean of Northeastern University's College of Criminal Justice, says including so wide an array of crimes confuses debate over the causes of workplace violence. "You start broadening it and talking about your run-of-the-mill thieves, you're talking about a different problem. When you have police officers getting killed, they're not getting killed over employment issues."

The Northwestern Survey

Northwestern National Life, however, wanted as broad a definition as possible for its survey in order "to capture anything that makes people begin to feel unsafe in the workplace," says Susan Braverman, executive vice president of Crisis Management Group Inc., Newton, Massachusetts, who helped design the survey.

Northwestern found that one in four workers was harassed, threatened or physically attacked in the 12 months preceding July 1993. Seeming to confirm that mayhem rules the workplace, the survey garnered immediate and widespread attention in the nation's press—but little scrutiny of its underpinnings.

The company built the survey on the replies of 600 workers, a skimpy sample by social-research standards. The survey also had a low "response rate," that portion of an initially targeted population or "sample" who actually respond to a surveyor's questions. Researchers are happiest when they get usable responses from 75% to 80% of the target sample, but the response rate for this survey was far lower. Northwestern didn't disclose its response rate in any of its public communications but, at the *Wall Street Journal*'s request, Peggy Lawless, a former Northwestern market-research manager who directed the survey effort, calculated a rate of 29%, meaning that the 600 people in the final sample represented less than a third of the initially targeted sample.

NORC's Mr. Smith, using data that Northwestern supplied to the *Journal*, calculated a more favorable 42%. The rates vary because both researchers used different assumptions in defining the initial target sample. But both rates are low, says Mr. Smith, suggesting the reported results may reflect "response bias." Such low rates, he explains, increase the chances "that the people you interviewed are not representative of all people in the group you're trying to generalize to."

Yet Northwestern used the results to estimate that 2.2 million people had been physically attacked at work in the 12 months preceding the survey. It based this finding on the replies of only 15 people.

"It's unbelievable," says Ronet Bachman, a statistician with the Bureau of Justice Statistics. "People can just say what they want." Dawn Castillo, an epidemiologist with the National Institute for Occupational Safety and Health, or NIOSH, was a tad more circumspect when she wrote in a recent paper that the results "need to be interpreted with caution."

Findings Adrift

But the findings quickly became separated from their statistical moorings. News reporters accepted the results with little qualification. Most failed to note, for example, that co-workers, ex-employees and bosses caused only a third of the attacks.

Ms. Lawless defends the survey as being accurate and representative. "It was not necessarily the answer to all the questions, but to give direction to other researchers," she says. But she adds that she too was "appalled" at how some television and print media used the results. She recalls one story that appeared in *USA Today* under the headline, "Survey: Homicides at Work on the Rise."

The survey, however, never even mentioned homicide. A spokesman for the newspaper says: "Clearly, it wasn't a good headline." He wouldn't comment further on the story.

Fanning Fears

Such statistics have armed a cadre of workplace-violence experts who in turn may also be fanning company fears. Typically they concentrate on co-worker violence to the exclusion of far more common robbery-related murders. Antiviolence seminars for corporate executives have proliferated, and can convey the impression that massacres are almost commonplace. . . .

But officials occupying positions uniquely suited to gauging the incidence of violence by workers say it doesn't happen very often. The New York State Public Employees Federation, a union representing 56,000 white-collar professionals working for state corrections and health facilities, has since 1989 provided its members with Assault, Trauma and Captivity Insurance—ATAC for short. Of the 50 to 60 claims filed each year, says Richard Doucette, administrator of the program, two-thirds stem from assaults by patients at state mental-health institutions, including three hospitals for the criminally insane. At most, he says, he sees one claim a year involving violence by a co-worker or ex-worker.

David Frances, head of EAP Systems, Woburn, Massachusetts, which provides employee counseling services to some 60 companies, says, "Offhand, I can't even think of a single case in my personal experience of an employee being violent in the workplace."

Nonetheless, the prospect of killings by workers continues to frighten companies far out of proportion to their true incidence. "If this were purely on the basis of statistics in our work force, we couldn't justify the time we're spending on it," says Ann Leibowitz, labor counsel for Polaroid Corp., Cambridge, Massachusetts, which is now drafting a violence prevention and response plan. But she likens workplace attacks to airplane crashes. "There are not many of those either, but the ones that happen scare the pants off everybody."

> "Law-enforcement and public-health officials describe a virtual 'epidemic' of youth violence spreading from the inner cities to the suburbs."

Youths Are Increasingly Violent

Barbara Kantrowitz

In the following viewpoint, Barbara Kantrowitz describes several incidents of youth violence that she says are part of a growing trend in America. According to Kantrowitz, the number of murders and other violent crimes committed by teenagers has increased dramatically in recent years. She writes that young people—especially inner-city youths—have become inured to, and traumatized by, the violence that pervades society. Kantrowitz is a former senior writer for *Newsweek*.

As you read, consider the following questions:

1. According to the author, by what percentage did the number of teenagers arrested for murder increase between 1987 and 1991?
2. In what ways has prison become the dominant institution of inner-city culture, according to Kantrowitz?
3. According to the author, how are violent teens unlike adult criminals?

Charles Conrad didn't have a chance. He was 55 years old, crippled by multiple sclerosis and needed a walker or wheelchair to get around. The boys who allegedly attacked him in July 1993 were young—17, 15 and 14—and they were ruthless. Police say that when Conrad returned to his suburban Atlanta condominium while they were burgling it, the boys did what they had to do. They got rid of him. Permanently.

Torture

Over a period of many hours—stretching from dusk on July 17 until dawn of the next day—they stabbed him with a kitchen knife and a barbecue fork, strangled him with a rope, and hit him on the head with a hammer and the barrel of a shotgun, according to a statement one of the boys, 14-year-old Carlos Alexander Nevarez, reportedly gave to police. At one point they realized they were hungry. So they heated up the macaroni and cheese they found in Conrad's kitchen, and washed it down with Dr Pepper.

Despite this torture, Conrad survived. According to the statement published by *The Atlanta Journal-Constitution*, a grievously wounded Conrad begged the boys to shoot him and put a swift end to his agony. But, Nevarez said, the boys were afraid people would hear the gunshots. So they allegedly beat him some more, and then poured salt into his wounds to see if he was still alive. When his body twitched in response to the pain, they threw household knickknacks at him. After he was struck in the back by a brass eagle, "he stopped breathing," Nevarez told police. The boys then took off in Conrad's wheelchair-equipped van with their hard-earned loot: a stereo, a VCR, a camcorder and a shotgun, according to an indictment. Even law-enforcement officials were shocked when they arrested the boys the next day. The DeKalb County District Attorney, J. Tom Morgan, calls it "the worst crime scene I've ever seen."

An Epidemic of Youth Violence

Conrad's death was particularly gory, but it was not an isolated incident. Each day seems to bring a new horror story of vicious crimes by boys—and a few girls. Near Ft. Lauderdale, Florida, on July 14, 1993, a group of teenagers allegedly beat and stabbed a friend to death. . . . A few days earlier in New York, a Brooklyn mother made the front pages for the saddest of distinctions: losing all three of her young sons to street violence. Some victims, such as the mentally retarded girl sexually assaulted by high-school football players in Glen Ridge, New Jersey in 1993, get whole forests of publicity. But most victims are mourned only by the people who loved them. In February 1993, Margaret Ensley's 17-year-old son Michael caught a bullet in the hallway of his high school in Reseda, California. She says a teen shot her son because he thought Michael gave him a funny look. The shooter, she says, is now serving 10 years in a youth-authority camp. "But I have life imprisonment without the possibility of parole," says Ensley, 'because I won't ever have my son back again. . . . When they were filling his crypt, I said, 'Lord, let me crawl up there with him,' because the pain was so unbearable."

Children Who Witness Violence

In a recently published book, J. Barbarino and colleagues make comparisons between the children they have studied in Chicago and children of war in Mozambique, the West Bank, and Cambodia. Exposure to violence adversely affects children's development in many areas, including their ability to function in school, emotional stability, and orientation toward the future. These effects may be long lasting. The severity of a child's reactions to trauma is related to the proximity to the violent event, the victim's relationship with the child, and the presence of a parent or caretaker to mediate the intensity of the event. Children who have been exposed to violence may also display symptoms associated with posttraumatic stress disorder, such as diminished ability to concentrate in school, persistent sleep disturbances, flashbacks, disordered attachment behaviors with significant caretakers, sudden startling and hypervigilance, and a nihilistic, fatalistic orientation to the future, which leads to increased risk-taking behaviors.

Betsy McAlister Groves, *JAMA*, January 13, 1993.

Law-enforcement and public-health officials describe a virtual "epidemic" of youth violence spreading from the inner cities to the suburbs. "We're talking about younger and younger kids committing more and more serious crimes," says Indianapolis Prosecuting Attorney Jeff Modisett. "Violence is becoming a way of life." Much of it, but by no means all, can be found in poor neighborhoods, where a disproportionate number of victims and victimizers live side by side. But what separates one group from another is complex: being neglected or abused by parents; witnessing violence at an early age on the street or in the house; living in a culture that glamorizes youth violence in decades of movies from *A Clockwork Orange* to *Menace II Society*; the continuing mystery of evil. To that list add the most dangerous ingredient: the widespread availability of guns to kids. In a Harvard School of Public Health survey released in July 1993, 59 percent of children in the sixth through the 12th grades said they "could get a handgun if they wanted one." More than a third of the students surveyed said they thought guns made it less likely that they would live to "a ripe old age." Cindy Rodriguez, a 14-year-old living in gang-riddled South-Central Los Angeles, is a testament to the ferocity of unrestrained firepower. Two and a half years ago, a gang bullet ripped through her body as she was talking to the mailman outside her house. Now she's paralyzed for life. And the bullets keep coming. "We hear gunshots every day," she says. "Sometimes I get scared. I'm in the shower and I hear it and I get all scared. But you have to live with the reality."

Violence is devastating this generation, as surely as polio cut down young people 40 years ago. Attorney General Janet Reno says youth violence is "the greatest single crime problem in America today." Between 1987 and 1991, the number of teenagers arrested for murder around the country increased by an astounding 85 percent, according to the Department of Justice. In 1991, 10- to 17-year-olds accounted for 17 percent of all violent-crime arrests; law-enforcement officials believe that figure is even higher now. Teenagers are not just the perpetrators; they're also the victims. According to the FBI, more than 2,200 murder victims in 1991 were under 18—an average of more than six young people killed every day. The Justice Department estimates that each year, nearly a million young people between 12 and 19 are raped, robbed or assaulted, often by their peers.

Unmeasured Violence

That's the official count. The true number of injuries from teen violence could be even higher. When emergency medical technicians in Boston recently addressed a class of fifth graders, they were astonished to find that nearly three quarters of the children knew someone who had been shot or stabbed. "A lot of violence goes unmeasured," says Dr. Deborah Prothrow-Stith, assistant dean of the Harvard School of Public Health and author of *Deadly Consequences*, a book about teen violence. Paramedic Richard Serino, who is a supervisor in the emergency room at Boston City Hospital, estimates that doctors save seven or eight wounded teens for every one who dies. Many of the "lucky ones," Serino says, end up paralyzed or with colostomy bags.

The statistics are shocking—and so is the way some teenagers react when they're caught and accused of brutal crimes. "Hey, great! We've hit the big time," 17-year-old defendant Raul Omar Villareal allegedly boasted to another boy after hearing that they might be charged with murder. Villareal was one of six Houston teens arrested and charged in the brutal rape and strangulation of two young girls who made the fatal mistake of taking a shortcut through a wooded area where, police say, the boys were initiating two new members into their gang. In Dartmouth, Massachusetts, in April 1993, two 16-year-olds and one 15-year-old armed with clubs and knives barged into a high-school social-studies class and, police say, fatally stabbed a 16-year-old. One of the accused killers reportedly claimed that cult leader David Koresh was his idol and laughed about the killing afterward.

Dartmouth is a suburb of New Bedford, the sort of place city dwellers flee to, thinking they'll find a respite from city crime. While the odds may be a bit better, a picket fence and a driveway is no guarantee. Indeed, even suburban police departments around the nation have taken to keeping watch on groups they worry may develop into youth gangs. Thus far, most of these kids seem like extras from *West Side Story*, bunches of boys content to deface walls and fight with clubs and chains.

The casual attitude toward violence is most acute in inner-city neighborhoods, where many youngsters have grown up to the sounds of sirens and gunshots in the night and the sight of blood-spattered sidewalks in the morning. After so many years in a war zone, trauma begins to seem normal. This is how Shaakara, a sweet-faced 6-year-old who lives in Uptown, one of Chicago's most dangerous areas, calmly describes one terrible scene she witnessed at a neighbor's apartment: "This lady, she got shot and her little baby had got cut. This man, he took the baby and cut her. He cut her on the throat. He killed the baby. All blood came out. This little boy, when he saw the baby, he called his grandmother and she came over. And you know, his grandmother got killed, but the little boy didn't get killed. He comes over to my house. That man, he took the grandmother and put her on the ground, and slammed her, and shut her in the door. Her whole body, shut in the door." After telling her tale, Shaakara smiles. "You know what I want to be when I grow up? A ballerina or a mermaid."

Drugs, Prisons, and Guns

In this heightened atmosphere of violence, normal rules of behavior don't apply. As traditional social supports—home, school, community—have fallen away, new role models have taken their place. "It takes an entire village to raise a child, but the village isn't there for the children anymore," says Modisett, the Indianapolis prosecutor. "The only direction these kids receive is from their peers on the street, the local drug dealers and other role models who engage in criminal conduct." Katie Buckland, a Los Angeles prosecutor who volunteers in the city's schools, says the kids she sees have already given up the idea of conventional success and seize the opportunities available. "The kids that are selling crack when they're in the fifth grade are not the dumb kids," she says. "They're the smart kids. They're the ambitious kids . . . trying to climb up their own corporate ladder. And the only corporate ladder they see has to do with gangs and drugs."

With drugs the route to easy money, prison is the dominant institution shaping the culture, replacing church and school. In the last few years, more young black men have gone to jail than to college. Fathers, uncles, brothers, cousins have all done time. April Allen, a 15-year-old who lives in Boston's Roxbury section, has friends who think of jail as a kind of sleep-away camp. "The boys I know think it's fun to be in jail because other boys they know are in jail, too," she says. Prison is a way of looking; the dropped-waist, baggy-pants look is even called "jailing" in Miami. And prison is a way of acting. "In prison, the baddest, meanest guy runs the cell," says H. T. Smith, a lawyer and African-American activist who practices in Miami's Overtown ghetto. "Your neighborhood, your school—it's the same. You've got to show him you're crazy enough so he won't mess with you."

Street Mentality

If prison provides the method of social interaction, guns provide the means. Alexis Vega, a 19-year-old New Yorker, explains the mentality on the streets where she grew up: "If a man threatens me, that's a threat to my life. So I go get a gun and make sure I shoot him first before he shoots me. Even though he might not mean it. Just by saying it, it may scare me so much that I'm going to get him first." Vega has seen run-of-the-mill arguments turn into tragedies. "A bullet doesn't have anybody's name on it," says Vega. "Somebody shoots, they're so nervous, they'll catch you even though you don't have anything to do with it."

One kid with a gun is a finite danger; a gang equipped with Uzis, AK-47s and sawed-off shotguns means carnage. Unlike adult criminals, who usually act alone, violent teens normally move in a pack. That's typical teen behavior: hanging together. But these are well-equipped armies, not just a few kids milling outside a pizza parlor. There's a synergistic effect: one particularly aggressive kid can spur others to commit crimes they might not think of on their own. The victims are often chosen because they are perceived as weak or vulnerable, say social scientists who study children and aggression. As horrible as some of the crimes are, kids go along with the crowd rather than go it alone.

A New and Dangerous Breed

Some social scientists argue that teenage aggression is natural. In another era, they say, that aggression might have been channeled in a socially acceptable way—into the military, or hard physical labor—options that are still available to putative linebackers and soldiers. But other researchers who have studied today's violent teens say they are a new and dangerous breed. At a conference on teen-violence prevention in Washington, D.C., in July 1993, psychologists and social workers discussed the causes of skyrocketing teen-crime rates. In one of the largest longitudinal studies of violent youth, scientists followed about 4,000 youngsters in Denver, Pittsburgh and Rochester, New York, for five years. By the age of 16, more than half admitted to some form of violent criminal behavior, says Terence P. Thornberry, the principal investigator in Rochester and a psychologist at the State University of New York in Albany. "Violence among teenagers is almost normative in our society," Thornberry told the conference.

"Adults murder 10 times more children under age 15 than are killed by other children, and 2.5 times more than are killed by teenagers."

Youths Are Unfairly Blamed for Violence

Mike Males

Government officials have called for policies and programs designed to combat youth violence in America, including adult punishments, more prisons, and boot camps. In the following viewpoint, Mike Males argues that such measures are ineffective and that they amount to a campaign to incarcerate minority males. He contends that politicians focus on youth violence in order to divert attention from their failure to address the underlying problems of poverty, racism, and child abuse in American society. Males is a regular contributor to *In These Times*, a liberal weekly magazine, and a Ph.D. candidate in social ecology at the University of California at Irvine.

As you read, consider the following questions:

1. How often is a teenager arrested for murder in Los Angeles, according to Males?
2. According to the author, what proportion of juveniles incarcerated in 1993 consisted of minorities?
3. How many youths are reported abused every day in Los Angeles, according to Males?

Mike Males, "Willie Horton, Jr.," *In These Times*, December 27, 1993. Reprinted with permission.

It was no small irony: President Clinton invoking the images of Martin Luther King in Memphis and Cesar Chavez in Los Angeles to announce a get-tough anti-crime campaign certain to inflict its worst punishments upon the young and non-white.

In Memphis and L.A. in November 1993, Clinton declared that King didn't die for the freedom of "children to have children" or for "13-year-olds gunning down 9-year-olds with automatic weapons."

Familiar Stereotypes

These images are familiar: they are the same stereotypes of rampant violence and sexual immorality once openly directed at the very same minority groups whose heroes Clinton invoked. In truth, juvenile boys and girls account for fewer than 1 percent of all births in the United States; 85 percent of all child murder victims are slain by adults, not by children or teenagers.

L.A. served as the perfect symbolic backdrop for Clinton's message. On any given day, the *Los Angeles Times* is a chronicle of youth gone berserk: drive-by mayhem, pipe stabbings, schoolyard riots, rapist suburban "posses," endless gang warfare. One in seven teenage killers in the United States resides in Los Angeles County, and arrests of teenagers for violent crimes have doubled since the early 1980s. Of course, latter-day L.A. is a violent place in general: the cataclysmic 1992 uprisings added but a 60-corpse blip to the 2,600 killings recorded that year.

Federal anti-crime proposals include a ban on gun possession by juveniles, the transfer of violent kids from juvenile to adult courts, $500 million for new juvenile prisons, federal prosecution of a wider variety of youth offenses, expanded school and community "prevention" programs and militaresque "boot camps" for young first-time offenders.

These initiatives have won support not just from whites but from many black and other minority adults fed up with gang violence. Yet, in foundation and execution, the crime-prevention and punishment strategies proposed by Clinton are extensions of the same '80s logic that plunged us into the abyss of innercity youth violence extant today.

Refuting Punitive Measures

Though gang-laden L.A. provides stark photo-ops and audiences eager for get-tough oratory, a careful examination of California's anti-crime programs provides the refutation, not the affirmation, of the punitive measures Clinton officials and Congress aim to train on youth.

Gun laws? California already has some of the nation's stiffest anti-firearm laws: 14,000 youths were arrested in 1992 for carrying guns, one-fourth of all such arrests in the nation. Prisons?

California has for 20 years incarcerated a higher percentage of its youths than any other state—450 per 100,000 juveniles, a rate eight times higher than alternative-sentencing states such as Massachusetts. Tougher sentences? California already imprisons youth for longer terms than adults convicted of the same crimes. According to the California Department of Corrections, a youth convicted of murder spends an average of 60 months behind bars—compared to 41 months for adult murderers. The statistics are similar for other violent crimes.

Boot camps? California has pioneered similar alternatives: chiefly, the California Conservation Corps—in which non-dangerous youth convicts labor on outdoor work projects—as well as juvenile diversion and community treatment programs. These have been moderately successful with lesser offenders but are not panaceas for the AK-47–toting gang-bangers Clinton decries.

California's get-tough policy (even with its liberal attachments) has hardly proven a success. Youth homicide arrests rocketed from 350 in 1970 (below the national average) to 1,396 in 1992—a rate now double the national average. In L.A., a teenager is arrested for murder every 18 hours, a per-capita rate five times that elsewhere.

Bitter Irony

Clinton's invocation of Chavez and King to support his law and order initiatives is bitterly ironic, given the pattern of arrests in California today. The state's 1992 *Crime and Delinquency* report shows that 89 percent of the youths arrested for murder and 80 percent of those arrested for violent crimes are blacks, Latinos or other minorities.

Although white non-Latinos are by far the state's largest racial group, only 82 white California teenagers were arrested for murder in 1992, compared to 665 non-whites. The homicide rate among black youth is 12 times the rate among white youth. And Latinos, 35 percent of California's teenage population, account for 60 percent of its murders.

These rates vary inversely with rates of poverty: 15 percent of California's white youth lived on incomes below federal poverty guidelines in 1991, compared to 45 percent of its Latino youth and 51 percent of its black youth. To toss out emotional anecdotes of "youth violence" without citing the crucial contexts of racism, anti-immigrant bigotry and poverty is to obscure just how devastating these forms of societal violence against black and Latino adolescents remain, and how little progress has been made toward assuring non-white youth equality of opportunity in the 25 years since King was murdered.

A visit to the grounds of the Herman G. Stark Youth Training

School, or "Chino" as Californians call it, demonstrates better than any statistics the mass incarceration of minority males. Out of 2,000 young inmates held in this maximum-security prison for offenses ranging from drug sales to first-degree murder, white faces are a rare sight; a typical counseling group consists of eight blacks, three Latinos and an Asian.

Non-white youth imprisonment is accelerating nationwide as well: two-thirds of all juveniles behind bars in 1993 were minorities, up from less than half in 1985. Instead of facing and publicizing the implications of this alarming trend, Clinton officials and congressional Democrats have resorted to evoking the inflammatory Willie Hortonism of Reagan-Bush politics: not crude portraits of sinister-looking black murderers but emotion-laden images of Uzi-toting seventh-graders, children having sex with children, killer kids set free by bleeding-heart judges—all symbols of what is politely labeled a "youth problem" to mask its roots in disparities of color and class. [Willie Horton is a black convicted murderer whom George Bush featured in his anti-crime TV ads during the 1988 presidential election campaign.]

Superficial Blather

The dismissive—indeed, moronic and often vindictive—coverage of the terrifying rise of violence in America, especially in the lives of our nation's children, is itself nothing short of criminal. The pundits, most of whom are clueless about the status of children in America, spew a lot of superficial blather about "values" and two-parent families while failing to discuss even one concrete proposal that would help prevent kids beset by violence and poverty from turning into murderers.

Susan Douglas, *The Progressive*, November 1993.

Like the issues of race and class, the issue of gender is a troubling one for politicians bent on exploiting "youth crime." How can the issue be "youth violence" when juvenile girls account for only 2 percent of all violent crime and fewer than 1 percent of all murders? Given that boys and men account for nine out of 10 violent crimes, violence is more honestly framed as a "male issue" rather than as a "youth issue.". . .

Adult Violence Against Children

One major contributing factor to youth violence—the pervasiveness of adult violence against children—has gotten surprisingly little attention from officials and the media. In a city in which 400 youths are reported abused every day, Clinton didn't refer to violence against children by adults, even though his topic was violent crime.

The Los Angeles Council on Child Abuse and Neglect reported 140,000 cases of beating, killing, rape, molestation and criminal neglect inflicted on children and youths in the county in 1992—a rise of 15 percent over 1991 and a rate well above the national average. "Our children continue to suffer terribly in the hands of adults," L.A. County Sheriff Sherman Block told the *Los Angeles Times*. "They are victimized at a terribly alarming rate."

In a California Department of Justice sample of 1,596 murder cases in 1992 for which the offender's and victim's ages are known, 1,266 involved murderers over age 20. Adults murder 10 times more children under age 15 than are killed by other children, and 2.5 times more than are killed by teenagers.

But prevailing official solutions to youth problems focus not on initiatives to alleviate social conditions, which deteriorated alarmingly in the '80s, but on stepping up '80s-style repressions: more laws, tougher sentences, more censorship, more psychiatric confinement. These kinds of programs Clinton and his advisers term "prevention," an appealing concept that, in practice, has been a windfall for myriad law enforcement, education, consulting and treatment interests—and a disaster for youth and society.

"Prevention" Failures

Consider a few major, unpublicized '80s "prevention" failures. Though the multi-billion-dollar "war on drugs" doubled the number of young drug arrestees and drastically expanded school and community efforts against drug use, drug-related death rates among teenagers, which had declined considerably from 1974 to 1984, rose drastically in the latter half of the '80s. Similarly, in the mid- and late '80s, "teen pregnancy" became the focus of toughened laws and stigmatizing publicity. But birthrates among teenage mothers, which had declined by 47 percent from 1957 to 1984, rose 20 percent from 1984 to 1991.

Punitive attempts to prevent teen violence have been similarly unsuccessful. Teenage murder arrests declined by 11 percent from 1974 to 1984. From 1984 to 1992, in the wake of the Reagan-era get-tough approach, teenage murder rates rose by a staggering 95 percent, the fastest, steepest increase ever.

A Policy Disaster

Surely, by now, health and law-enforcement policy-makers must be getting the picture: youth-targeted "prevention," as framed in '80s-'90s context, not only does not work, it represents a policy disaster of major proportions. Nor has it ever worked. As researcher Barry Krisberg has noted, studies of more than 100 prevention programs (from the intensive Cambridge-

Somerville and Boston Midcity projects of the '30s and '50s to modern efforts) have shown that "regardless of type . . . of program or intervention techniques . . . there is little evidence that they are effective in preventing delinquency."

Krisberg's findings have been repeatedly confirmed: there is no magic youth-targeted crime-prevention formula. Because of its failures, "prevention" has become an excuse for punitive policies and popular rhetoric such as have overtaken the U.S. Senate and the Clinton administration.

Periodical Bibliography

The following articles have been selected to supplement the diverse views presented in this chapter.

Jerry Adler "Kids Growing Up Scared," *Newsweek*, January 10, 1994.

Victoria J. Barnett "Growing Up in America: Children as Targets of Violence," *Commonweal*, February 10, 1993.

Michael Barrier "The Enemy Within," *Nation's Business*, February 1995.

Mark Braverman and Susan R. Braverman "Seeking Solutions to Violence on the Job," *USA Today*, May 1994.

John J. DiIulio Jr. "The Question of Black Crime," *Public Interest*, Fall 1994.

Robert Elias "Official Stories: Media Coverage of American Crime Policy," *Humanist*, January/February 1994.

James Alan Fox and Glenn Pierce "American Killers Are Getting Younger," *USA Today*, January 1994.

Ted Gest and Dorian Friedman "The New Crime Wave," *U.S. News & World Report*, August 29–September 5, 1994.

Michele Ingrassia et al. "Life Means Nothing," *Newsweek*, July 19, 1993.

Beverly Roberson Jackson "Children in the Midst of Violence," *Christian Social Action*, December 1993. Available from 100 Maryland Ave. NE, Washington, DC 20002.

JAMA: The Journal of the American Medical Association "Silent Victims: Children Who Witness Violence," January 13, 1993. Available from 515 N. State St., Chicago, IL 60610.

Constance Johnson "'Silent Victims' Who Witness Violence," *U.S. News & World Report*, March 27, 1995.

Andrea N. Jones "Fighting for Respect," *In These Times*, August 23, 1993.

Mike Males "Bashing Youth: Media Myths About Teenagers," *Extra!* March/April 1994. Available from Fairness and Accuracy in Reporting, PO Box 911, Pearl River, NY 10965-0911.

Michelle Marriott   "Living in 'Lockdown,'" *Newsweek*, January
                        23, 1995.

Newsweek   "Murder: A Week in the Death of America,"
                        August 15, 1994.

Jill Smolowe   "Danger in the Safety Zone," *Time*, August
                        23, 1993.

Nancy Traver   "Children Without Pity," *Time*, October 26,
                        1992.

USA Today   "The United States of Violence," May 1994.
                        Entire issue on violence.

Janice Windau and   "Murder Inc.—Homicide in the American
Guy Toscano   Workplace," *Business and Society Review*,
                        Spring 1994. Available from Management
                        Reports, Inc., 25-13 Old Kings Hwy. N.,
                        Suite 107, Darien, CT 06820.

2 CHAPTER

What Causes Violence?

Chapter Preface

Many parents, politicians, and media commentators argue that violence on television, in movies, in video games, and in music contributes to high rates of violent crime among teenagers. In his 1995 State of the Union address, President Clinton asked Hollywood moviemakers to "assess the impact of your work and to understand the damage that comes from the incessant, repetitive, mindless violence and irresponsible conduct that permeates our media." A June 1995 *Time* magazine poll echoed the president's concern about the effects of media violence. Seventy-five percent of those surveyed believe that the depiction of violence in the media "inspires young people to violence."

Other critics, however, maintain that attacks on media violence are misplaced and politically motivated. They argue that there is no way to link media violence to actual incidents of violence. These critics contend that for every John Hinckley, who tried to assassinate President Reagan in 1981 after watching the movie *Taxi Driver,* there were thousands, perhaps millions, of others on whom the film had no such violent effect. Todd Gitlin, a professor of sociology and the director of the mass communications program at the University of California, Berkeley, asserts, "In the case of violence, there are plenty of real smoking guns and I persist in thinking that the current crusade [against media violence] is choosing easy politics and an easy target—Hollywood amorality—over the far tougher project of chipping away at the motives and means of murder."

Whether or not media violence is responsible for societal violence is just one of the questions addressed in the following chapter examining a variety of causes of violence.

"*A vast amount of scientific research proves that watching violence on the screen is causally related to real-life aggression.*"

Violence in the Media Causes Youth Violence

Barbara Hattemer

In the following viewpoint, Barbara Hattemer argues that the violence that children see every day on television and in the movies teaches them to be violent as they become teenagers. She contends that the increase in violent crime—rape, assault, and murder—in the United States, especially that committed by teenagers, relates directly to increasing amounts of violence portrayed in the media. Hattemer is the president of the National Family Foundation, an organization that promotes ways to strengthen families, and the author of *Don't Touch That Dial: Impact of the Media on Children and the Family*.

As you read, consider the following questions:

1. According to the author, what messages does movie and television violence send?
2. How has the behavior of young people changed in recent years, according to the author?
3. How did the introduction of television affect rates of violence in the United States, Canada, and South Africa, according to Hattemer?

Excerpted from "Cause and Violent Effect" by Barbara Hattemer. This article appeared in the July 1994 issue and is reprinted with permission from *The World & I*, a publication of The Washington Times Corporation, copyright ©1994.

Recent headlines proclaim increasing youth violence: "4 Teenagers Charged in Murder of Tourist," "Pupils Told To Run for Their Lives—Teacher Describes Terror in Classroom," "FSU Student Murdered, Sister Raped—18-year-old Beaten to Death, Sister Tied to Tree in Ocala National Forest."

Youth crime is on everyone's mind. It was the focus of virtually every political campaign of 1994. There is talk of boot camps, stricter laws, trying children as adults for committing serious crimes, larger prisons, harsher sentences, gun control, curfews. Take the kids off the streets so we can feel safe again! Keep them home! Why? So they can watch more murder and rape on television and video?

How weary we have grown of the statistics on how many murders every high school graduate has seen. According to the American Psychological Association, even before leaving elementary school, the average child has seen eight thousand murders and one hundred thousand acts of violence on television.

Social science, clinical concepts, and common sense all agree that what children watch affects who they become, what they believe, what they value, and how they behave.

The Early Influence of TV

Television's influence on our children starts earlier than most of us realize. Andrew Meltzoff found that fourteen-month-old infants can watch an unfamiliar toy being dismantled and reassembled on television and repeat the actions twenty-four hours later. Even at this early age, television acts as a guide to real-life behavior. Throughout childhood, children learn by imitating what they see others doing.

Two- to six-year-old children cannot evaluate the messages they receive from the media they watch. They simply accept what they see as normal behavior. Children cannot tell the difference between reality and fantasy until the fifth or sixth grade. Six- to twelve-year-olds imitate what they see and hear without fully understanding the consequences of what they are doing. Most adolescents do not have a fully developed, internal set of morals and values. They accept the conduct they see in the media as the social norm and integrate it into their own behavior patterns.

What are the predominant messages of television, movies, and other media that our children are accepting and imitating? That violence is an everyday occurrence and an acceptable way of solving problems and that promiscuous sex is normal and expected of everyone, including younger and younger children. These two messages merge as the philosophy of pornography, once thought to be limited to sleazy adult bookstores and out-of-the-way art cinemas, has been mainstreamed. The rape myth—that women secretly want to be raped and that they enjoy forced sex—has so permeated our children's minds that 65 percent of boys and 47 percent of girls agreed with a survey question that "it was acceptable for a man to force sex with a woman if he had been dating her more than 6 months."

While television has unlimited potential for good, at the present time its influence on children's lives is largely negative. Television programming, according to Dr. Paul Howard, a prominent Boston psychiatrist, is so hostile and aggressive it produces tremendous anxiety in young watchers. "One weekend of children watching television," he declared, "undoes a whole week of psychotherapy for my young patients."

Television and Violence

Television and violence have been almost synonymous since television became a part of nearly every home. As far back as 1977, nine of every ten TV programs contained violence. Today, while there is more variety, there are more sources of violence than ever before. In addition to violent action-adventure movies and television dramas, violence pervades music videos, rap songs, documentaries, commercials, and news broadcasts. The networks provide up to 10 violent acts per hour; cable, up to 18 violent acts per hour; and children's cartoons, 32 violent acts per hour. Movies like *Teenage Mutant Ninja Turtles* raise the count to 133 violent acts per hour. The body count is rising, too: *Total Recall*, 74 dead; *Robocop 2*, 81 dead; *Rambo III*, 106 dead; and *Die Hard 2*, 264 dead.

Mass-produced, cheap industrial violence is something quite new in our culture. The new heroes glamorize violence for its own sake. The violence is the story, not an element necessary to the telling of a story. Add to this the influence of violent video games and fantasy games that encourage children to spend hours planning how to kill or maim more successfully. Mix in violent comic books and serial-killer trading cards, and you have a culture that gives its children a steady diet of violent role models but very little old-fashioned nurture and direction from parents.

Violent Youth

For nearly a decade, judges and police officers have been exclaiming that they have never before seen rapists and murderers who are so young. The news, in its promotion of the sensational, keeps the tragic headlines ever before us. What some feared might one day happen is indeed happening. The subculture that has long been singing about beating up women, killing parents, and murdering for fun has surfaced.

One-half of the sex offenders in this country are now under the age of eighteen! A 1988 Michigan crime report stated that

681 juveniles who averaged fourteen years of age were convicted of sexually assaulting children who averaged seven years of age. These are not always violent or deeply troubled children; they are children who have been exposed too early to material they cannot process without imitating. They see it on cable in their own homes, they hear it on the telephone. Dial-a-porn companies have admitted that 75–85 percent of their customers are children. Overstimulated by what they see and hear, they act it out on younger siblings or playmates.

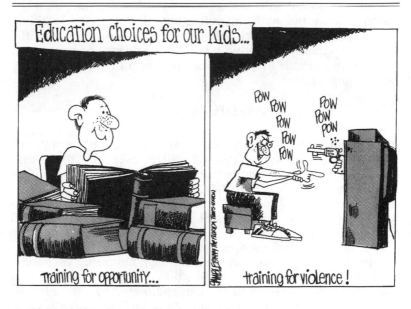

Education choices for our kids...

training for opportunity...   training for violence!

Gamble/*Florida Times-Union*. Used by permission.

Violent crime is up 560 percent since 1960 and is rising. There are three million incidents of school crime every year. In 1993 alone, the rate of violent encounters in schools rose 34 percent in the state of Florida. Rape, assault, and murder have replaced chewing gum, talking in class, and throwing wads of paper, the greatest school problems in the forties. From 1987 to 1991, teenagers arrested for murder increased 85 percent. In 1990, 4,200 teenagers were killed by guns. In New York City, one in five teenagers carries a weapon to school; and one in twenty, a gun. On any one day, 135,000 children carry guns to school across the nation.

It is said that we have always been a violent society, but there is a new callousness among our young people. Many studies have found that using pornography increases men's callousness toward and distrust of women, as well as their inclination to rape. Research also has revealed that 100 percent of our high schoolers have seen soft-core pornography, and 90 percent of high school boys and 80 percent of girls have seen hard-core pornography. The younger they are when they see it, the more likely they are to want to imitate it.

Horror movies aimed at young teens desensitize them to violence and create an ever-increasing appetite for it. If the camera angle allows the child to see the action through the eyes of the madman, a subtle shift takes place. He identifies not with the passive victim but with the active perpetrator. In his imagination, it is the child himself who wields the knife, the ax, or the deadly weapon. Identifying with the aggressor, he senses the thrill of momentary power over another and learns to enjoy committing a crime. . . .

Real-Life Aggression

No one today doubts that our children are seeing massive amounts of violence in a wide variety of media presentations. Moreover, a vast amount of scientific research proves that watching violence on the screen is causally related to real-life aggression. Since the 1968 National Commission on the Causes and Prevention of Violence, a series of government commissions and reports and a consensus of medical associations have all found a link between screen violence and violent behavior.

The television and motion picture industries have been successful in casting doubt on such findings by saying that some studies show an effect and others do not, but the studies that show the fewest effects have been sponsored by the industry. We now have over three thousand studies telling us that watching violent films increases violent behavior. Research has found that preschool children who frequently watch violent cartoons behave aggressively. First graders who watch aggressive cartoons exhibit more hostile behavior in school than first graders who watch neutral programming or even a football game. Because the impact is greater the more realistic the violent scenes are, researchers fear the more realistic human characters in today's cartoons may have an even greater influence on children.

Leonard Eron and Rowell Huesman conducted an important longitudinal study, following eight-year-olds for twenty-two years. They found that children who watched large amounts of violent television at age eight were more likely to be engaged in criminal behavior at age thirty. Not only did they commit serious crimes, they also punished their children more harshly and were much more aggressive when drinking.

Studies before and after the introduction of television in an area reveal an increase in aggressive behavior after the arrival of television. Two years after television was introduced into Notel, Canada, physical aggression among children increased 160 percent.

Childhood Exposure to Violence

A study by Brandon Centerwall focused on the effects of childhood exposure to television violence on adult criminal behavior in larger populations, comparing the effect of television on the roughly comparable white populations of the United States, Canada, and South Africa. Fifteen years after television was introduced into the United States and Canada, white homicide deaths had risen 93 percent and 92 percent, respectively. At the same time, in South Africa, where there was no TV, the white homicide rate had dropped 7 percent. Yet, eight years after South Africa received TV, the rate had already increased 56 percent, indicating that, in fifteen years, it would be close to that of the United States and Canada. In fact, by 1987, twelve years after television had been introduced into South Africa, the white homicide rate had risen by 130 percent.

Centerwall looked for every possible alternative explanation, completing another eleven studies on factors such as the baby boom, urbanization, economic trends, alcohol consumption, capital punishment, civil unrest, and the availability of firearms, but he could find none. He ruled out such factors as the U.S. civil rights movement and the Vietnam War because these did not affect Canada. He concluded that exposure to violent programming on television is causally related to roughly one-half the twenty thousand yearly homicides in the United States and one-half the rapes and assaults as well.

His conclusions held up when he looked at populations within the United States that acquired television at different times. When television appeared in the early 1950s, it was an expensive luxury. Since blacks tended to lag behind whites by about five years in acquiring television sets, he predicted that the white homicide rate would rise before the black homicide rate in the United States. In fact, the white homicide rate began to rise in 1958, while the black homicide rate dropped consistently throughout the next four years. Similarly, those regions of the United States like New York and New Jersey that acquired television before other sections of the country were also found to have an earlier increase in the homicide rate.

Centerwall believes that the lag of ten to fifteen years between the introduction of television and the rise in the homicide rate indicates that the greatest effect is on children under the age of twelve. In the past, it took these children ten to fifteen years to grow up before they were old enough to commit homicide.

Today, however, children are not waiting to become adults to begin committing adult crimes. Youth crime is growing at a much faster rate than adult crime. The past ten years have seen an increase of 55 percent in the number of children arrested for murder. Centerwall explains this as the snowballing effect. The first generation raised on television learned values from the adults in their lives as well as from the TV set. With the increasing dominance of the media in society, the passing on of values from the older generation has diminished, while the second and third generations raised on TV have increasingly taken their values from the media culture.

Lethal Violence

The increase in the seriousness of juvenile crime may be explained further by the fact that violence has become increasingly graphic and gory. According to journalist David Barry, the juvenile delinquency portrayed in 1950s' movies "consisted almost entirely of assaults with fists and weapons which left victims injured, but alive. It was nonlethal violence. The notion of American teenagers as killers was beyond the threshold of credibility."

Since then, he says, the level of criminal violence reported in everyday news stories has become almost unrecognizable. He offers the following statistics as evidence of the effect of the first twenty-nine years of television on crime in the United States. In 1951, there were 6,820 murders, 16,800 rapes, and 52,090 robberies. By 1980, these had increased to 23,000 murders, 78,920 rapes, and 548,220 robberies—vastly more than the 47 percent population increase from 150 million to 220 million. The murder rate is increasing six times faster than the rate of population growth. It is now the leading cause of death for black youths and the second leading cause of death of all fifteen- to twenty-four-year-olds. Violence is the leading cause of injury to fifteen- to forty-four-year-old women. The U.S. Centers for Disease Control calls it both a leading public health issue and an epidemic.

From Media Violence to Real Violence

Researchers offer numerous explanations of how and why media violence translates into real-life violence. They theorize that when a child observes violence used as a means of solving conflicts, the event is recorded in his brain and stored in his memory bank. This scene can be reinforced by subsequent violent scenes, which eventually blend into a general script of how to react to conflict. The more graphic the violence, the more likely it will catch the child's attention and become part of a script stored in his memory, waiting to be retrieved when he faces a similar conflict situation in real life.

Older children are particularly responsive to violence that is realistic or close to their personal experience and thus seems likely to happen in real life. Younger children are more likely to identify with and imitate violent behavior if the character is attractively portrayed. The more that children of all ages identify with a violent character, the more likely they are to be aggressive themselves.

Watching violence primes the pump and starts a network of associations. As media violence is absorbed into a person's thoughts, it activates related aggressive ideas and emotions that eventually lead to aggressive behavior. What a child observes as the associative networks in his brain are developing is of paramount importance.

Violence that is rewarded or left unpunished appears to be sanctioned in a child's mind. It is, therefore, much more likely to be imitated. Violence that appears to be justified or portrayed as necessary for a good cause is even more likely to be imitated. One reason the large amount of violence in Japanese films does not produce as much real-life violence as in the United States is the way that Japanese films portray violence, highlighting the pain, suffering, and tragic consequences that follow. They teach an altogether different lesson than America's glamorized violence.

Not everyone reacts the same way to violence. Poorly nurtured children with few inner strengths and without internalized boundaries are more susceptible to its influence than well-nurtured children who have received a strong value system from their parents. Children who are undersupplied with parental love are often angry and chaotic inside. They are drawn to violent films, heavy metal music, and gangster rap because it reflects their inner turmoil. It both reinforces and offers approval for their negative attitudes. The combination of being undersupplied with parental nurture and overstimulated by violent media can be deadly.

"Violence on the screens, however loathsome, does not make a significant contribution to violence on the streets."

Media Violence Does Not Cause Societal Violence

Todd Gitlin

The media, from lurid nineteenth-century billboards and tabloids to today's television cartoons and blockbuster movies, have been blamed for episodes of violence in society, according to Todd Gitlin. In the following viewpoint, Gitlin asserts that despite more than a century of speculation about the link between media violence and real-life aggression, there is little evidence that more than a handful of "impressionable people" have been so influenced that they have committed violent acts based directly on what they have seen. He does concur, however, that media violence can contribute to an atmosphere that legitimizes violence as a method of resolving conflict. Gitlin is a professor of sociology and the director of the mass communications program at the University of California, Berkeley.

As you read, consider the following questions:

1. What historical examples does Gitlin use to argue that the media has long been blamed for violence in society?
2. According to the author, what does cause violence?
3. What does Gitlin mean when he calls efforts to blame the media for violence a "confession of despair"?

Excerpted from "Imagebusters" by Todd Gitlin. Reprinted with permission from *The American Prospect*, Winter 1994; ©1994 New Prospect Inc.

Guns don't kill people, picture tubes do. Or at least that seems to be the message behind the clangor of current alarms about television violence. Don't misunderstand: I have denounced movie violence for more than two decades, all the way back to *The Wild Bunch* and *The Godfather*. I consider Hollywood's slashes, splatters, chainsaws, and car crashes a disgrace, a degradation of culture, and a wound to the souls of producers and consumers alike.

A Weak Link

But I also think liberals are making a serious mistake by pursuing their vigorous campaign against violence in the media. However morally and aesthetically reprehensible today's screen violence, the crusades of Illinois senator Paul Simon and Attorney General Janet Reno against television violence, as well as Catharine MacKinnon's war against pornography, are cheap shots. There are indeed reasons to attribute violence to the media, but the links are weaker than recent headlines would have one believe. The attempt to demonize the media distracts attention from the real causes of—and the serious remedies for—the epidemic of violence.

The sheer volume of alarm can't be explained by the actual violence generated by the media's awful images. Rather, Simon, Reno, and MacKinnon—not to mention [former vice president] Dan Quayle and the Reverend Donald Wildmon—have signed up for a traditional American pastime. The campaign against the devil's images threads through the history of middle-class reform movements. For a nation that styles itself practical, at least in technical pursuits, we have always been a playground of moral prohibitions and symbolic crusades.

Even before the technology of movies made savagery so vivid, middle-class uplifters in America and England have been variously enthralled and disgusted by media violence and blamed it for inciting working-class youth. In his study of the 1888 Jack the Ripper phenomenon, cultural historian Christopher Frayling notes that London's penny comic weekly *Illustrated Police News* regaled readers with detailed accounts and artists' renditions of the Ripper crime scenes, compiling 184 cover pictures during the four years after the last murder. The high-minded were quick to link the Ripper crimes to the excesses of popular culture. *Punch* magazine asked rhetorically:

> Is it not within the bounds of probability that to the highly-coloured pictorial advertisements to be seen on almost all the hoardings [billboards] in London, vividly representing sensational scenes of murder exhibited as "the great attractions of certain dramas, the public may be to a certain extent indebted for the horrible crimes in Whitechapel [an area in London]?

We say it most seriously—imagine the effect of gigantic pictures of violence and assassination by knife and pistol on the morbid imagination of an unbalanced mind.

In his excellent new history of American entertainment, *Going Out: The Rise and Fall of Public Amusements*, David Nasaw tells us that comparable fears about the impact of moving pictures on children's impressionable minds cropped up in the movies' first decade. Of the 250 films it screened in 1910, the Ohio Humane Society found 40 percent to be "unfit for children's eyes," identifying working-class and immigrant children as particularly vulnerable to the message that crime paid. "In 1907," Nasaw writes, "Chicago passed a censorship ordinance requiring police permits for films shown in nickel and dime theaters." When Jane Addams' Hull House opened a theater to show wholesome alternatives—*Cinderella* and travelogues—very few children showed up, and one of them, a 12-year-old, explained to the reformers: "Things has got ter have some hustle. I don't say it's right, but people likes to see fights, 'n' fellows getting hurt, 'n' love makin', 'n' robbers, and all that stuff."

In the 1930s, the Payne Foundation funded studies attributing juvenile crime to movie violence, complete with testimonials of youthful offenders that they had gotten larcenous ideas from the silver screen. Legions of censors from the Hays Office monitored Hollywood output to make sure that, at the least, crime didn't pay. In the 1950s, Dr. Fredric Wertham made a name for himself by attributing all manner of delinquencies to the mayhem depicted in comic books. Congressmen unable to find sufficient domestic threat in Communism were able to find it in comic books.

Increasing Screen Violence

If today's censorious forces smell smoke, it is not in the absence of fire. In recent years, market forces have driven screen violence to an amazing pitch. As the movies lost much of their audience—especially adults—to television, the studios learned that the way to make their killing, so to speak, was to offer on big screens what the networks would not permit on the small. This meant, among other things, grisly violence—aimed to attract the teenagers who were the demographic category most eager to flee the family room. At the same time, the technologies of special effects steadily advanced to permit more graphic representations. We have witnessed the burgeoning of a genre unknown two decades ago: the "action movie," a euphemism for the debased choreography that budding auteurs throughout the world aspire to imitate. Aiming to recoup losses and better compete with cable, television programmers struck back: the networks lowered their censorship standards and pruned their "standards and practices" staffs; the deregulatory Federal Communications Commission clammed up; and local news fell all over itself cramming snippets of gore between commercials.

The financiers, executives, directors, writers, make-up artists, distributors, and others responsible should be covered with shame. But leave aside, for the moment, the aesthetic and moral cost and consider the arguments about the practical consequences of violent images. There is as much evidence as social science is capable of compiling that violence on the screen inspires and expedites *some* aggression in *some* children. After watching violent programs, many children become hostile, push each other around, stop cooperating, become more fearful, and become desensitized.

America's Violent Culture

We were a violent culture before TV, from Wounded Knee to the lynching bee, and we'll be one after all our children have disappeared by video game into the pixels of cyberspace. Before TV, we blamed public schools for what went wrong with the Little People back when classrooms weren't overcrowded in buildings that weren't falling down in neighborhoods that didn't resemble Beirut, and whose fault is that? *The A-Team?* We can't control guns, or drugs, and each year 2 million American women are assaulted by their male partners, who are usually in an alcoholic rage, and whose fault is that? *Miami Vice?* The gangs that menace our streets aren't home watching Cinemax, and neither are the sociopaths who make bonfires, in our parks, from our homeless, of whom there are at least a million, a supply-side migratory tide of the deindustrialized and dispossessed, of angry beggars, refugee children and catatonic nomads, none of them traumatized by *Twin Peaks.* So cut Medicare, kick around the Brady bill and animadvert Amy Fisher movies. But children who are loved and protected long enough to grow up to have homes and respect and lucky enough to have jobs don't riot in the streets. Ours is a tantrum culture that measures everyone by his or her ability to produce wealth, and morally condemns anybody who fails to prosper, and now blames Burbank for its angry incoherence. Why not recessive genes, angry gods, lousy weather? The mafia, the zodiac, the *Protocols of the Elders of Zion?* Probability theory, demonic possession, Original Sin? George Steinbrenner? Sunspots?

John Leonard, *The Nation,* December 27, 1993.

All these conclusions are contained in a recently published report, *Violence and Youth,* by the American Psychological Association's Commission on Violence and Youth—a report that Attorney General Reno has recommended. "Depictions of violence in the mass media . . . may reinforce the tendency toward aggression in a young child who is already exhibiting aggressive behavior," says this report. "There is absolutely no doubt that higher levels of viewing violence on television are correlated with increased acceptance of aggressive attitudes and increased aggressive behavior." *Absolutely no doubt*: strong words coming from a professional association. The report continues: "Aggressive children who have trouble in school and in relating to peers tend to watch more television; the violence they see there, in turn, reinforces their tendency toward aggression, compounding their academic and social failure. These effects are both short-term and long-lasting." If this were not strong enough, the report goes on to say: "In explicit depictions of sexual violence, it is the message about violence, more than the sexual nature of the materials, that appears to affect the attitudes of adolescents about rape and violence toward women." The report also notes that "children from low-income families are the heaviest viewers of television." That is, the children who have the least stable families, the fewest life prospects, the most violent environments, and the greatest potential for race and class resentment are the ones most exposed not only to images of violence but to the glaring contrast between the things available in their own lives and the things available in the programs and commercials of television.

Sometimes Movies Teach

And once in a while—meaning far too often—some grotesque image inspires emulation. Both big and small screens have taught impressionable people—or at least reinforced their propensity to practice—thrilling new ways to lacerate flesh. In 1982, after the cable television broadcast of *The Deer Hunter*, several people killed themselves playing Russian roulette, which was featured in the movie. American youths recently were killed and maimed when they lay down on the center strip of a highway, imitating a scene from Disney's movie *The Program*. A few months ago, a 17-year-old French youth blew himself up after learning from an episode of *MacGyver* how to build a bomb in a bicycle handle, at least according to his mother, who is suing the head of the channel for manslaughter.

But correlation is not necessarily cause. The notorious 5-year-old *Beavis and Butthead* fan who started a fire and killed his 2-year-old sister may have been starting fires long before these loathsome characters were smudges in their creator's eye. In the end, it is not possible to know with precision whether these victims would have found some other way to commit mayhem in the absence of the images.

The question the liberal crusaders fail to address is not whether these images are wholesome but just how much real-world violence can be blamed on the media. Assume, for the sake of argument, that *every* copycat crime reported in the media can be plausibly traced to television and movies. Let us make an exceedingly high estimate that the resulting carnage results in 100 deaths per year that would not otherwise have taken place. These would amount to 0.28 percent of the total of 36,000 murders, accidents, and suicides committed by gunshot in the United States in 1992.

That media violence contributes to a climate in which violence is legitimate—and there can be no doubt of this—does not make it an urgent social problem. Violence on the screens, however loathsome, does not make a significant contribution to violence on the streets. Images don't spill blood. Rage, equipped with guns, does. Desperation does. Revenge does. As liberals say, the drug trade does; poverty does; unemployment does. It seems likely that a given percent increase in decently paying jobs will save thousands of times more lives than the same percent decrease in media bang-bang.

A Disposition to Aggression

Now I also give conservative arguments about the sources of violence their due. A culture that despises and disrespects authority is disposed to aggression, so people look to violence to resolve conflict. The absence of legitimate parental authority also feeds a culture of aggression. But aggression per se, however unpleasant, is not the decisive murderous element. A child who shoves another child after watching a fist fight on TV is not committing a drive-by shooting. Violence plays on big screens around the world without generating epidemics of carnage. The necessary condition permitting a culture of aggression to flare into a culture of violence is access to lethal weapons.

Thus when Senator Simon and Attorney General Reno denounce TV violence, I am reminded of the story of the fool who is found on his hands and knees searching the sidewalk under a streetlight.

What are you looking for?" asks a passerby.

"My watch."

"Where did you lose it?"

"Over there," says the fool, pointing to the other side of the street.

"Then why are you looking over here?" asks the passerby.

"Because it's dark over there."

It's dark over there in the world of real violence, hopelessness, drugs, and guns. There is little political will for a war on poverty, guns, or family breakdown. Here, under the light, we are offered instead a crusade against media violence. This is largely a feel-good exercise, a moral panic substituting for practicality. But in the language of media consultants, the panic "resonates." The obsession offers frissons of horror while denying that the moralist is also attracted. It appeals to an American propensity that sociologist Philip Slater called the Toilet Assumption: once the appearance of a social problem is swept out of sight, so is the problem. And the crusade costs nothing. . . .

A Confession of Despair

The symbolic crusade against media violence is a confession of despair. Those who embrace it are saying, in effect, that they either do not know how to, or do not dare, do anything serious about American violence. They are tilting at images. If Janet Reno cites the APA report, she also should take note of the following statements within it: "Many social science disciplines, in addition to psychology, have firmly established that poverty and its contextual life circumstances are major determinants of violence. . . . It is very likely that socioeconomic inequality—not race—facilitates higher rates of violence among ethnic minority groups. . . . There is considerable evidence that the alarming rise in youth homicides is related to the availability of firearms." The phrase "major determinant" does not appear whenever the report turns to the subject of media violence.

The question for reformers, then, is one of proportion and focus. If there were nothing else to do about deadly violence in America, then the passionate crusade against TV violence might be more justifiable, even though First Amendment absolutists would still have strong counterarguments. But the imagebusting campaign permits politicians to fulminate photogenically without having to take on the National Rifle Association, or for that matter, the drug epidemic, the crisis of the family, or the shortage of serious jobs. To the astonishment of the rest of the known world, we inhabit a political culture in which advocates of gun control must congratulate themselves for imposing restrictions on the purchase of certain semi-automatic weapons, or a five-day waiting period before the purchase of a handgun. . . .

Sweeping Away the First Amendment

Imagebusters may claim that the causes of violence in America are so intractable that an outraged, frightened public has no better expedient than to cleanse the media. This counsel of desperation not only promises very little practical good but also presumes that the First Amendment can and should be swept away cavalierly. This is always a dangerous course. Censorship is a blunderbuss, not a scalpel. Just which violence is supposed to be cleansed anyway? The number of drops of blood spilled is scarcely the test of an image's vileness or perniciousness. Context is, by definition, unmeasurable. Moreover, Hollywood's history of self-regulation is hardly impressive. The self-imposed movie ratings system that replaced the old Hays Office production code in 1966 has steadily ratcheted up the mayhem it permits in the PG-13 and R categories. Even modest advisory notices backfire, often attracting precisely those they are meant to warn off. The only television program that warns viewers to watch with care before each episode, *N.Y.P.D. Blue*, has actually depicted the pain and fear that devastate friends and coworkers after the shooter does his shooting.

Self-restraint is certainly desirable. Public shaming of those who produce grisly images is defensible (though it may prove paradoxically self-defeating). But even in the short run there is far better public policy to be made. Senator Daniel Patrick Moynihan of New York, for example, has proposed an efficient and ingenious means: prohibitive taxes on bullets, with the most damaging bullets taxed the most. His point is that the guns already loosed into a desperate world (200 million, by some estimates) are out there and hard to recall. But bullets may well be the weak link in the violence chain. If we cut off the manufacture of bullets, except those used for hunting, or tax them prohibitively, then the bullets already out in the world will be harder to replace.

With the NRA losing steam, this is the time to generate a serious debate about guns and bullets. The NRA would make a bully enemy. A country choked with the fear of crime might well rally to Moynihan's proposal against the gun lobby if the stakes were explained to them. Ballots Against Bullets would be a dandy organization. . . .

Criticism for the Right Reasons

There is no space here to address properly the plague of real-world violence. But let that discussion proceed with proper respect for the gravity of the situation. As for *media* violence, let it be criticized for the right reasons and in the right spirit. To be loathsome, popular culture doesn't have to be murderous. To disapprove of media violence, we don't need a threat of government action to rectify morals by fiat. The proper disapproval would have recourse to categories of judgment that make Americans nervous: aesthetic and moral standards and the intersection of the two. The democracy of taste has not been hospitable to judgments of this order. We aren't content to condemn trash on the grounds that it is stupid, wasteful, morally bankrupt; that it coarsens taste; that it shrivels the capacity to feel and know the whole of human experience.

Let a thousand criticisms bloom. Let reformers flood the networks and cable companies and, yes, advertisers, with protests against the gross overabundance of the stupid, the tawdry, and the ugly. Let them demand of local TV stations that the news cameras find something else to photograph besides corpses. To the Hollywood defense that Shakespeare also piled the stage with bodies, let reformers reply that *Timon of Athens* was not piped into the living room several times nightly, that revenge plays were not filling the seats of the Globe Theatre during the rest of the day—not to mention every other theater as well—and that close-ups of Elizabethan sword thrusts and resultant gore were not available in living color. If it be objected that Goethe's *Sorrows of Young Werther* may have prompted more than one suicide by a spurned lover, as did Pablo Neruda's *Twenty Love Poems and a Desperate Song*, or that more than one nineteenth-century Russian youth (not to mention Ted Bundy, or so he claimed) learned murderous technique from *Crime and Punishment*, let reformers ask whether the questioner seriously asks us to rank the makers of *The Texas Chainsaw Massacre* with Goethe, Neruda, or Dostoevski, and if the answer is yes, let that serve as the cinching of the case as to what television has done to popular culture.

Not least, let the reformers not only turn off the set, but criticize the form of life that has led so many to turn, and keep, it on.

"It stands to reason that genes might contribute to violent activity."

Genes May Contribute to Violence

Anastasia Toufexis

In the following viewpoint, Anastasia Toufexis, an associate editor for *Time* magazine, examines the possibility that genes may predispose some people to violence. Toufexis describes current research projects that suggest that a link between genes and violence may indeed exist. Although heredity may dispose an individual to violence, according to Toufexis, other environmental factors—education and family background, for example—influence whether a predisposition to violence will translate into acts of violence.

As you read, consider the following questions:

1. Why is it now possible to do accurate scientific research on the possible biological causes of violence, according to Toufexis?
2. What cultural factors does the author list that may also contribute to the incidence of violence in the United States?
3. According to Toufexis, why do some people oppose current research on the genetic component to violence?

Anastasia Toufexis, "Seeking the Roots of Violence," *Time*, April 19, 1993; ©1993 Time Inc. Reprinted by permission.

It's tempting to make excuses for violence. The mugger came from a broken home and was trying to lift himself out of poverty. The wife beater was himself abused as a child. The juvenile murderer was exposed to Mötley Crüe records and *Terminator* movies. But do environmental factors wholly account for the seven-year-old child who tortures frogs? The teenager who knifes a teacher? The employee who slaughters workmates with an AK-47? Can society's ills really be responsible for all the savagery that is sweeping America? Or could some people be predisposed to violence by their genes?

Until recently, scientists had no good way to explore such questions—and little incentive: the issue was seen as so politically inflammatory that it was best left alone. But advances in genetics and biochemistry have given researchers new tools to search for biological clues to criminality. Though answers remain a long way off, advocates of the work believe science could help shed light on the roots of violence and offer new solutions for society.

But not if the research is suppressed. Investigators of the link between biology and crime find themselves caught in one of the most bitter controversies to hit the scientific community in years. The subject has become so politically incorrect that even raising it requires more bravery than many scientists can muster. Critics from the social sciences have denounced biological research efforts as intellectually unjustified and politically motivated. African-American scholars and politicians are particularly incensed; they fear that because of the high crime rates in inner cities, blacks will be wrongly branded as a group programmed for violence.

The backlash has taken a toll. . . . A proposed federal research initiative that would have included biological studies has been assailed, and a scheduled conference on genetics and crime has been canceled. A session on heredity and violence at February's meeting of the American Association for the Advancement of Science turned into a politically correct critique of the research; no defenders of such studies showed up on the panel. "One is basically under attack in this field," observes one federal researcher, who like many is increasingly hesitant to talk about his work publicly.

Some of the distrust is understandable, given the tawdry history of earlier efforts to link biology and crime. A century ago, Italian physician Cesare Lombroso claimed that sloping foreheads, jutting chins and long arms were signs of born criminals. In the 1960s, scientists advanced the now discounted notion that men who carry an XYY chromosome pattern, rather than the normal XY pattern, were predisposed to becoming violent criminals.

Fresh interest in the field reflects a recognition that violence has become one of the country's worst public-health threats. The U.S. is the most violent nation in the industrialized world. Homicide is the second most frequent cause of death among Americans between the ages of 15 and 24 (after accidents) and the most common among young black men and women. More than 2 million people are beaten, knifed, shot or otherwise assaulted each year, 23,000 of them fatally. No other industrialized nation comes close: Scotland, which ranked second in homicides, has less than one-fourth the U.S. rate.

This cultural disparity indicates that there are factors in American society—such as the availability of guns, economic inequity and a violence-saturated culture—that are not rooted in human biology. Nevertheless, a susceptibility to violence might partly be genetic. Errant genes play a role in many behavioral disorders, including schizophrenia and manic depression. "In virtually every behavior we look at, genes have an influence—one person will behave one way, another person will behave another way," observes Gregory Carey, assistant professor at the University of Colorado's Institute for Behavioral Genetics. It stands to reason that genes might contribute to violent activity as well.

Some studies of identical twins who have been reared apart suggest that when one twin has a criminal conviction, the other twin is more likely to have committed a crime than is the case with fraternal twins. Other research with adopted children indicates that those whose biological parents broke the law are more likely to become criminals than are adoptees whose natural parents were law-abiding.

No one believes there is a single "criminal gene" that programs people to maim or murder. Rather, a person's genetic makeup may give a subtle nudge toward violent actions. For one thing, genes help control production of behavior-regulating chemicals. One suspect substance is the neurotransmitter serotonin. Experiments at the Bowman Gray School of Medicine in North Carolina suggest that extremely aggressive monkeys have lower levels of serotonin than do more passive peers. Animals with low serotonin are more likely to bite, slap or chase other monkeys. Such animals also seem less social: they spend more time alone and less in close body contact with peers.

A similar chemical variation appears to exist in humans. Studies at the National Institute on Alcohol Abuse and Alcoholism conclude that men who commit impulsive crimes, such as murdering strangers, have low amounts of serotonin. Men convicted of premeditated violence, however, show normal levels. As for aggressive behavior in women, some researchers speculate that it might be tied to a drop in serotonin level that normally occurs just before the menstrual period. Drugs that increase serotonin, researchers suggest, may make people less violent.

Scientists are also trying to find inborn personality traits that might make people more physically aggressive. The tendency to be a thrill seeker may be one such characteristic. So might "a restless impulsiveness, an inability to defer gratification," says psychologist Richard Herrnstein of Harvard, whose theories about the hereditary nature of intelligence stirred up a political storm in the 1970s. A high threshold for anxiety or fear may be another key trait. According to psychologist Jerome Kagan, also of Harvard, such people tend to have a "special biology," with lower-than-average heart rates and blood pressure.

'Forgive my father, for I have sinned.'

Kippen Williams/*The Spectator*. Used by permission.

Findings like these may be essential to understanding—and perhaps eventually controlling—chronic wrongdoers, argue proponents of this research. "Most youth or adults who commit a violent crime will not commit a second," observes Kagan. "The group we are concerned with are the recidivists—those who have been arrested many times. This is the group for whom there might be some biological contribution." Kagan predicts that within 25 years, biological and genetic tests will be able to pick out about 15 children of every thousand who may have violent tendencies. But only one of those 15 children will actually *become* violent, he notes. "Do we tell the mothers of all 15 that their kids might be violent? How are the mothers then going to react to their children if we do that?"

It is just such dilemmas that have so alarmed critics. How will the information be used? Some opponents believe the research runs the danger of making women seem to be "prisoners of their hormones." Many black scholars are especially concerned. "Seeking the biological and genetic aspects of violence is dangerous to African-American youth," maintains Ronald Walters, a political science professor at Howard University. "When you consider the perception that black people have always been the violent people in this society, it is a short step from this stereotype to using this kind of research for social control."

The controversy began simmering . . . when Louis Sullivan, then Secretary of Health and Human Services, proposed a $400 million federal research program on violence; 5% of the budget would have been devoted to the study of biochemical anomalies linked to aggressive behavior. The program was shelved before being submitted to Congress, and one reason may have been the reaction to an unfortunate statement by Dr. Frederick Goodwin, then director of the Alcohol, Drug Abuse and Mental Health Administration. Commenting about research on violence in monkeys, Goodwin said, "Maybe it isn't just the careless use of the word when people call certain areas of certain cities 'jungles.'" African Americans were outraged. The ensuing furor forced Goodwin to resign, though Secretary Sullivan then appointed him to head the National Institute of Mental Health. . . .

Soon after that episode, the federally endowed Human Genome Project agreed to provide the University of Maryland with $78,000 for a conference on violence. When the program's organizers announced that the session would look at genetic factors in crime, opponents torpedoed the meeting. "A scandalous episode," charges Harvard's Herrnstein. "It is beneath contempt for the National Institutes of Health to be running for cover when scholars are trying to share their views."

Dr. Peter Breggin, director of the Center for the Study of Psychiatry in Bethesda, Maryland, who led the opposition that scuttled the conference, has no apologies. "The primary problems that afflict human beings are not due to their bodies or brains, they are due to the environment," he declares. "Redefining social problems as public health problems is exactly what was done in Nazi Germany."

Some critics see the current interest in heredity as part of an ugly political trend. "In socially conservative times," argues political scientist Diane Paul of the University of Massachusetts at Boston, "we tend to say crime and poverty are not our fault and put the blame not on society but on genes."

Even staunch believers in heredity's influence do not discount environment. In fact, the two are intimately entwined, and separating cause and effect is not easy. Biology may affect behavior, but behavior and experience also influence biology. Serotonin levels, for example, are not only controlled by genes but, according to research in monkeys, they can be lowered by regular exposure to alcohol. By the same token, says Kagan, a child with a fearless personality may turn into a criminal if reared in a chaotic home, but given a stable upbringing, "he could well become a CEO, test pilot, entrepreneur or the next Bill Clinton."

No one thinks that discovering the roots of violence will be simple. There may be as many causes as there are crimes. The issue is whether to explore all possibilities—to search for clues in both society and biology.

"There is a clear correlation between the surge in criminal violence in . . . largely urban communities and the collapse of marriage."

The Breakdown of Families Causes Violence

Patrick F. Fagan

The breakdown of the traditional family over the last thirty years has left a legacy of violence and chaos in America's urban neighborhoods that must be reversed, argues Patrick F. Fagan in the following viewpoint. Fagan, a senior policy analyst at the Heritage Foundation, a well-known conservative think tank in Washington, D.C., enumerates the consequences of this violence and chaos that he says continues to spread throughout America's urban areas. He contends that children who come from single-parent families headed by teenage mothers are far more likely than others to live in abusive, neglectful homes and, as a consequence, are more likely to become violent teenagers and adults. Thus, Fagan concludes, the breakdown of families and communities is one of the "root causes" of social violence.

As you read, consider the following questions:

1. What statistics does Fagan use to support his conclusion that the collapse of America's families leads to increased rates of violence?
2. How does the hostility in broken families translate into violence in children, according to Fagan?
3. On what basis does the author discount race as a factor in violence?

Excerpted from "The Real Root Causes of Violent Crime" by Patrick F. Fagan, Heritage Foundation *Backgrounder*, March 17, 1995; ©1995 The Heritage Foundation. Reprinted by permission.

Policymakers at last are coming to recognize the connection between the breakdown of American families and various social problems. The unfolding debate over welfare reform, for instance, has been shaped by the wide acceptance in recent years that children born into single-parent families are much more likely than children of intact families to fall into poverty and welfare dependence themselves in later years. These children, in fact, face a daunting array of problems.

While this link between illegitimacy and chronic welfare dependency now is better understood, policymakers also need to appreciate another strong and disturbing pattern evident in scholarly studies: the link between illegitimacy and violent crime and between the lack of parental attachment and violent crime. Without an understanding of the root causes of criminal behavior—how criminals are formed—members of Congress and state legislators cannot understand why whole sectors of society, particularly in urban areas, are being torn apart by crime. And without that knowledge, sound policymaking is impossible.

A review of the empirical evidence in the professional literature of the social sciences gives policymakers an insight into the root causes of crime. Consider, for instance:

- Over the past thirty years, the rise in violent crime parallels the rise in families abandoned by fathers.
- High-crime neighborhoods are characterized by high concentrations of families abandoned by fathers.
- State-by-state analysis by Heritage Foundation scholars indicates that a 10 percent increase in the percentage of children living in single-parent homes leads typically to a 17 percent increase in juvenile crime.
- The rate of violent teenage crime corresponds with the number of families abandoned by fathers.
- The type of aggression and hostility demonstrated by a future criminal often is foreshadowed in unusual aggressiveness as early as age five or six.
- The future criminal tends to be an individual rejected by other children as early as the first grade who goes on to form his own group of friends, often the future delinquent gang.

On the other hand:

- Neighborhoods with a high degree of religious practice are not high-crime neighborhoods.
- Even in high-crime inner-city neighborhoods, well over 90 percent of children from safe, stable homes do not become delinquents. By contrast only 10 percent of children from unsafe, unstable homes in these neighborhoods avoid crime.
- Criminals capable of sustaining marriage gradually move away from a life of crime after they get married.
- The mother's strong affectionate attachment to her child is

the child's best buffer against a life of crime.
- The father's authority and involvement in raising his children are also a great buffer against a life of crime.

The scholarly evidence, in short, suggests that at the heart of the explosion of crime in America is the loss of the capacity of fathers and mothers to be responsible in caring for the children they bring into the world. This loss of love and guidance at the intimate levels of marriage and family has broad social consequences for children and for the wider community. The empirical evidence shows that too many young men and women from broken families tend to have a much weaker sense of connection with their neighborhood and are prone to exploit its members to satisfy their unmet needs or desires. This contributes to a loss of a sense of community and to the disintegration of neighborhoods into social chaos and violent crime. If policymakers are to deal with the root causes of crime, therefore, they must deal with the rapid rise of illegitimacy. . . .

The Broken Family

The evidence of the professional literature is overwhelming: Teenage criminal behavior has its roots in habitual deprivation of parental love and affection going back to early infancy. Future delinquents invariably have a chaotic, disintegrating family life. This frequently leads to aggression and hostility toward others outside the family. Most delinquents are not withdrawn or depressed. Quite the opposite: They are actively involved in their neighborhood, but often in a violent fashion. This hostility is established in the first few years of life. By age six, habits of aggression and free-floating anger typically are already formed. By way of contrast, normal children enjoy a sense of personal security derived from their natural attachment to their mother. The future criminal is often denied that natural attachment.

The relationship between parents, not just the relationship between mother and child, has a powerful effect on very young children. Children react to quarreling parents by disobeying, crying, hitting other children, and in general being much more antisocial than their peers. And, significantly, quarreling or abusive parents do not generally vent their anger equally on all their children. Such parents tend to vent their anger on their more difficult children. This parental hostility and physical and emotional abuse of the child shapes the future delinquent.

Most delinquents are children who have been abandoned by their fathers. They are often deprived also of the love and affection they need from their mother. Inconsistent parenting, family turmoil, and multiple other stresses (such as economic hardship and psychiatric illnesses) that flow from these disagreements compound the rejection of these children by these parents, many of whom became criminals during childhood. With all these factors working against the child's normal development, by age five the future criminal already will tend to be aggressive, hostile, and hyperactive. Four-fifths of children destined to be criminals will be "antisocial" by 11 years of age, and fully two-thirds of antisocial 5-year-olds will be delinquent by age 15.

Broken Families and Violence
Teenage Violent Crime Rate: 1965–1992

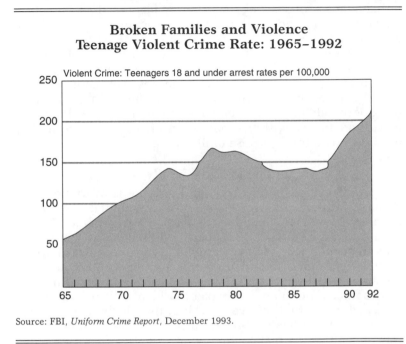

Source: FBI, *Uniform Crime Report*, December 1993.

Summing up the findings of the professional literature on juvenile delinquency, Kevin Wright, professor of criminal justice at the State University of New York at Binghamton, writes: "Research confirms that children raised in supportive, affectionate, and accepting homes are less likely to become deviant. Children rejected by parents are among the most likely to become delinquent."

Fatherless Families

According to the professional literature, the absence of the father is the single most important cause of poverty. The same is true for crime. According to Kevin and Karen Wright,

> Research into the idea that single-parent homes may produce more delinquents dates back to the early 19th century. . . . [O]fficials at New York State's Auburn Penitentiary, in an attempt to discern the causes of crime, studied the biographies

of incarcerated men. Reports to the legislature in 1829 and 1830 suggested that family disintegration resulting from the death, desertion, or divorce of parents led to undisciplined children who eventually became criminals. Now well over a century later, researchers continue to examine the family background of unique populations and reach similar conclusions.

The growth of the poverty-ridden family today is linked directly with the growth of the family headed by the always-single mother. And this modern form of family disintegration—or more accurately non-formation—has its consequences for criminal behavior. The growth in crime is paralleled by the growth in families abandoned by fathers.

The rate of juvenile crime within each state is closely linked to the percentage of children raised in single-parent families. States with a lower percentage of single-parent families, on average, will have lower rates of juvenile crime. State-by-state analysis indicates that, in general, a 10 percent increase in the number of children living in single-parent homes (including divorces) accompanies a 17 percent increase in juvenile crime.

Along with the increased probability of family poverty and heightened risk of delinquency, a father's absence is associated with a host of other social problems. The three most prominent effects are lower intellectual development, high levels of illegitimate parenting in the teenage years, and higher levels of welfare dependency. According to a 1990 report from the Department of Justice, more often than not, missing and "throwaway" children come from single-parent families, families with stepparents, and cohabiting-adult families.

In normal families a father gives support to his wife, particularly during the period surrounding birth and in the early childhood years when children make heavy demands on her. In popular parlance, he is her "burn-out" prevention. But a single mother does not have this support, and the added emotional and physical stress may result in fatigue and less parent availability to the child, increasing the risk of a relationship with the child that is emotionally more distant. The single mother generally is less able to attend to all of her child's needs as quickly or as fully as she could if she were well taken care of by a husband. These factors tend to affect the mother's emotional attachment to her child and in turn reduce the child's lifelong capacity for emotional attachment to others and empathy for others. Such empathy helps restrain a person from acting against others' well-being. Violent criminals obviously lack this. At the extreme, and a more common situation in America's inner cities, the distant relationship between a mother and child can become an abusing and neglectful relationship. Under such conditions the child is at risk of becoming a psychopath.

These observations have disturbing implications for society. If the conditions in which psychopathy is bred continue to increase, then America will have proportionately more psychopaths, and society is at an increased risk of suffering in unpredictable ways.

A father's attention to his son has enormous positive effects on a boy's emotional and social development. But a boy abandoned by his father is deprived of a deep sense of personal security. According to Rolf Loeber, professor of psychiatry, psychology and epidemiology at the Western Psychiatric Institute in the University of Pittsburgh School of Medicine, "A close and intense relationship between a boy and his father prevents hostility and inappropriate aggressiveness." This inappropriate aggressiveness is an early indication of potential delinquency later on, particularly in boys. Furthermore, such bad behavior is a barrier to the child's finding a place among his more normal peers, and aggressiveness usually is the precursor of a hostile and violent "street" attitude. Elijah Anderson, professor of sociology at the University of Pennsylvania, observes that these young men, very sensitive in their demands for "respect," display a demeanor which communicates "deterrent aggression" not unlike the behavior that causes normal peers to reject and isolate aggressive boys in grade school. The message of this body language, of course, triggers rejection by the normal adult community. . . .

The Absence of a Mother's Love

According to Professor Rolf Loeber of the University of Pittsburgh School of Medicine: "There is increasing evidence for an important critical period that occurs early in children's lives. At that time, youngsters' attachment to adult caretakers is formed. This helps them to learn prosocial skills and to unlearn any aggressive or acting out behaviors."

The early experience of intense maternal affection is the basis for the development of a conscience and moral empathy with others.

If a child's emotional attachment to his mother is disrupted during the first few years, permanent harm can be done to his capacity for emotional attachment to others. He will be less able to trust others and throughout his life will stay more distant emotionally from others. Having many different caretakers during the first few years can lead to a loss of this sense of attachment for life and to antisocial behavior. Separation from the mother, especially between six months and three years of age, can lead to long-lasting negative effects on behavior and emotional development. Severe maternal deprivation is a critical ingredient of juvenile delinquency: As John Bowlby, the father of attachment research, puts it, "Theft, like rheumatic fever, is a disease of childhood, and as in rheumatic fever, attacks in later life are frequently in the nature of recurrences." A child's emotional attachment to his mother is powerful in other ways. For example, even after a period of juvenile delinquency, a young man's ability to become emotionally attached to his wife can make it possible for him to turn away from crime. This capacity is rooted in the very early attachment to his mother. We also know that a weak marital attachment resulting in separation or divorce accompanies a continuing life of crime. . . .

Parental Fighting and Domestic Violence

The empirical evidence shows that, for a growing child, the happiest and most tranquil family situation is the intact primary marriage. But even within intact two-parent families, serious parental conflict has bad effects. The famous studies of Harvard professors Sheldon and Eleanor Glueck in the 1950s found that one-third of delinquent boys in their sample came from homes with spouse abuse. The Cambridge-Somerville Youth Study observed that the incidence of delinquent behavior was higher in intact homes characterized by a high degree of conflict and neglect than it was in broken homes without conflict. Dr. Travis Hirschi, professor of criminology at Arizona State University, in a study of junior and senior high school children in northern California, replicated these findings a decade later. As these and other studies have shown, the lack of emotional attachment to parents is more strongly related to delinquency than is an intact home. Professor Kevin N. Wright, in his review of the literature for the Department of Justice, lists twenty-one other major studies that clearly show the link between parental conflict and delinquency. The lesson is clear: Conflict between parents hurts the child. The more frequent or intense the conflict, the more the child is hurt emotionally. In sharp contrast, tranquillity and peace in the family and in the marriage help prevent delinquency. . . .

Parental Neglect

The children of single teenage mothers are more at risk for later criminal behavior. One reason is that teenage single mothers monitor their children less than older married mothers do. They are more inclined to have an inconsistent, explosively angry approach to disciplining their children. In such homes family members, including children, generally use aggressive, coercive methods to make sure their needs are met by others in the family. The parent's inability to monitor a child's behavior compounds the hostility between parent and child and leads to the first of the two major stages in delinquency described by the Oregon Group:

> [The first stage is a] breakdown in family management procedures, producing an increase in antisocial behavior and an im-

pairment in social skills and application at school. [In] the second stage, during adolescence, these conditions continue and the disruptions in the parents' monitoring practices and the adolescent's own poor social skills place him further at risk for finding his community in a deviant peer group.

. . . The professional literature is replete with findings of a connection between future delinquency and criminal behavior and the abuse and neglect visited upon children by their parents. This abuse can be physical, emotional, or sexual. "Overwhelmingly," observes Patricia Koski, "studies conducted since 1964 have found a positive correlation between parent-child aggression-violence-abuse-physical punishment and aggression on the part of the child." Or, as summarized by Cathy Spatz Widom, professor of Criminal Justice and Psychology at Indiana University, Bloomington, "Violence begets violence."

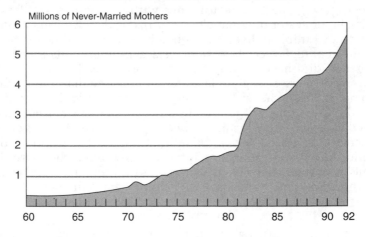

1960–1992: Undeviating Growth in Abandoned Mothers and Children

Source: Bureau of the Census, *Current Population Reports—Marital Status and Living Arrangements*, March 1992.

Studies of the official records of abused children and arrested offenders put this connection in the range of 14 percent to 26 percent. But the connection triples to a range of 50 percent to 70 percent once researchers go beyond official reports of investigated cases of child abuse to reports of abuse by the delinquents themselves.

Significantly, west coast Crips and Blood gang members almost without exception grew up in dangerous family environments. Typically, they left home to escape the violence or drifted away because they were abandoned or neglected by their parents. Consequently, these young men have developed a defensive worldview characterized by a feeling of vulnerability and a need to protect oneself, a belief that no one can be trusted, a need to maintain social distance, a willingness to use violence and intimidation to repel others, an attraction to similarly defensive people, and an expectation that no one will come to their aid. Young women delinquents who run away from home are also frequently victims of sexual abuse.

The close connection between child abuse and violent crime is highlighted also in a 1988 study of the fourteen juveniles then condemned to death in the United States: twelve had been brutally abused, and five had been sodomized by relatives. . . .

The Collapse of Community

Criminal youth tend to live in high-crime neighborhoods. Each reinforces the other in a destructive relationship, spiraling downward into violence and social chaos. The 1980s witnessed an extraordinary increase in community violence in most major American cities. In 1990, homicide in Boston increased by over 40 percent over the previous year; in Denver, it rose by 29 percent; in Chicago, Dallas, and New Orleans, by more than 20 percent; in Los Angeles, by 16 percent; in New York, by 11 percent. In 1988, nationwide firearm death rates for all teenagers for the first time exceeded the total for all other natural causes of death combined, and black male teens were 11 times more likely than their white counterparts to be killed by guns.

According to the national survey data, there is a clear correlation between the surge in criminal violence in these largely urban communities and the collapse of marriage. Professional research in criminology also supports this conclusion.

Tragically for these communities, single-parent neighborhoods tend to be high-crime neighborhoods. Researchers long ago observed that violent crime, among both teenagers and adults, is concentrated most heavily in urban neighborhoods characterized by a very high proportion of single-parent families. More recent figures indicate the illegitimate birth rate in many urban neighborhoods is a staggering 80 percent. And today's researchers, like those before them, find that a neighborhood composed mainly of single-parent families invariably is a chaotic, crime-ridden community in which assaults are high and the gang—"the delinquent subcommunity"—assumes control. In these chaotic conditions, parental supervision of adolescent and pre-adolescent children is almost impossible. In turn, children living in these neighborhoods are more likely to learn, accept, and use physical violence to satisfy their wants and needs.

While serious crime is highest in these socially disorganized, largely urban neighborhoods, however, its frequency is not a function of race. The determining factor is absence of marriage. Among broken families, with their chaotic, "dysfunctional" relationships, whether white or black, the crime rate is very high. Among married two-parent families, whether white or black, the crime rate is very low. The capacity and determination to maintain stable married relationships, not race, is the pivotal factor. The chaotic, broken community stems from these chaotic, broken families. The reason race appears to be an important factor in crime is the wide differences in marriage rates among ethnic groups.

While the crime rate among blacks has risen sharply, so has the disappearance of marriage. The same holds true for whites.

A recent report from the state of Wisconsin further illustrates the same relationship.

A high concentration of broken families without husbands and fathers is the danger signal for future crime.

Violent Families, Violent Youth, and Violent Communities

Violent youth often come from violent parents. Violent youth are the most likely to have witnessed conflict and violence between their parents. They also are the most likely to commit serious violent crime and to become "versatile" criminals—those engaged in a variety of crimes, including, theft, fraud, and drugs. Among these youths, physically or sexually abused boys commit the most violent offenses.

Internal family violence is only one major contributor to adolescent violence in these socially disorganized neighborhoods. The neighborhood itself (which includes the youth's violent peers, also rooted in their own broken families) is the other powerful contributor, especially to violent delinquency, and its culture of aggression and violence is imported into the school. Consider a recent report from the Centers for Disease Control:

> More than 4 percent of high school students in grades 9-12 had carried a firearm at least once in the past 30 days, and 35.5 percent of those had carried six or more times during that period. Thus, about 1.4 percent of high school students might be considered regular gun carriers. Furthermore, more than 60 percent of the students surveyed in Baltimore reported knowing someone who had carried a gun to school.

Given the level of violence in their neighborhoods, for young people to carry guns for self-defense is perhaps understandable. And the youth most likely to feel the need for defense is the member of a street gang in a violent neighborhood. After he has committed his first violent crime, the evidence shows that he is likely to commit further crimes and more than twice as likely as other criminal youths to commit more violence. . . .

Two researchers from the National Institute of Mental Health, John E. Richters and Pedro Martinez, have studied families in high-risk inner-city neighborhoods. Their study indicates that only 6 percent of children from stable, safe homes become delinquent. Meanwhile, 18 percent of children from homes rated as either unstable or unsafe (broken marriage or lack of supervision) became delinquent, but 90 percent of children from homes rated as *both* unstable and unsafe became delinquent. Only 10 percent did not.

Such studies show that the family is fighting desperately with the violent neighborhood for the future of its children. The good news is that even in violent and crime-ridden neighborhoods, "good families" are winning the battle, though a 6 percent juvenile delinquency failure rate is still a tragedy for them. Even the troubled family is winning, with its 82 percent success rate, though the one-in-five delinquency rate means that every second family has had a family member in jail. Remarkably, even 10 percent of children from the most unstable and unsafe families somehow survive and escape a life of crime. The 90 percent delinquency rate among their siblings may be inevitable, for these are the families with the highest concentration of neglectful and abusive parents who would warp any child. . . .

The Breakdown of the Family

The professional literature of criminology is surprisingly consistent on the real root causes of violent crime: the breakdown of the family and community stability. The sequence has its deepest roots in the absence of stable marriage.

Despite the good news that overall crime rates have dropped in recent years, the frightening news is that both the level and viciousness of teenage violent crime have been rising steadily. More ominous still, this was set in motion sixteen to eighteen years ago, when these violent teenagers were born into chaotic family and social conditions. Since then these conditions have become more prevalent, and we will see a continued rise in violent teenage crime. Furthermore, America is headed toward a 50 percent out-of-wedlock birth rate sometime in the next twelve to twenty years, inching more and more of the country closer to today's inner-city illegitimacy rate. If this trend is not reversed, Americans must prepare for extensive and serious erosion of public safety and practical freedoms.

"Violence will not significantly diminish until we are willing to accept that something is very wrong in our society and are willing to correct it."

Lack of Moral Purpose Causes Violence

Douglas Mattern

In the following viewpoint, Douglas Mattern asserts that a century of wars and political corruption and scandals, along with the rise of greedy multinational corporations, has fostered an extreme decline in moral values in the United States. At the same time, he argues, the United States has seen a corresponding increase in societal violence. Unless the slide into moral chaos is halted and reversed, he contends, violence will continue to increase. Mattern is the president of the Association of World Citizens, an organization that promotes peace and a global spirit of community. He is also a contributing editor of the *Human Quest*, a journal of religious humanism.

As you read, consider the following questions:

1. How does Mattern characterize popular television interview programs?
2. What did a three-year study by the General Accounting Office (GAO) reveal about the Pentagon, according to Mattern?
3. According to the author, how can the moral vacuum in the United States be filled?

Douglas Mattern, "The Plague of National Violence," *The Human Quest*, March/April 1994. Reprinted by permission.

Many factors contribute to the violence rampant in the United States, other than the nightly mayhem of murder on the television screen and in the movies. Nearly 50 years of an economy that depends on war or the constant preparation for war is a factor.

A Moral Vacuum

The increasingly superficial nature of society is another, because it undermines real values and produces a moral vacuum. For example, we have reached an absurd level of celebrity worship centering around movie stars, TV personalities, sports figures, etc., many of whom have little of substance to give either the present or the future.

It is also common for petty gangsters, white collar criminals, and the totally bizarre to receive vast media attention. At the same time, people dedicated to improving the quality of life in this country—and peace and justice in the world—are ignored; virtually shut out of the establishment media

This is sadly evident in popular television interview programs such as Donahue, Oprah Winfrey, Geraldo, etc. These programs have degenerated to a degree of bad taste and utter idiocy not dreamed of in former times. In this context, the role of the establishment media is dismal. This includes political-type interview programs which feature the same conservative and right-wing guests time and again. When, for example, is the last time a person with a new idea or vision of the future appeared on a national television program? This sterile reporting and presentation of views by the media and its favored guests, along with the obsession with escapism and celebrity worship, significantly contributes to the moral vacuum and confused values of today.

The problem is that the media is owned and run by Corporate America for the sole purpose of selling products, and this entity views the entire country as one giant marketplace where the only thing that counts is what sells. This selling idea has become so pervasive that even individuals seeking employment are told they must "sell themselves" to prospective employers, as if human worth is nothing more than a piece of merchandise.

The Drug Problem

We have 25 million Americans taking illegal drugs. We had a war on drugs. We had a war on poverty. We are obsessed with war on everything, including small Third World countries. A step forward is to develop constructive programs to deal with our problems rather than waging more useless wars. On drugs the most important question is why are so many people taking illegal drugs? What is missing in our society that a significant percentage of the population depends on this type of extreme escapism? Only when we face up to "why," can we hope to resolve this problem.

Corruption also plays a role in the overall decline of values, thus contributing to senseless violence—Watergate, Irangate, the Wall Street scandals, the Savings and Loan debacle, etc. In addition to the above add the military-industrial complex. Along with being an insidious business, it is rife with corruption. For decades this industry has robbed American taxpayers of millions of dollars through fraud. In 1986 alone, 59 of the top 100 defense contractors in this country were under federal investigation for fraud.

Violence Seems Normal

In 1966, when Charles Whitman took his hunting rifle up into the tower at the University of Texas and sniper-killed 16 people at random, the nation was mesmerized. Today, we have come to think that violence is normal. We are numb, desensitized, inured to the steady bombardment of cases and imagery. Office shoot-ups, carjackings, stalkers, drive-by shootings, children who kill, courtroom murders, child abductions, Jeffrey Dahmer, Joel Rifkin . . . ho-hum, that's life in the '90s.

I am not into America-bashing. I'd rather live here than anywhere else. But something is wrong. Very wrong.

Michael Rustigan, *Los Angeles Times*, August 2, 1993.

Add the Pentagon. After a three-year study federal investigators for the Government Accounting Office concluded what knowledgeable peace activists have been saying for years; namely, that military officials in the Pentagon purposely lied to Congress regarding the cost and necessity of weapons systems built in the 1980's. They found the Pentagon understated by "billions" of dollars the cost of nuclear missiles, and exaggerated the threat posed by the Soviet Union. All of these scandals revealed that the menace of organized crime in this country is not confined to the Mafia, that criminals are not only dressed in black shirts and white ties, but also in Wall Street business suits, military uniforms, industrial lab coats, and the garb of government officials.

There is no excuse for this level of corruption, or the type and frequency of violence that has swept across the country. We need strong anti-gun laws to curtail the availability of handguns and to eliminate the availability of military-type weapons. But this requires politicians who have the courage and conviction to stand up to the National Rifle Association and enact these laws. More fundamentally, the violence will not significantly diminish until we are willing to accept that something is very wrong in our society and are willing to correct it. The focus and obsession with violence as entertainment, the decades of militarism in our foreign policy, the focus on self-interest rather than concern for the whole society, the exaggerated quest for material possessions, the corruption of politics and national ideals, the greed and abuse of the environment are all contributing factors to the new violence in the country.

A New Idealism

What we need are teachers, the churches, school administrators, parents, and politicians, labor unions, peace organizations, and others to help install a new sense of idealism and purpose in our society, including such fundamentals as respect for life and the environment, social justice, racial equality, and common kindness and concern for others. We might even add basic good manners which are disappearing at a considerable pace. In short, a civilized society.

As the two main political parties are becoming a mirror image of each other, we must create a new political/social movement—perhaps even a new political party to achieve these goals. The democrats and republicans are so similar—almost identical in foreign policy, that people must vote on personalities rather than a real difference on issues.

We must rapidly develop this new movement with the dynamism, the ethics, and the leaders who can instill the new values and purpose the country needs. And by working together, both here and around the world, with an intense level of commitment, a courageous determination in the face of all obstacles, and a passionate vision for the future, the prevalent cynicism and violence will be overcome, and replaced with a foundation for a better, safer, environmentally sound, and progressively governed world for the new millennium.

"Thirty-two percent of all the murders solved by police are committed by criminals out on bail, probation or parole."

The Criminal Justice System Contributes to Violence

Robert James Bidinotto

Robert James Bidinotto writes on criminal justice topics for *Reader's Digest*, a monthly general interest magazine. In the following viewpoint, Bidinotto argues that the criminal justice system in the United States allows dangerous, violent criminals to be out on the street where they commit many of the violent crimes that citizens fear. Such practices as plea bargaining and lenient paroling of all criminals, he contends, keep criminals from serving the prison sentences they deserve and keep rates of violence high.

As you read, consider the following questions:

1. According to the Bureau of Justice Statistics figures cited by the author, how did the time criminals spent in prison in 1960 and 1990 differ?
2. How does Bidinotto describe the "reality" of the parole system?
3. What examples does the author cite to support his argument that alternatives to prison sentences are ineffective?

The career of Morris Bud Vroman is a stark testament to why Americans no longer feel safe. This Michigan native had a long criminal record—including assault, larceny and a weapons charge—when he was convicted of breaking and entering in 1983 and sentenced to six to 15 years. In prison, he amassed dozens of major violations for habitually disobeying orders, refusing to work, threatening to kill a guard and fighting with other inmates.

When Vroman's case came before the parole board in 1988, he was turned down. Notes from the proceeding described him as "a wild-eyed guy" whose behavior while incarcerated had been "frankly downhill."

"Rehabilitation"

Then Vroman took classes in "impulse control," and a prison report noted "a positive change in his behavior." After three state declarations of prison "overcrowding emergencies," Vroman was paroled to a Detroit halfway house in February 1989.

He was employed briefly but was fired for fighting. After that he lasted only two days in job-training sessions, then refused to take part in a mental-health program. Finally, he stopped reporting to his parole officer altogether and disappeared.

Vroman surfaced over a year and a half later. Spotting a 16-year-old Detroit girl waiting for a bus to school, he forced her into a vacant building, repeatedly assaulted her sexually, then tried to strangle her. He was arrested for criminal sexual conduct and larceny.

At his trial, Vroman sat sketching bullets blasting through the prosecutor's head. When the jury pronounced him guilty, the parolee glared at his victim and said, "You're dead, bitch."

Dangerous Compromises

In recent years, states have enacted some of the stiffest criminal sentences in the world, yet we are losing the war against crime. One key reason is that tough penalties aimed at hardened criminals are being systematically undermined. Plea bargains permit criminals to escape punishment for the crimes they actually commit. And because there is not enough space to house them, convicts are hustled out of prisons as fast as harried cops, prosecutors and judges shove them in. Parole is granted to individuals who should never receive it; parole violations are ignored. "Good behavior" credits shave months, even years, off time served.

Virginia's parole-board chairman, Clarence L. Jackson, acknowledges that many convicts in his state serve as little as one-sixth of their sentence. In Massachusetts, ten years may actually mean an inmate must do only 12 months.

National figures reveal an astonishing fact: the time prisoners spend behind bars has been *declining*. In 1960, according to the federal Bureau of Justice Statistics (BJS), the mean time served in prison for all offenses was 28 months; by 1990, it had fallen to just 22. Violent offenders will do, on average, less than 4 years. The mean time served by murderers released in 1990 was only 7½ years.

Hidden Crimes

The undermining of public safety begins with plea bargaining. This practice allows prosecutors to recommend a lighter sentence if a defendant will plead guilty to a lesser charge. This "bargain" spares everyone the bother of a trial.

Because criminals often don't get charged with their most serious crimes, plea bargaining lets them evade serious punishment. In a recent investigation, *The Record* newspaper in Hackensack, New Jersey, also exposed how plea bargaining can make a criminal seem much less dangerous than he really is.

Conrad Jeffrey was arrested in 1985 for kidnapping and attempted aggravated sexual assault on a 12-year-old boy in Newark, New Jersey. The initial charges of kidnapping, terroristic threats, child endangering and attempted aggravated sexual assault were reduced through a plea bargain to attempted kidnapping. He was sentenced to five years and paroled in less than two.

Next Jeffrey was charged with aggravated assault, auto theft, resisting arrest, drunken driving, leaving the scene of an accident and eluding the police. He was able to plead the charges down to burglary of a motor vehicle and aggravated assault. Jeffrey was given concurrent sentences of four years for the two charges, but was paroled again. Then he pulled a knife on a 14-year-old Hackensack girl.

Reduced Charges

Jeffrey could have gone to prison for a long time under New Jersey's habitual-offender law. But partly because a presentencing report was vague about the circumstances of his earlier record, he was allowed once more to plead guilty to reduced charges.

Jeffrey spent the mandatory minimum 2½ years in prison before he was again released in March 1993. Two weeks later, he was arrested for threatening a man in Newark. His parole was not revoked.

On May 5, 1993, seven-year-old Divina Genao was abducted from the courtyard of her Passaic apartment building. An informant's tip sent police to a boardinghouse. Hearing screams in a room, they kicked in the door. According to pending charges,

Conrad Jeffrey lunged out at them. Inside, little Divina's body was on the bed. Jeffrey has been indicted for her murder.

Worthless Pledges

"Parole" originally meant "word"—in the sense of "giving one's word." It is the conditional early release of an inmate from confinement, on his pledge that he will behave himself. In theory, a parolee is still under state supervision. If he commits a crime or violates parole, he can be "flopped," or sent back to prison to serve the remainder of his sentence. The reality is very different. "Parole has become a population valve to control prison overcrowding," explains Kenneth Babick, a parole and probation officer in Multnomah County, Oregon. "It bears little relation to behavior behind bars or on the outside."

Michigan's lax parole system was further highlighted by a series of articles in the Detroit *Free Press* in the wake of the chilling case of Leslie Allen Williams.

Williams was first paroled in 1972 after serving one year of a one- to five-year sentence for breaking into a store in Novi, Michigan. A plea bargain had reduced the charge to attempted breaking and entering. On parole, he broke into a home in Wixom where a 15-year-old girl was sleeping and tried to choke her. Charged with breaking and entering, and assault with intent to commit great bodily harm, he was once again allowed to plea bargain—this time to breaking and entering.

Since Williams was on parole, he should have been returned to prison for the remainder of his previous five-year sentence. Instead, he got a sentence of 18 months to ten years.

After two years he was paroled in July 1975, and within weeks he abducted a teen-ager at gunpoint and raped her. Williams was sentenced for this crime to a reassuring 14 to 25 years. Yet he was paroled *again* in January 1983.

Two weeks after his release, Williams kidnapped a woman and threatened her with a screwdriver. He had once again broken parole, and he had up to 18 years left on the meter for his previous crime. He received a new sentence of 7 to 30 years.

Williams was out on the streets a fourth time in 1990. "Your granting a parole so swiftly, your belief in my efforts and progress has been an inspiration," he wrote to the parole-board member who had urged his release.

In 1991, he went on a rampage. Kidnapping Kami Villanueva, 18, from her South Lyon, Michigan, home, he raped and then strangled her. When he encountered sisters Michelle and Melissa Urbin—teen-age honor students out for a walk—they, too, were murdered.

A few months later, he attacked Cynthia Marie Jones, 15, and her boyfriend in a Milford park. After tying the young man to a tree at knifepoint, Williams raped the girl, then stabbed her to death. Meanwhile, his parole officer reported that Williams was having "no problems."

The reign of terror finally ended in May 1992. Williams was captured after kidnapping a woman at gunpoint as she placed flowers on her mother's grave. He is now serving multiple life sentences.

Murray Burley denounced the parole system that had freed the killer of his granddaughter, Cynthia Marie Jones. "I am more frightened of that system and the people who operate it than I am of Williams," he told reporters. "We don't know how many Williamses they have let out."

Releasing Killers

Throughout the country, many of the most celebrated murder cases involve killers who were once in the hands of the law, once in prison, but were released and put back onto the streets.

Consider the case of Wayne Lamar Harvey, which is all too typical. Harvey participated in the brutal shotgun killing of two people in a Detroit bar in December 1975. A plea bargain reduced his two first-degree murder charges to second degree, and he was given a 20- to 40-year prison sentence. On the day he entered prison, he was automatically granted nine and a half years of "good-time" credits, which he was allowed to keep despite 24 major prison rule violations during his incarceration. His minimum sentence was further reduced by two years under Michigan's "Prison Overcrowding Emergency Powers Act."

Harvey was paroled to a halfway house in July 1984 after serving eight and a half years of his original minimum sentence. On October 25, 1984, Harvey and a female halfway-house escapee killed a 41-year-old East Lansing police officer and father of 6, then proceeded to a nearby home where Harvey shot and killed a 33-year-old woman as she opened the door.

Allan Brownfeld, *Washington Inquirer*, September 1, 1989.

In fact, parole horror stories are anything but unusual. One federal study that tracked 109,000 former prisoners found that 63 percent of them were rearrested for serious crimes—including 2300 homicides, 3900 forcible sex crimes, 17,000 robberies and 23,000 assaults. Today, well over half a million convicts are out on parole.

A study by the National Council on Crime and Delinquency discovered that half of all the new prison admissions in California in 1987 were parole violators. And BJS statistics reveal that

32 percent of all the murders solved by police are committed by criminals out on bail, probation or parole.

Questionable Incentives

By far the most widely used tool for reducing the time criminals spend behind bars is so-called good-behavior credit. In most states, inmates are granted generous early-release credits for such things as participating in prison rehabilitation programs or not being a discipline problem, or simply to ease crowding.

Even the most serious felons may go free. As a teen-age "enforcer" for a Chicago street gang, Stanley Davis was convicted in 1971 of shooting a young Army private in the face with a shotgun. For this murder, he was sentenced to 35 to 100 years. Despite this sentence, Davis was released after serving only 20 years. He was paroled in May 1991. "He behaved himself very well in the institution," state Prison Review Board chairman James K. Williams later explained. "We thought he was a good risk."

Less than a year after Davis's release, Chicago police officer Robert Perkins got a tip about a burglary suspect and confronted Davis, who pulled out a gun and fired four times. Perkins, an 18-year veteran, was struck in the head and died soon after, leaving a wife and three daughters.

Davis was captured a week later and confessed. Convicted of first-degree murder, he is now serving a sentence of natural life without parole.

Experts report that problems with this form of early release exist in almost every state. "'Good time' has become little more than a bribe to entice inmates' good behavior," says Edward Leddy, a professor of criminology at St. Leo College in Norfolk, Virginia. "It's designed to make life easier for prison authorities—but too often at the expense of public safety."

Alternatives to Incarceration

To avoid the costs of building and operating more prisons, many states dump thousands of convicts into halfway houses and work-release programs. As a consequence, felons who shouldn't be free end up in programs designed for much less dangerous offenders. In Georgia, William Lamar Bonner was finishing a sentence in a Macon work-release program. Each day, a man picked up Bonner at a halfway house, supposedly to take him to a job at a nearby drywall firm. Every evening, Bonner returned promptly to the halfway house.

Bonner and the other man were arrested for burglary during a police stakeout on December 29, 1992. According to police, guns were found in the van they were driving. They have since been charged with 22 daytime burglaries. The biggest surprise to authorities was that the man checking Bonner out of the halfway house each day was his cousin, Sammy Arthur Dixon—himself free on parole.

In Orlando, Florida, vacationers, including families with children visiting Walt Disney World, were reporting scores of hotel-room thefts to police. A reporter from Orlando television station WFTV decided to investigate. A hidden camera revealed that two of the burglars were hotel maids. One of the maids turned out to be a state prisoner participating in a work-release program.

Solving the Problem

As was recently noted by the *Washington Post*, citizens must "have confidence that punishment will bear some reasonable relationship to the severity of the crime." Here is how we can ensure that it does.

1. *Build more prisons.* Overcrowding is universally acknowledged to be a driving force behind the early release of dangerous convicts. Constructing more cells to isolate such criminals from society should be a top priority.

"Most of our predatory violence is committed by chronic offenders who are cycled in and out of corrections facilities," notes former U.S. attorney general William Barr, who now heads the First Freedom Coalition, a nationwide organization to strengthen the criminal-justice system. "If you put additional police on the street with no prison space behind them, all you're going to do is spin the revolving door faster."

Prisons more than pay for themselves. Several investigations have confirmed that the crimes committed by the average offender cost society at least twice as much as their cells do.

2. *Restrict plea bargaining.* Many officials protest that without plea bargaining, courts would become hopelessly clogged. But Oakland County, Michigan, has virtually eliminated plea bargaining without the predicted problems.

"Actually, our court dockets and waiting time are getting shorter because of our no-plea-bargain policy," says Oakland prosecutor Richard Thompson. "Once you say you're ready to deal, defense attorneys stall, waiting for the most lenient deal. Here, they know they're not going to manipulate the system."

3. *Truth in sentencing.* Public safety demands that current parole and good-behavior systems be tightened dramatically.

"At a minimum, parole violators should be sent back to prison to serve their full terms," declares George Ward, chief assistant prosecutor in Wayne County, Michigan. More than a dozen states and the federal government have gone even further, abolishing parole entirely.

Other states are tightening up the "good-time" system. Arizona limits good-time credits to no more than 15 percent of an inmate's sentence. Says Steve Twist, the state's former chief assistant attorney general, "The public needs to know that a sentence means what it says."

Keeping the Public Safe

It was broad daylight when Cecile Ham, 48, was abducted from a Houston drugstore parking lot. The assailant, Spencer Corey Goodman, killed Ham and then used her credit cards for shopping.

The crime occurred one day after Goodman got out of prison, where he had been sent for auto theft, burglary—and for violating a previous probation. He was released early, on parole, and was supposed to report to a halfway house. He never showed up.

Cecile Ham's husband, Bill, was present when the jury sentenced Goodman for the murder. He later released this statement:

"The goodness that was Cecile will never again touch our lives. The sweetness of her smile and humor in adversity will never strengthen us again except as a memory."

Ham made one final appeal. "The charge," he declared, "is to work toward a system dedicated to the freedom to live our lives unharmed and safe."

"Sixty-nine percent of the youths who had been maltreated as children reported involvement in violence as compared to 56 percent of those who had not."

Family Violence Causes Youth Violence

Terence P. Thornberry

In the following viewpoint, Terence P. Thornberry presents statistics to argue that children who grow up in violent families are more likely than other children to be violent as teenagers. Children who are maltreated are more likely to become violent than those who are not maltreated, according to Thornberry, and children who experience multiple forms of violence are twice as likely to become violent as those who experience no violence. Thornberry is a professor at the school of criminal justice at the State University of New York in Albany and the director of the Rochester Youth Development Study, which is done in conjunction with the Justice Department's Office of Juvenile Justice and Delinquency Prevention's research program on the causes of delinquency.

As you read, consider the following questions:

1. What was the Rochester Youth Development Study set up to measure, according to Thornberry?
2. According to the author, what statistics correlate with the four different degrees of family violence the researchers measured?

Terence P. Thornberry, "Violent Families and Youth Violence," Office of Juvenile Justice and Delinquency Prevention *Fact Sheet*, no. 21, December 1994. (References and a graph in the original publication have been deleted here.) Reprinted courtesy of the U.S. Justice Department and the author.

Compared to other industrialized nations, America's rates of criminal violence are unacceptably high. Pervasive violence adversely affects our streets, schools, work places, and even our homes.

While we have come to recognize the extent of family violence, we know much less about its consequences, particularly its effects on children growing up in violent families. This viewpoint examines this issue for one outcome, involvement in violent behavior during adolescence. It addresses two questions.

First, are children who are victims of maltreatment and abuse during childhood more apt to be violent when they are adolescents? And second, are children who are exposed to multiple forms of family violence—not just maltreatment—more likely to be violent?

Studying Delinquency

Data from the Rochester Youth Development Study are used in this analysis. This ongoing study of delinquency and drug use began with 1,000 7th and 8th grade students attending the public schools of Rochester, New York, in 1988. . . . The youths and their primary caretaker were interviewed every six months until the adolescents were in the 11th and 12th grades. Students who left the Rochester schools were also contacted. The overall retention rate was 88 percent. In addition to personal interviews, the project collected data from schools, police, social services, and related agencies.

Delinquency is measured by self-reports of violent behavior. Every six months the interviewed youths indicated their involvement in six forms of violent behavior, ranging from simple assault to armed robbery and aggravated assault. The measure used in this analysis is the cumulative prevalence of such behavior over the course of the interviews.

Child Maltreatment and Delinquency

Practitioners and researchers have long been interested in whether early childhood victimization is a significant risk factor for later involvement in violence. To examine this issue, information was collected on maltreatment from the Child Protective Service files of the Monroe County, New York, Department of Social Services for all study subjects. Maltreatment includes substantiated cases of physical or sexual abuse or neglect. To examine prior victimization as a risk factor for later violence, we have considered only those instances of maltreatment that occurred before age 12.

Sixty-nine percent of the youths who had been maltreated as children reported involvement in violence as compared to 56 percent of those who had not been maltreated. In other words, a history of maltreatment increases the chances of youth violence by 24 percent.

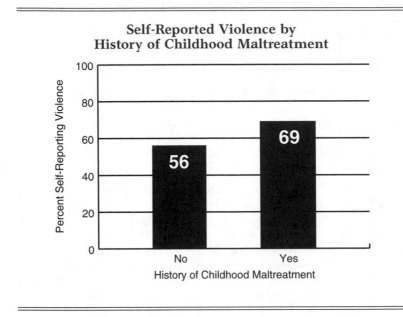

**Self-Reported Violence by
History of Childhood Maltreatment**

Other analyses of these data indicate that maltreatment is also a significant risk factor for official delinquency and other forms of self-reported delinquency; for the prevalence and frequency of delinquency; and for all these indicators when gender, race/ethnicity, family structure, and social class are held constant.

Multiple Family Violence

If direct childhood victimization increases the likelihood of later youth violence, does more general exposure to family violence also increase the risk? To address this question, three different indicators of family violence were examined: partner violence, family climate of hostility, and child maltreatment.

Partner violence was measured . . . based on parent interview data and indicates the level of violence between the subject's parent and his or her spouse. The family climate of hostility scale—also taken from the parent interview—measures the extent to which there was generalized conflict in the family, and to which family members physically fought with one another. The child maltreatment measure is similar to the one used earlier, but now includes cases of maltreatment in which any children in the subject's family are victimized, not just the study participant.

For each type of family violence, adolescents who live in violent families have higher rates of self-reported violence than do youngsters from non-violent families. The results for partner violence illustrate this finding. Seventy percent of the adolescents who grew up in families where the parents fought with one another self-reported violent delinquency as compared to 49 percent of the adolescents who grew up in families without this type of conflict. Similar patterns can be seen for the other two indicators of family violence.

The Consequences of Violence

The final issue we examined was the consequences of growing up in families experiencing multiple forms of violence. While 38 percent of the youngsters from non-violent families reported involvement in violent delinquency, this rate increased to 60 percent for youngsters whose family engaged in one of these forms of violence, to 73 percent for those exposed to two forms of family violence, and further increased to 78 percent for adolescents exposed to all three forms of family violence. Exposure to multiple forms of family violence, therefore, doubles the risk of self-reported youth violence.

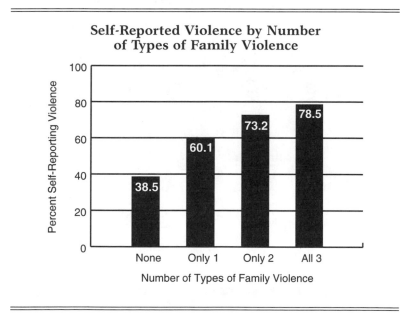

Self-Reported Violence by Number of Types of Family Violence

This analysis examined the relationship between family violence and youth violence. Adolescents who had been direct victims of child maltreatment are more likely to report involvement in youth violence than non-maltreated subjects. Similarly, adolescents growing up in homes exhibiting partner violence, generalized hostility, or child maltreatment also have higher rates of self-reported violence. The highest rates were reported by youngsters from multiple violent families. In these families, more than three-quarters of the adolescents self-reported violent behavior. In other words, children exposed to multiple forms of family violence report more than twice the rate of youth violence as those from non-violent families.

"Crack has been like a bullet wound to the communities that were already suffering."

The Drug Trade Causes Violence

Isabel Wilkerson

Turf wars, drive-by shootings, and executions are the legacy of the crack cocaine epidemic of the late 1980s and early 1990s, argues Isabel Wilkerson in the following viewpoint. She maintains that as the popularity of crack increased so did the number of guns and the incidence of violence perpetrated by drug dealers trying to expand their markets. Despite the waning of crack sales in many urban areas, she contends, the violence associated with the drug trade continues. Wilkerson is the Chicago bureau chief for the *New York Times* and a 1994 Pulitzer prize winner.

As you read, consider the following questions:

1. Why did Jovan Rogers say he needed to carry a gun, according to the author?
2. How did Jovan Rogers get started in the drug trade, according to Wilkerson?
3. According to Wilkerson, what effect did getting shot have on Jovan Rogers's attitudes toward others in his neighborhood?

On a spring morning in 1990 in a dead-end neighborhood in Chicago, it was Jovan Rogers's turn to sell a little bag of crack that, added to the bags that he figured were sure to follow, could buy him gym shoes and girlfriends and maybe keep the electric company from turning off the lights at his mother's apartment again.

He was 14, and not sure he was ready to be out there on his own. He had been playing lookout for the older boys, watching for police cars and yelling "Five-O" when he thought he saw one. He had not yet had to look a customer in the eye and wonder if this was an undercover police officer trying to make an arrest or a rival dealer there to rob him.

In another time and place, he might be doing something safer to get money, like cutting people's grass or bagging groceries. But there are mostly dirt lawns where he lives, and there are no supermarkets.

Employment in the Drug Business

He was too young to work at McDonald's. And anyway, in his neighborhood, the biggest employer is the drug business, which pays more in a day than flipping hamburgers would in a month.

Jovan stood nervously by the curb in front of his apartment building and waited for people old enough to be his parents to line up to buy his merchandise. "I was shaking, man, hearing noises," he said. "Everybody who came up to me, I was asking, 'Man, you ain't the police, are you?' I kept jumping every time a car would pull out of the alley."

Jovan soon found that he had more than just the police to worry about. With crack came violence. And before he was finally arrested for drug dealing and put on probation in 1992, he had lost a half-dozen friends to gunfire, witnessed executions and fired on rival gang members in turf wars. In his business, it was understood that there would be casualties.

Drug Violence

Violence caught up with Jovan when he was shot in an early morning rampage by rival gang members when he was barely 17. After that, he never left home without his .38. Without it, "you feel empty, bare, naked," he said, "because you ain't got your friend with you."

Crack was not the only reason Jovan carried a gun—he says he needed it for protection—but crack was his passport to violence. Rock, as people here call it, and the scattered street market it feeds, gives teen-agers like Jovan a dangerous way to make fast money in a world without stock clerks or paperboys.

Crack, the highly addictive, smokable form of cocaine, became widely available on the streets of many American cities in the 1980's when dealers began to market the drug at relatively cheap prices. It became widespread in Chicago by 1990. Consumption leveled off in 1994 as heroin made a comeback.

But the corrosive effects of crack and its role in youthful violence are only now being understood by criminologists and police departments.

Drug Violence

Homicides each year and the year crack was introduced into each city (●).

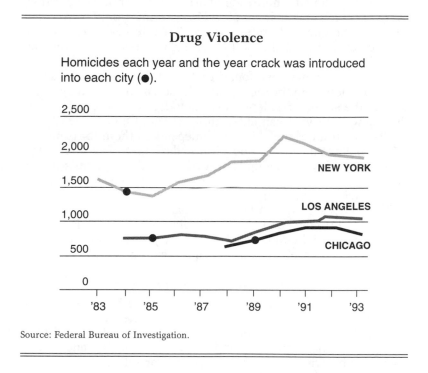

Source: Federal Bureau of Investigation.

Crack has been like a bullet wound to the communities that were already suffering. Even if the bullet can safely be extracted, it has left these neighborhoods deeply scarred.

Crack and Guns

The most visible signs are the guns that crack dealers started to carry the way accountants carry calculators. "Guns multiplied right after crack came," said Jeffrey Fagan, a professor of criminal justice at Rutgers University, who has studied the connection between crack and violence. "They filtered down into the hands of kids and are still in circulation. When the epidemic subsided, the guns stayed behind."

Wherever it landed, crack took a definable course: The drug's fleeting highs and long, desolate lows created a frenetic field of customers who again and again had to come back for more. In all the chaos, small-time dealers could set up shop practically anywhere, and did.

Teen-agers who might have otherwise stuck to hustling or shoplifting suddenly had a shot at the big time. As kingpins and upstarts competed for prime locations, disputes were settled with violence. With more guns on the street, homicides skyrocketed.

No matter the city, homicide charts tell the same story. Whatever year crack took hold, in New York, Washington, Los Angeles, Chicago, the homicide rates soared. The rate has leveled off in these cities, but the toll is still much higher than before crack arrived, because the guns remained, even as crack use declined.

And the survivors have found that crack has turned the social order of their neighborhoods upside down. Armed teen-agers control the streets, residents say. They decide who can stroll on the sidewalk or who can enter an apartment building, while the adults are afraid of the children or depend on them for drugs.

"The boys stand there and almost dare us to say anything," said Gwen Clay, a resident of North Lawndale, Jovan's neighborhood, where teen-agers had removed her gates so they could cut through her yard when they wanted.

"The adults seem powerless," said Barry Krisberg, president of the National Council on Crime and Delinquency in San Francisco. "That is very frightening to kids. So they jump in on the side of what they see as the strength, which is the drug dealers."

Winning Money, Girls and Status

Ask Jovan Rogers why he got into the drug business and he will tell you about the three younger sisters he has to take care of, about his mother, an on-again, off-again welfare recipient who gave birth to him at 14 and had trouble making ends meet, about her boyfriend who went to prison for selling drugs, about the family refrigerator that did not have enough food in it and an apartment with no electricity because his mother lacked money to pay the light bill.

"You feel so sorry," Jovan said of the times his mother had asked him for help. "If there's nothing to eat at night, who's going to go buy something to make sure something is there? I was the only man in the house, and they had to eat. They knew I was out there hustling for us."

Ask him about crack, and he will also tell you about the seductive idea of being somebody when you have nothing. "If you weren't selling drugs, you weren't nobody," Jovan said. "If you sell drugs, you had anything you wanted. Any girl, any friend, money, status. If you didn't, you got no girlfriend, no friends, no money. You're a nothing."

To make money, he used to take out the neighbors' trash and run to the store for them. They didn't have much money either,

116

and the 50 cents they would give him didn't go far. But the dealers were hiring.

Jovan had to compete to get a job with them. He would wake up early and stand outside his building hoping one of the older boys, most of them members of the Vice Lords street gang, would choose him to be a lookout. He could make $75 a day just watching for the police.

Over time, Jovan got used to the job, became good at it and started selling drugs himself, independently of the gang. He learned that all he had to do was to stand at his spot, and grownups in the neighborhood would flock to him for a 20-minute high. Mothers would bring their children with them, offering food stamps for crack. Men, who in another day and place would tell boys like him to go inside and behave themselves, would give him their cars as collateral for a few bags of crack.

He began as a sidewalk dealer but had to move whenever the bigger fish decided to take his spot. He found fighting the gangs over street corners a losing battle. Unable to beat them, he joined with the Vice Lords, in drug-dealing terms entering the big leagues. Soon he was making $800 a day. It was not a lot of money for people in his business, he said.

Jovan was a retailer, not a drug lord. He was never one of the wildly successful ones who had lines outside a crack house of his own, pulling in hundreds of thousands of dollars a week. But crack did to him what it had to thousands of inner-city boys. It transported him into the violent orbit of gangs and guns.

Watching Killing and Taking a Bullet

In an urban rite of passage, Jovan got his first gun at 15 after he had proved himself as a dealer and lookout man. It was a training weapon, so to speak, a small .22-caliber pistol that gang sergeants barely in their 20's give the younger boys when they are ready for greater responsibility.

More powerful guns would come in time—.45's, 9 millimeters, Glocks and Techs. But for now, the boys would have to content themselves with the smaller guns.

Whenever gang members went to parties or other social events, younger boys were assigned to stand guard so the older ones could enjoy themselves without having to watch their backs.

"While the rest are partying, I'm the one in the back of the crowd with my hood on my head and my hand in my pocket," Jovan said, describing his duties.

There was little instruction on how to use a gun. "You just grow into it," Jovan said. "Once you get a gun, it's your responsibility. Don't get caught without it. That's the first thing they tell you."

The gang imposed a $500 fine for losing a gun.

It was after one of those parties at the neighborhood hangout that he first used his gun, he said. Some rival gang members ambushed members of Jovan's gang outside. There was no time to be scared or to think. At times like this, he said, when it was shoot or be shot, he did not think about right or wrong, about how a victim might feel as a bullet pierced his body or about somebody's grieving mother at a funeral.

"Either we had to shoot them things or get shot," Jovan said. "I didn't wait to see if somebody got hit. I don't know what happened."

That year, the drug spots in the neighborhood were plagued by a string of holdups by a certain crack addict. The word was that the man was wanted by the gangs and should be shot on sight. The day the man was caught, Jovan said, he stood frozen as older gang members cornered the robber and exacted street justice with 17 bullets from a semiautomatic.

"You could see sparks flying, jumping from the body," Jovan said, cupping his hands over his face and shaking his head.

In 1992, in the dark hours of a December Sunday morning, Jovan lay on a cold pavement in a pool of his own blood after a party outside the same makeshift hangout where he had fired his first shot. Members of a rival gang had opened fire as Jovan and his fellow gang members fled.

A bullet from a .45-caliber semiautomatic hit one boy's leg and scraped the hand of another before striking Jovan in the left buttocks and emerging above his pelvic bone.

A friend named Boo-Boo ran the few blocks to get Jovan's mother, Verna. "Oh, my God! They took my boy from me!" Ms. Rogers wailed as she rushed toward her son to await the ambulance.

The wound has now healed, but Jovan still carries the memory of that night. When it is cold or rainy outside, his left leg aches, and he walks with the limp of an old man.

The family is saving the two-inch bullet as a symbol of his survival. His mother keeps it in her bedroom drawer.

Wielding Power and Seeking Control

The shooting only pulled Jovan deeper into the cave. He started packing a .38 wherever he went. He said he no longer cared who was hurt in the streets as long as he survived. And until his arrest for trying to sell heroin to an undercover officer, he wielded great power in his small world made up mostly of drug addicts, choosing who would get drugs and who would not. He had his own kind of street logic and morality.

For instance, he said he would sell to anybody except pregnant women and mothers who brought their children. "You can't buy nothing with your shorty with you," he would tell them.

"I'm sorry, baby," the customers would say, then leave their children at the corner and come right back to make their purchase.

The customers had to do what the dealers told them because of their obsession with crack. "They have to be nice," Jovan said. "They need it. You don't."

Jovan is a melancholy figure, tightly contained. Off the streets and away from the drug world, he is an obliging and quiet-spoken teen-ager who rarely smiles, who opens doors for people or reaches over to help pick up something they have dropped. He always looks as if he is in the middle of a difficult chess game.

His father died of an overdose when Jovan was 5. Jovan met his father only once. "I thought I was bad luck," Jovan said, "because right after I saw him, he died."

With only his mother's boyfriends as guides—one beat him, another sold drugs—Jovan learned to be a man on his own. "I've never called a man 'daddy,'" Jovan said. "I've never used that word. I don't even know what a daddy is."

Jovan's mother, who is 33, has had her own struggle with drugs, pleading guilty in 1993 to trying to buy cocaine from an undercover officer.

His grandmother Ida Sherrod, who has lived off and on with the family, does what she can. "I can't give them what they want," Mrs. Sherrod said. "All I can do is pray to God and hope I don't get that phone call that he's in jail or hurt."

Jovan is fatalistic. Asked where he thought he would be 10 years from now, he said, "To tell you the truth, dead. The way the streets are now, I think I'll be out of here. History."

Getting Control

For now, though, he is trying to gain control of his life. He no longer wears the gang colors of black and gold or the $100 gym shoes and gold chains that were part of his uniform as a drug dealer. He says he leaves his .44-caliber automatic with an aunt on the South Side.

He was on probation until 1993, and his case worker, Bill Glover, said Jovan had abandoned drug dealing as far as he could tell. Mr. Glover has become a mentor for Jovan. He picks up his report cards and lends him a couple of dollars when he can.

After being kicked out of school for a year because of his involvement in the gang, Jovan is now a senior in high school. He should do well this time, Mr. Glover said, because he got A's and B's without even trying before. Mr. Glover wants him to go to college.

Jovan's dream is less grandiose. He says he would be happy to find a job paying $6 or $7 an hour. But so far, he said, no one but the drug dealers seem willing to hire him.

"It is the capitalist system and U.S. imperialism that is the basic cause of crime and violence, at home and in the world."

Capitalism Causes Violence

Gus Hall

Gus Hall has been a member of the Communist Party USA, of which he is currently the chair, since 1934. He is the author of several books, including *Fighting Racism* and *Karl Marx: Beacon for Our Times*. In the following viewpoint, Hall contends that capitalism, characterized by private or corporate ownership of capital goods and the exchange of goods and services in a free-market economic system, is responsible for a culture of violence in the United States. According to Hall, capitalism, a system unfair to all but the wealthy, fosters alienation, poverty, anger, hopelessness, and cruelty, all of which contribute to increasing levels of violence.

As you read, consider the following questions:

1. What are the two classes that Hall describes and how does he describe them?
2. What role does "Corporate America" play in causing violence, according to the author?
3. According to the author, what can solve America's violence problem?

Excerpted from "Crime and Violence: It's a Class Question" by Gus Hall, *People's Weekly World*, January 15, 1994. Reprinted with permission.

The Long Island Railroad (LIRR) shooting was only one of the many inhuman crimes occurring across the country in late 1993. [On December 7, 1993, Colin Ferguson shot and killed 6 people and injured 19 others on a commuter train in New York.] Just in the first weeks of December a computer engineer opened fire in an unemployment office in Oxnard, California, killing 4 before he was killed by police, and 2 children were slain in St. Louis. In Petaluma, California, a 12-year-old girl abducted from her bedroom was found dead.

A murder-suicide left three dead in San Diego and a teenage sniper fired randomly at a lunchtime crowd in the Chicago Loop. There were countless other crimes including incidents of battered women and abused children that will never make the headlines, but nonetheless spark fear and anger in communities across our land.

In spite of the shocking statistics, all the talk and half-baked efforts for restricting guns—e.g., exchanging guns for toys or cash—the gun business is booming. There are nearly as many guns in this country as people. In 1992, when the population was 255 million, there were 211 million guns.

Blaming the Victims

There is a debate raging in our country about the crime and gun epidemic. Newsmen, politicians and the "authorities" blame guns, crack, gangs, poor schools, television violence and poverty—and the victims themselves.

On nationwide TV recently New York senator Daniel Moynihan, the infamous advocate of "benign neglect," blamed "teen-age mothers who are having all those illegitimate babies" who grow up to be "unstable and violent." In almost every political debate on crime, racist stereotypes, code-words and themes are injected into the discussion.

One example is President Clinton's racist diatribe on crime delivered in Memphis. The president went public with almost every stereotype and concept of inferiority that blames the victims of poverty and racism. If they would only "pull themselves up by the bootstraps" and put an end to "crime in their own communities," things would get better.

This is official racism that says crime and violence are confined to Black and other minority communities. This is part of the effort to criminalize racially and nationally oppressed peoples with the ideology that drugs, crime and violence, and anti-social behavior are caused by inherited characteristics that produce inferior people.

The crime issue is being used to promote racism and perpetuate racist ideology. Particularly in the LIRR incident the use of racism has become a serious problem in itself.

After the shooting, TV reporters interviewed one of the victims. Answering a reporter's question about the senselessness of the attack, the victim's wife cried out, "We don't just kill Black people. My family didn't kill any Black people. Why did that Black man shoot my husband. Why?" Reporters conducted dozens of such inflammatory interviews.

We can never justify or condone—we condemn—mass murder, or any murder. But at the same time, we have to look for the causes and the circumstances in our society that contribute to such insanity. It is not enough to say that it is insane, although it is at least temporary insanity that pushes a human being to commit such atrocities.

The Roots of the Crisis

Communists start from the premise that it is the capitalist system and U.S. imperialism that is the basic cause of crime and violence, at home and in the world.

In fact, U.S. development, production, research and use of atomic weapons to annihilate innocent men, women and children, the Cold War and the race for nuclear superiority are the ultimate violence. As part of the New World Order, the only superpower is once again menacing the world with the nuclear threat, this time without the restraining counterforce of the Soviet Union.

The causes of this seemingly senselessly violent society elude most of us because those who own and run everything in our society have a stake in making it look as if we are simply a society run amok—a country filled with violent people who have abandoned "family values," "religious guiding principles" and our "duty and obligations" to society.

Thus, it is said, in order to protect the law-abiding citizens the authorities have to toughen the laws, increase police, build more and bigger prisons, sweep the homeless, the jobless and the poor into nightmare shelters or mental institutions and throw people off the welfare rolls and into the street.

The simple truth is that we live under the most violent and criminal social system in history. It is the socioeconomic system that has run amok. In its effort to salvage itself and its profits by tightening all the screws on working people, the poor, the racially and nationally oppressed, it commits the most violent crimes and abuses.

To carry out this effort, monopoly capital maintains a vast army, a national network of penal and criminal control systems, backed up by the force of law. It uses the FBI, the national guard and other enforcement agencies to keep the people under surveillance and under control.

There are huge think-tank institutions, like the Heritage

Foundation, that are paid by the government and corporations to come up with schemes to diffuse militancy and class struggle trade unionism, to destroy the trade unions and slow down the development of class consciousness.

Racism is the weapon of choice of the ruling class. It spares no cost and uses every form of brutality and violence to keep the working class divided. Unity—Black, Brown, white working-class unity—is feared more than almost anything else by Corporate America which uses every form of coercion, manipulation and violence to keep the working class from coming together to fight their common enemy.

A Passion for Violence

American society is gripped by a passion for violence and death that borders on the pathological.

This deeply disturbing trend has not, of course, gone unnoticed. Editorialists, political commentators, cultural critics, religious leaders—all join in a chorus of anguish over violence in America. And many do accurately identify the reasons for the violence epidemic. . . .

Frustrated, angry, hopeless, stressed out—people lash out violently at the individuals they imagine are responsible for their distress, or even randomly at people they don't even know.

While identifying the causes of violence, the commentators are nevertheless at a loss to find a solution for it. It's not because no solution exists. It's because they all—liberal and conservative alike—share an allegiance to the profit economy, an allegiance that is a prerequisite for being a recognized "expert." Intellectually chained to the status quo, they are prohibited from acknowledging that the social breakdown they describe is the inevitable product of the competitive system and can only be reversed by building a new economic system.

New Unionist, March 1993.

There are two main classes in our society. And there are essentially two kinds of crime: the officially sanctioned criminality of Corporate America and its state-monopoly government, including organized crime, the FBI and CIA. There are the racist, anti-Semitic hate groups backed and tolerated by Corporate America to promote and provoke division between peoples.

Then there are the crimes of the working and poor people who for one reason or another lose all hope and commit crimes. Sadly, the crimes of ordinary people are usually committed against each other.

Crime and violence in the United States is a unique problem. There are killings and other crimes of violence elsewhere, but the depth and scope do not compare to the United States. To seek root causes we have to ask: what is there about our society that provokes, promotes and perpetuates criminal behavior?

We live in a society in which the huge, impersonal and all-powerful corporations can throw people out of work, out of their homes and onto the streets, onto welfare, into jails without reason except profits.

The calls for more extreme laws against crimes of violence— for example, former New York governor Mario Cuomo's "three strikes and you're out," the concept of putting a three-time offender in jail for life, while calling for tax giveaways to the rich and real estate interests, but no new jobs—will go nowhere.

When people, especially people and their unions, challenge unjust, anti-labor laws, when they strike and protest bourgeois justice and the legal system, punishment is swift and severe. No one knows this better than the Communist Party, the labor movement and people's movements. . . .

The Gap Between Rich and Poor

There are unique features of capitalism which make people vent their rage against society and those they see as their oppressors. One is the widening gap between the rich and poor in the United States—the widest in the world. Another is hopelessness, which lays the basis for terrible anger, frustration and thus, deviations from socially acceptable and normal behavior.

There are large sectors of people who see no future for themselves. This is especially true for those millions suffering in the ghettos, barrios, reservations and Appalachias of our country. Economic and environmental racism is destroying their lives. Many of our young people see drugs, gangs and anti-social behavior as a way to get back at a system that sees them as expendable.

Alienation, common to all capitalist societies, is unique in the United States. It is the deepest kind of alienation. The description you hear so often to describe alleged murderers is "loners." Hopelessness and anger turns people inward, into brooding loners and potentially violent—against themselves and others. . . .

Economic Mayhem

There can be no solutions or diminishing of these problems of crime, violence and brutality without an approach to the economic destruction of people, families and cities; without attacking the economic and environmental racism that is decimating the lives of 80 million racially and nationally oppressed.

Crime and violence must be put into the framework of U.S.

capitalism and class warfare against the people. Lack of work means instability, fear, anger and frustration. The question of jobs and equality is an emergency one. Until the economic crisis is eased, all kinds of crime and violence will continue and even intensify.

It is impossible to understand what's going on unless we look at everything through the prism of class, the working class and the class struggle. Racism is perpetuated for superprofits. Class division, disunity is fostered to ensure those profits.

For Clinton, the answers to crime and violence are more prison sentences, jails, street sweeps and police. This is no surprise, for Clinton has been backtracking and caving in on every campaign promise he made.

The government takes no responsibility to force the corporations to cease and desist downsizing, privatizing and closing down America. On the contrary, the government promotes it with schemes like NAFTA [North American Free Trade Agreement] and GATT [General Agreement on Tariffs and Trade] agreements that are disasters for the workers of all the countries involved.

The working class has been betrayed by Clinton and Corporate America. The American people have come to expect crime and corruption—especially on Wall Street and Capitol Hill. They have no confidence in the Democratic or Republican parties or in politics in general. They now believe that politicians and their votes are bought and paid for. It will take independent politics, a new people's party of labor and workers—Black, Brown and white—to rebuild trust and confidence in government.

We all know that you have to take the money from where it is—from the corporations and the military budget—to initiate huge "rebuild America" projects and create millions of jobs. To achieve this requires a united working class in struggle.

We cannot speak about crime without connecting it to unemployment and poverty. Whenever there is severe unemployment and poverty, there is crime, drugs and violence. Even still, the great majority of working people, including the unemployed, do not commit crimes.

Crime, like joblessness, is a national disease. When people— any people—lose hope, when poverty and despair is the only view of the future, crime, drugs and violence are the results.

Ultimately, the long-term solution has to be a direct, revolutionary challenge to the capitalist system itself. Because lasting solutions cannot be found within a system in crisis, socialism will inevitably be seen as the only rational, viable, humane way to end class exploitation and oppression.

Crime and violence, inhumanity, competition and dog-eat-dog individualism will be replaced by a sound system that allows the full flowering of every individual's potential: a socialist system.

Periodical Bibliography

The following articles have been selected to supplement the diverse views presented in this chapter.

Nick Alexander	"On the Front Lines in Chicago," *Third Force*, vol. 2, no. 5, November/December 1994.
Natalie Angier	"Elementary, Dr. Watson, the Neurotransmitters Did It," *New York Times*, January 23, 1994.
Charles S. Clark	"TV Violence," *CQ Researcher*, March 26, 1993. Available from 1414 22nd St. NW, Washington, DC 20037.
Theodore Dalrymple	"Beyond Sympathy, Beneath Contempt," *Spectator*, June 20, 1992. Available from 56 Doughty St., London WC1N 2LL, UK.
Paul John Edge	"Paternal Legacy," *Ms.*, May/June 1993.
David Gelman	"The Violence in Our Heads," *Newsweek*, August 2, 1993.
Henry A. Giroux	"White Panic," *Z Magazine*, March 1995.
Walter Goodman	"How Harmful Is Viewing Violence?" *New York Times*, March 22, 1994.
Elizabeth Kolbert	"Television Gets Closer Look as a Factor in Real Violence," *New York Times*, December 14, 1994.
Richard Lacayo	"Violent Reaction," *Time*, June 12, 1995.
Lewis H. Lapham	"Burnt Offerings," *Harper's Magazine*, April 1994.
George Lardner	"Getting Serious About Crime," *Washington Post National Weekly Edition*, November 29–December 5, 1993. Available from 1150 15th St. NW, Washington, DC 20071.
Richard G. Malloy	"Media Violations," *America*, February 6, 1993.
Salim Muwakkil	"Do Genes Cause Crime?" *In These Times*, December 28, 1992.
Ron Nixon	"Crusade Against Gangsta Rap," *Third Force*, vol. 2, no. 2, May/June 1994.
Edward T. Oakes	"Why Has American Society Become So Violent?" *America*, September 5, 1992.

William Raspberry   "Television Violence Begets Real Violence," *Liberal Opinion Week*, February 14, 1994. Available from PO Box 468, Vinton, IA 52349-0468.

Sarah Richardson   "A Violence in the Blood," *Discover*, October 1993.

Brian Siano   "Frankenstein Must Be Destroyed: Chasing the Monster of TV Violence," *Humanist*, January/February 1994.

Chi Chi Sileo   "Violent Offenders Get High on Crime," *Insight*, May 2, 1994. Available from 3600 New York Ave. NE, Washington, DC 20002.

George Sweeting   "Coping with Conflict," *Moody*, February 1994. Available from 820 N. LaSalle Blvd., Chicago, IL 60610.

Nancy Touchette   "Biochemical Factors in Impulsive and Violent Behavior," *Journal of NIH Research*, vol. 6, February 1994. Available from 1444 I St. NW, Suite 1000, Washington, DC 20005.

Peter Tulupman   "Video Games: The School of Hard Knocks, Knives, and Numchaks," *Business and Society Review*, Fall 1993. Available from Management Reports, Inc., 25-13 Old Kings Hwy. N., Suite 107, Darien, CT 06820.

David Wasserman   "Science and Social Harm: Genetic Research into Crime and Violence," *Report from the Institute for Philosophy and Public Policy*, Winter 1995. Available from the University of Maryland, College Park, MD 20742.

Juan Williams   "Violence, Genes, and Prejudice," *Discover*, November 1994.

How Serious a Problem Is Domestic Violence?

Chapter Preface

Domestic violence is usually described by the media and others as male violence against female victims. Advocates for victims of domestic violence often focus on providing shelter and legal assistance for battered women. Some critics, however, contend that this focus on women as victims ignores the fact that men are often victims of domestic violence.

These critics assert that statistics show that husbands are victims of domestic attacks more frequently than are wives. For example, well-known family violence researcher Murray A. Straus of the University of New Hampshire reviewed the National Family Violence Surveys of 1975 and 1985 and concluded that "in both surveys, the rate of wife-to-husband assault was about the same (actually slightly higher) than the husband-to-wife assault rate."

Others disagree with the view that men are equally victimized by domestic violence. While men may often be victims, these commentators argue, they usually do not suffer from the brutal, debilitating, and ongoing violence that many women experience. Instead, they contend, men most often experience minor violence such as slaps and pushes. Even Straus found that violence by men produced a much greater number of injuries than violence by women.

The viewpoints in the following chapter debate the seriousness of domestic violence for both men and women.

"Most experts agree that the battering of women has reached epidemic proportions."

Domestic Violence Against Women Is a Serious Problem

R. Barri Flowers

In the following viewpoint, R. Barri Flowers asserts that domestic violence has been a problem for women throughout history and continues to cause suffering and hardship today. Flowers contends that domestic violence, which affects women of every socioeconomic group, often makes battered women so desperate that they actually kill their abusers to prevent further abuse. Flowers is a criminologist and social scientist from Lake Oswego, Oregon, and is the author of *The Victimization and Exploitation of Women and Children*, from which this viewpoint was taken.

As you read, consider the following questions:

1. What historical situations does Flowers discuss to demonstrate that domestic violence has long existed?
2. According to the author, how does a battered woman typically view herself?
3. What are the three stages in the cycle of violence, according to the author, and how do they apply to wife abuse?

From: *The Victimization and Exploitation of Women and Children: A Study of Physical, Mental, and Sexual Maltreatment in the United States* by R. Barri Flowers; ©1994 by Ronald B. Flowers. Reprinted by permission of McFarland & Company, Inc., Publishers, Jefferson, NC 28640.

Perhaps the classic symbolization of the victimization of women is the battered woman. Not only have women been the victims of abusive husbands or boyfriends throughout history, but this form of victimization and domestic violence continues to be amongst the most hidden and painfully prevalent issues of our time. A recent study of domestic violence found women to be victims of intimates at a rate three times as often as men. In this viewpoint, we will examine the problem of battered women and its implications for women and our society.

A Dark History of Wife Abuse

Wife battering has been in existence since ancient times, often thought of as an acceptable and even expected practice. Historical literature is replete with examples of the cruelties inflicted upon women by their spouses. One article recounts the "scalding death of Fausta ordered by her husband, the Emperor Constantine, which was to serve as a precedent for the next fourteen centuries."

Friedrich Engels postulated that wife abuse began "with the emergence of the first monogamous pairing relationship which replaced group marriage and the extended family of early promiscuous societies." Another theory advanced that the historical condoning of violence against women is rooted in the "subjugation and oppression of women through the male partner exercising his authority as head of the family."

In western society, wife battering has flourished since the Middle Ages. The rampant violence towards wives in Europe came to America with the colonists. "During one period, a husband was permitted by law to beat his wife so long as his weaponry was not bigger than his thumb." Such laws remained on the books until the end of the nineteenth century.

Defining the Battered Woman

For many, a battered woman continues to reflect physical abuse of some nature. One study, by Mildred D. Pagelow, defined battered women as

> adult women who were intentionally physically abused in ways that caused pain or injury, or who were forced into involuntary action or restrained by force from voluntary action by adult men with whom they have or had established relationships, usually involving sexual intimacy.

With advances in understanding relationships and the effects of behavior, the definition of the battered woman has broadened in recent years. The term now reflects not only physical abuse of women such as beatings with fists or other objects, choking, whipping, but also psychological or emotional abuse, including threats, insults, intimidation and degradation. The perpetrators of battering include not only husbands, ex-husbands, or lovers, but children and grandchildren as well.

Referring to battered women has also taken on many now common phrases such as "the battered wife or woman syndrome," "wife abuse," "woman battering," and "conjugal violence." Most important is the recognition that women can be victimized by their mates in many ways, each of which can be devastating to the woman's physical and emotional well being.

Society Sanctions Domestic Violence

For too long societies have behaved as if they were helpless to stop the violence done to women in the home. Worse, societies have sanctioned the violence, by blaming the women ("Why did she stay?" "What did she do to provoke him?"), by excusing men's actions, by saying that he had the right to physically chastise "his" woman, by taking too little action or none at all, by leaving women with nowhere to turn, no place to go, no protection.

Marcia Ann Gillespie, *Ms.*, September/October 1994.

While most experts agree that the battering of women has reached epidemic proportions, researchers have found that women actually reporting this occurrence is far less frequent. A recent study estimated that only 1 out of every 270 incidents of wife abuse is ever reported to law enforcement. In a study of women victims of battering, Denver psychologist Lenore Walker, who has done extensive research on the subject and authored several books on family violence, indicated that less than 10 percent ever reported serious violence to the police. The severe underreporting of domestically violated women can generally be attributed to the following reasons:

- Victim denial.
- Protection of the batterer.
- Disavowal techniques to keep it in the family.
- Silent desire to be abused.
- Fear of alternatives (i.e., continued abuse, loss of support).
- Shame.

Despite the cloak of silence that greatly hampers efforts at discovering and assisting battered women, researchers have found the problem to be staggering. Over a five-year period (1987–1991), the *National Crime Victimization Survey* found that 2.9 million women were the victims of violence by intimates, for an average of 572,032 victimizations per year. Diana Russell, a professor of sociology and author of *Rape in Marriage*, recently completed a survey of sexual assault of San Francisco women.

Twenty-one percent of the respondents who had ever been married reported being physically abused by a husband at some stage in their lives. According to a National Family Violence Survey conducted by sociologists Murray Straus and Richard Gelles, in 1985 1.7 million women were seriously physically abused by husbands or partners.

Estimates of battered women have soared as high as 1 woman out of every 2. Social scientists contend that every year as many as 2 million women in the United States are beaten by their spouses. According to FBI statistics, woman battering is one of the most frequently occurring crimes in the nation, with a beating taking place every 18 seconds. In 1992, 29 percent of the women murdered in the United States were killed by husbands or boyfriends.

Who Is the Battered Woman?

The popular myth is that battered women are of the lower class, undereducated, and minority segments of our population. However, these groups are overrepresented in the statistics because of their greater dependency (and therefore visibility) on society's institutions for their basic survival needs.

Recent studies indicate that as many as 80 percent of the cases of battering have gone undiagnosed because of the more privileged environment in which they occur. Women of every age, race, ethnicity, and social class are being battered by their husbands and lovers. What these women have in common is a low self-esteem that is usually related to repeated victimization. For some victims, this characteristic is limited only to their relationship with men; for others, low self-esteem pervades their entire existence.

Battered women typically view themselves and all women as inferior to men, have a tendency to cope with anger through denial or turning it inward, and suffer from depression, psychosomatic illnesses, and feelings of guilt. According to Terry Davidson, author of *Conjugal Crime: Understanding and Changing the Wife Beating Pattern*, victims of spousal abuse "may exemplify society's old image of ideal womanhood—submissive, religious, nonassertive, accepting of whatever the husband's life brings. . . . The husband comes first for these women, who perceive themselves as having little control over many areas of their own lives.". . .

Why Do Women Remain with an Abusive Mate?

The question of why physically or emotionally battered women tolerate mistreatment has been probed perhaps more than any other question associated with wife abuse. On the surface it would seem to walk away from this anguish would be as simple as the front door. Some women do just that. And yet all too often, escaping an abusive spouse or boyfriend is far more difficult to do. There are a number of typical reasons ascribed for this, including:

- *Fear*—of the abuser, being humiliated, having others find out, being left alone.
- *Finances*—losing money, the house, standard of living.
- *Children*—losing financial support for them and a father.
- *Social stigma*—shame, embarrassment, being labeled.
- *Guilt*—for bringing about the abuse or in believing that they are too needed by the abuser to leave.
- *Role expectations*—that abuse is a normal part of relationships; often based on learned experiences in childhood.

A cycle theory of violence has been developed by Lenore Walker as to why women remain in habitually abusive relationships. The tension reduction theory advances that three specific phases exist in a recurring cycle of battering: (1) tension building, (2) the acute battering incident, and (3) loving contrition.

The tension stage consists of a series of minor or verbal attacks. The woman manages to cope with these episodes by minimizing their significance and/or severity and using anger reduction techniques. She seeks to appease the batterer by doing whatever is necessary to calm him down, in the process becoming even more submissive.

The second stage, the acute battering incident, is characterized by "the uncontrollable discharge of the tensions that have been built up during stage one." Typically the batterer unleashes both physical and verbal aggression upon the wife, which she is unable to prevent. It is in this phase of the cycle that most injuries, sometimes severe, take place.

The third stage is that of loving contrition or the "honeymoon period." The abuser becomes at once charming, loving, apologetic, kind, remorseful—in short, he takes a 180 degree turn and is willing to do anything to be forgiven. "Suddenly he's giving her gifts, good sex, pampering," says marriage and family counselor Laura Schlessinger. "She wants to believe he's really sorry and that he will change this time. In the glow of all this attention, she does believe it." It is this contrition stage that provides the reinforcement for the woman remaining in the relationship. However, almost inevitably, stage one tension building resumes and a new cycle takes place.

Self-Defense for the Battered Woman

For many battered women the only means of dealing with an abusive mate is to strike back violently. There are few statistics on male victims of spouse abuse, yet some researchers have found the incidence of female batterers to be significant. Robert

Langley and Richard Levy estimated that 12 million men are physically abused by their wives in the United States during some point in their marriage. Suzanne Steinmetz, author of an article titled "The Battered Husband Syndrome," estimated that 280,000 men in this country are battered each year. Another study of spouse abuse findings approximated that 2 million husbands, compared to 1.8 million wives, had experienced at least one of the more serious forms of spouse abuse.

This data notwithstanding, few believe that female batterers can measure up to male batterers in numbers or severity of violence. Rebecca Dobash and Russell Dobash found the ratio of male-to-female spouse abuse to be 66 to 1.

Murders in Self-Defense In relatively rare instances, the battered woman is driven to the ultimate measure of self-defense— killing her abusive mate. Recent studies show that wives constitute more than half of the murdered spouses annually, with husbands being 6 to 7 times more likely to kill than be killed. Female perpetrators of spouse homicide have been documented. In a study of homicides and attempted homicides by females in Hungary, it was found that 40 percent of the victims were husbands, common-law husbands, and lovers. A similar finding was made by J. Totman in a study of 120 female murders in the United States, where 40 percent of the women had killed husbands and lovers. A study of females imprisoned for murder revealed that they were the sole perpetrators in 77 percent of the homicides, and in more than half of the homicides, the victim was an intimate or family member. According to FBI figures, 4 percent of the male murder victims in the United States in 1992 were killed by a wife or girlfriend.

Recent years have seen high profile cases of women killing their husbands or lovers with the motive often being self-defense after years of being the victim of spouse abuse. In a study of women charged with murder in Los Angeles County, Nancy Kaser-Boyd and Michael Maloney found that 42 percent of the women had killed a spouse or boyfriend. Three-quarters of the women cited years of physical and psychological abuse at the hands of the victims. Another study of females imprisoned in a California penitentiary for murder found that 28 of the 30 women convicted of killing their spouses had been victims of wife battering.

In *The Battered Woman Syndrome*, Walker gives a perspective on battered women turned murderers:

> Most women who killed their batterers have little memory of any cognitive processes other than an intense focus on their own survival. . . . Their description of the final incident indicates that they separate those angry feelings by the psychological process of a dissociative state. . . . This desperate attempt at remaining unaware of their own unacceptable feelings is a

measure of just how dangerous they perceive their situation. They fear showing anger will cause their own death, and indeed it could as batterers cannot tolerate the woman's expression of anger.

The battered woman who kills her abuser is often so consumed with hopelessness, helplessness, despair, and low self-esteem that she is unable to think beyond the desperation of the moment until the deed is done and the ramifications already set in motion as a consequence. In the article "Women and Homicide," writer Elissa Benedek speaks of the point of no return typical of many battered homicidal women: "The battered wife has turned to social agencies, police, prosecutors, friends, ministers, and family, but they have not offered meaningful support or advice. . . . Abused women who have murdered their spouses reveal that they feel that homicide was the only alternative left to them."

Sadly, battered women who kill their mates then become further victims as they often face murder charges, imprisonment, loss of their children, and lack of sympathy and understanding from the very social agencies that abandoned them in their hour of need.

Breaking the Cycle of Battering

Short of killing their abusers, breaking the cycle of abusive treatment at the hands of husbands and lovers is perhaps the most difficult aspect of the battered woman's syndrome. Psychologist Ann McClenahan explains: "The longer a woman stays and the harder she works to make the marriage work, the harder it is to leave."

Battered women's shelters have been established throughout the country as a first step in escaping the abuse and abuser. These shelters offer refuge, counseling, and protection for battered women. More efforts are needed to get abused women to use such facilities for their safety and more shelters are sorely needed.

Criminal justice system agencies are better equipped in the nineties to deal with issues of family violence, and abusive men are more likely to serve time if charges are pressed. Nevertheless, law enforcement continues to fall short as an effective intervention to domestic violence, particularly wife abuse, which is often still looked upon as a private spousal matter. Most such cases fail to come to the attention of law enforcement, while laws are inconsistent from state to state. In fact, battered women must often take the initiative to escape the violence which, unfortunately, many victims are unable or unwilling to do.

> *"The view that domestic violence is largely the doing of a minority of thugs and sociopaths is anathema to the highly politicized battered-women's advocacy movement."*

The Problem of Domestic Violence Has Been Exaggerated

Cathy Young

Cathy Young is the vice president of the Women's Freedom Network, a Washington, D.C.–based organization that discusses gender-related issues from the point of view that men and women share much common ground. In the following viewpoint, Young argues that many of the statistics used by advocates for battered women have been inflated to make the problem appear more serious than it really is. She contends that these advocates also ignore the incidence of women's violence toward men.

As you read, consider the following questions:

1. What are some of the statistics the author discusses? How does she follow up on the claims made in the media?
2. How does Young answer the question, "Is there an epidemic of domestic violence in America?"
3. What does the author claim is the agenda of advocates for battered women?

Cathy Young, "Abused Statistics," *National Review*, August 1, 1994; ©1994 by National Review, Inc., 150 E. 35th St., New York, NY 10016. Reprinted by permission.

It did not take long for advocacy groups and some commentators to claim that the O. J. Simpson case [in which Simpson was accused of murdering his former wife, Nicole Simpson] could do for domestic violence what Anita Hill did for sexual harassment [Hill sparked controversy in 1991 when she testified that Supreme Court nominee Clarence Thomas had harassed her years earlier]. If the Anita Hill analogy refers to gender politics eclipsing truth, common sense, and journalistic skepticism, then that is exactly what's happening.

We are barraged with horrendous figures. CNN's Sheryl Potts said at the end of a 3.5-minute segment on wife-abuse, "While you were watching this, 13 women were severely beaten by someone who claims to love them" (i.e., one every 15 seconds). According to the Associated Press, "4 million to 6 million women are beaten [each year]. That means once every 5 seconds . . . a woman is punched or kicked . . . or held down and pummeled." On *Crossfire*, Miami radio talk-show host Pat Stevens upped the count to 60 million by reasoning that "there are 6 million reported cases," and "the FBI estimates" that only 1 in 10 is reported. This went unchallenged.

One AP report ran somewhat counter to the general tone, noting that murders of women by male partners had dropped 18 per cent since the late 1970s; but it went on to temper this unduly optimistic message with the assertion that non-fatal violence was up: "From 1980 to 1990, federal figures show, reports of domestic assault . . . rose from 2 million to 4 million, according to Rita Smith, coordinator for the National Coalition Against Domestic Violence."

Statistics

Where do the numbers come from? One source for the 4-to-6-million figure is a 1993 Commonwealth Fund study, which included such acts as shoving, slapping, and throwing things in its definition of battering. The statistic of a woman beaten every 15 seconds is derived from the 1985 National Family Violence Survey by University of New Hampshire researchers Murray Straus and Richard Gelles, which estimated that about 1.8 million American women each year suffer at least one incident of "severe violence" by a partner—a punch, a kick, an assault with an object. But only 7 per cent of the victims required medical care. A study published in *Archives of Internal Medicine* in 1992 found that, based on reports by wives in marital therapy, 48 per cent of "severe marital aggression" by husbands caused no injury, and 31 per cent caused only a "superficial bruise." While these are still reprehensible acts, most people visualize something very different when they think of "severe violence."

And the reports of domestic assault rising from 2 to 4 million

138

a year over a decade? The figure, said Rita Smith, came from the Justice Department's Bureau of Justice Statistics. Were these assaults reported to police? "Either that, or to medical personnel," said Miss Smith. "I'm not exactly sure how they gathered it, but it was one of the statistics they put out in some publication." What publication? She didn't recall.

An information specialist at the BJS knew nothing of such figures. Most of the Bureau's publications are based on the National Crime Victimization Survey, which puts the number of female victims of assaults by partners at about 470,000 a year.

Shocking Claims

Another shocking claim was made in a *MacNeil/Lehrer NewsHour* segment by Connie McCall of Rainbow Services, a batteredwomen's assistance group in Los Angeles: "Over 50 per cent of women admitted to emergency rooms are admitted for an injury caused by a partner." In a pre–O.J. Simpson speech in March 1994, Health and Human Services Secretary Donna Shalala gave a more modest estimate: "In our hospital emergency rooms, some 20 to 30 per cent of women arrive because of physical abuse by their partner."

These numbers (whose implausibility ought to be evident to anyone who has ever been to a hospital) come in part from studies in which medical charts were reviewed and most unexplained or inadequately explained injuries to women were reclassified as related to abuse, and in part from a 1984 study based on questionnaires distributed to emergency-room patients in a Detroit hospital. About 25 per cent of the female patients answered "yes" to the statement, "At some time my boyfriend/husband or girlfriend/wife has pushed me around, hit me, kicked me, or hurt me"; so did about 20 per cent of the men. Most of the abuse did not seem to be directly related to the emergency-room visit. Moreover, a high percentage of the subjects were poor, unemployed, and cohabiting without marriage—factors strongly associated with the risk of domestic violence.

The same fallacy of projecting data obtained by studying the urban poor to the population at large is responsible for another widely reported figure—cited, for instance, in *Newsweek*'s July 4, 1994 cover story on battered women: "[I]n 1992 the U.S. Surgeon General ranked abuse by husbands and partners as the leading cause of injuries to women aged 15 to 44." In fact, in a 1992 column in the *Journal of the American Medical Association* on the medical response to domestic abuse, then-Surgeon General Antonia Novello mentioned that "One study found violence to be . . . the leading cause of injuries to women ages 15 through 44." This refers to *all* violence, not just violence by male partners. The article in which the finding was reported, titled "A Population-

Based Study of Injuries in Inner City Women," examines emergency-room visits by women "in a poor, urban, black community in western Philadelphia."

Domestic Murder Statistics

And how many women are killed by their current or former mates? CNN has cited the figure of 4,000 a year—even though the FBI statistic is 1,300 to 1,400. The higher number comes from activist groups and includes, Miss Smith told me, "a lot of suspicious deaths that aren't [officially] classified as a homicide." The higher the better: on *This Week with David Brinkley*, Lynne Gold-Bikin, incoming chairman of the American Bar Association's family-law section, claimed that "some 25 per cent of women who are abused ultimately get killed by their husbands." If, as *Newsweek* says, "1 woman in 4 will be physically assaulted in her lifetime," this would put a woman's risk of being murdered by a partner at 1 in 16. In fact, it's closer to 1 in 1,000.

A Media "Epidemic"

Numbers fed to the media are not just routinely exaggerated and massaged into an "epidemic" of violence; they are presented as somehow very different from the rest of the violence in a violent society: They are offered up as evidence of a gender war that implicates men in general, and the whole society, in the battering conducted by out-of-control males.

These days, it's fairly routine to see journalism endorsing the radical theory of domestic violence as gender warfare. Domestic violence can be portrayed as a war against women, but only if a lot of evidence is suppressed or explained away. . . .

The radical view of domestic violence (it's the patriarchy in action, oppressing women) simply doesn't fit the accumulating evidence. It's a highly ideological overlay, dividing the world unrealistically into brutish males and innocent, passive females. How long will this wrongheaded oppressor-victim framework dominate press coverage of the issue?

John Leo, *U.S. News & World Report*, July 11, 1994.

A widely cited statistic—which appeared in Sheryl Potts's CNN report—is that "women who leave their batterers are at a 75 per cent greater risk of being killed by the batterer than those who stay." This information was attributed to the NCADV; a brochure issued by the organization cites "Barbara Hart, 1988," as the source. When I asked Miss Smith about this, she said a bit hesitantly, "Barbara Hart is an attorney with the Pennsylvania Coalition Against Domestic Violence—and I have recently talked to her and she said, 'I didn't say that.' So, the figure—whether or not it's 75 per cent, I don't know. [But] most of the women who are murdered are either separated or in the process of leaving when they die." She assumed that all these women had been battered in the marriage. However, a number of experts such as criminologist Lawrence Sherman, president of the Crime Control Institute and author of *Policing Domestic Violence*, dispute the "escalation" theory. Sherman's study in Milwaukee over nearly two years revealed that in 33 domestic murders, 32 couples had no prior police record of battery—and there was 1 homicide among the roughly 6,500 couples with such records.

Epidemic Proportions?

Is there an epidemic of domestic violence in America? One could say that we have an epidemic of violence in general, and for all the talk about doctors and executives who beat their wives, domestic violence tends to affect primarily the same segments of society as street crime. Men and, to a lesser extent, women guilty of violence in the home are also much more likely than other people to commit violent acts outside the family. Yet the view that domestic violence is largely the doing of a minority of thugs and sociopaths is anathema to the highly politicized battered-women's advocacy movement. An NCADV pamphlet makes this clear: "A feminist-based analysis of battering [shifts] from a focus on the 'pathology' of individuals or families to the particular social policies, norms, and practices which tolerate woman-abuse."

The theme of supposed tolerance for woman-battering in our culture is reflected in the infamous tale of the "rule of thumb," repeated by Cokie Roberts on *This Week with David Brinkley*: "The rule of thumb, the expression we use . . . that was the size of the stick that was acceptable to beat your wife with under common law." Yet, as the scholar Christina Hoff Sommers shows in *Who Stole Feminism?* this origin of the phrase "rule of thumb" is a myth. While two American courts in the nineteenth century alluded to such an "ancient law" they never invoked it as a standard. The first legal code enacted by the Massachusetts colonists in 1652 *prohibited* wife-beating.

Women Batter, Too

Despite attempts to find the roots of wife-battering in the power of physical chastisement once given to husbands by law, few serious researchers believe that domestic violence is primarily a way to maintain patriarchal control. Even feminist scholar Elizabeth Schneider of Brooklyn Law School concedes, in a 1992 *New York University Law Review* article, that the "traditional model" of battering as a means of maintaining male dominance "is thrown into question when the violent partner is a woman, or the victim is a man." Though Professor Schneider is referring to same-sex couples, a wealth of research (notably the Straus-Gelles studies) has found that wives and girlfriends are the aggressors at least half the time, though they are five to six times less likely to cause physical damage. (On one *MacNeil/Lehrer* report, an L.A. police officer said that he had been on many calls where the woman was the assailant; but the panel discussion following the segment focused solely on male batterers and female victims.

For every two women killed by a male partner, there is at least one man killed by a wife or girlfriend—not including cases dismissed as self-defense. It is interesting to recall that in 1989, when San Diego housewife Betty Broderick fatally shot her ex-husband and his new wife after harassing them for months, the incident was not seen as emblematic of the epidemic of domestic violence by women. Indeed, Mrs. Broderick got a great deal of sympathy as a wronged wife (she claimed that Dan Broderick's alimony payments of only $16,000 *a month* amounted to a white-collar version of battery), and her first trial ended with a hung jury. Male violence toward women fits into the fashionable larger theme of oppression; female violence toward men does not.

With remarkable lack of compunction about exploiting a horrible tragedy for political gain, members of the National Organization for Women, with Patricia Schroeder and other congresswomen on hand, rallied on Capitol Hill to urge passage of the Violence Against Women Act—which, among other things, would redefine wife-beating as a gender-based hate crime and mandate sensitivity training for judges. (In Massachusetts, a similar media frenzy has already led to a situation in which, former Massachusetts Bar Association President Elaine Epstein wrote in 1993, "it has become essentially impossible to effectively represent a man against whom any allegation of domestic violence has been made.")

Beyond these immediate political goals, the advocates' real agenda is to promote their view that American women are routinely terrorized by men who are intent on keeping them subjugated. Why not just say that 5 out of 4 women are battered by men, and be done with it? Given their track records, the media would probably buy that one, too.

"Both the male and the female are bound in their dance of mutual destructiveness, their incapacity for intimacy and appreciation of differences."

Domestic Violence Against Men Is a Problem

Judith Sherven and James Sniechowski

Men are not alone in violently assaulting their mates, argue Judith Sherven and James Sniechowski in the following viewpoint. According to the authors, women assault their husbands in equal or greater numbers than men abuse their wives—a fact that undermines the myth that only men are violent. Sherven and Sniechowski contend that society should acknowledge that women share the responsibility for domestic violence. Sherven, a clinical psychologist, and Sniechowski, who holds a Ph.D. in human behavior, operate a consulting firm that works with corporations on gender issues.

As you read, consider the following questions:

1. Why are women much more likely than men to report being abused, according to Sherven and Sniechowski?
2. According to the authors, why is it so difficult for Americans to accept the fact that women abuse men?
3. What conclusions do the authors draw from their discussion of the "battered spouse syndrome"?

Judith Sherven and James Sniechowski, "Women Are Responsible, Too," *Los Angeles Times,* June 21, 1994. Reprinted by permission.

Once again, the myth of the evil, brutal male perpetrator and the perfect, innocent female victim is being broadcast and written about as gospel. The discussion is national. The rage and sorrow, palpable. Only when we come to terms with the fact that domestic violence is the responsibility of both men and women, however, can we put a stop to this horrible nightmare.

Mutual Destructiveness

Domestic violence is not an either-or phenomenon. It is not either the man's fault or the woman's. It is a both-and problem. Both the male and the female are bound in their dance of mutual destructiveness, their incapacity for intimacy and appreciation of differences. They need each other to perpetuate personal and collective dramas of victimization and lovelessness, and so, regrettably, neither can leave.

This is a very untidy idea for people who have grown up with movies in which the "good guy" triumphs over the "bad guy" and rescues the damsel from distress. But to tackle the plague of domestic violence, we must alter our perspective. Facts:

• Forty-one percent of spousal murders are committed by wives, according to a special report entitled, "Murder in Families," issued by the U.S. Department of Justice, Bureau of Justice Statistics in July 1994.

• The 1985 National Family Violence Survey, funded by the National Institute of Mental Health and supported by many other surveys, revealed that women and men were physically abusing one another in roughly equal numbers. Wives reported that they were more often the aggressors. Using weapons to make up for physical disadvantage, they were not just fighting back.

• While 1.8 million women annually suffered one or more assaults from a husband or boyfriend, 2 million men were assaulted by a wife or girlfriend, according to a 1986 study on U.S. family violence published in the *Journal of Marriage and Family*. That study also found that 54% of all violence termed "severe" was by women.

• The *Journal for the National Assn. of Social Workers* found in 1986 that among teen-agers who date, girls were violent more frequently than boys.

• Mothers abuse their children at a rate approaching twice that of fathers, according to state child-protective service agencies surveyed by the Children's Rights Coalition.

• Because men have been taught to "take it like a man" and are ridiculed when they reveal they have been battered by women, women are nine times more likely to report their abusers to the authorities.

In 1988, R.L. McNeeley, a professor at the School of Social Welfare of the University of Wisconsin, published "The Truth

About Domestic Violence: A Falsely Framed Issue" [in *Social Work*], again revealing the level of violence against men by women. Such facts, though, are "politically incorrect." Even 10 years earlier, Susan Steinmetz, director of the Family Research Institute at Indiana University–Purdue University received threats of harm to her children from radical women's groups after she published "The Battered Husband Syndrome" [in *Victimology*].

Why are we so surprised and appalled that men hit and abuse women who are physically smaller when women regularly hit and abuse small children?

Why are we, as a culture, loath to expose the responsibility of women in domestic abuse? Why do we cling to the pure and virginal image of the "sweet young thing" and the "damsel in distress"? If we are sincere about change, we must acknowledge the truth: Women are part and parcel of domestic violence.

Physical Assaults by Wives

Women initiate and carry out physical assaults on their partners as often as men do. . . . Despite the much lower probability of physical injury resulting from attacks by women, assaults by women are a serious social problem, just as it would be if men "only" slapped their wives or "only" slapped female fellow employees and produced no injury. One of the main reasons "minor" assaults by women are such an important problem is that they put women in danger of much more severe retaliation by men. They also help perpetuate the implicit cultural norms that make the marriage license a hitting license. . . . To end "wife beating," it is essential for women also to end the seemingly "harmless" pattern of slapping, kicking, or throwing things at male partners who persist in some outrageous behavior and "won't listen to reason."

Murray A. Straus in *Current Controversies on Family Violence*, 1993.

Why does our culture refuse to hold women as well as men accountable for their participation in domestic violence? All of such women's behavior, whether perpetrator or victim, is understood and passed off as the byproduct of socialization or poor economic status. On the other hand, men are held fully accountable for all of their behavior—despite the tough-guy stereotype all boys are encouraged to embody and the abuse many bear as a "normal and loving" part of their upbringing.

Some will argue that women fall into "spousal abuse syndrome," in which female passivity is explained as the result of the male brainwashing the female into believing that she is the cause of his violence. Consequently, she is powerless to alter the situation. But the truth is that all females receive some form of the following lessons: "You must cater to a man's ego," "You're nothing without a man" and "It's just as easy to love a rich man."

Girls often acquire this garbage from insecure mothers who believe that they are doing what is best for their daughters. If women are not expected to think and act for themselves, if their self-esteem is in shambles and their dependency is characterized as "feminine," the fault cannot be laid at the feet of men.

None of this is intended to exonerate O.J. Simpson [who was accused of murdering his former wife, Nicole Simpson, in June 1994]. If he is guilty of the murders with which he has been charged, he must answer for his actions. The point is that, in the reaction to this sensational case, we do ourselves a grave disservice to slip into a gender-biased frenzy, vilifying and accusing only men as abusers.

The women's movement claims its goal to be equal rights for women. If that is so, then women must share responsibility for their behavior and their contribution to domestic violence. Otherwise, we remain in a distortion that overshadows the truth. Only the truth will show us the way out of the epidemic of violence that is destroying our families and our nation.

"In their rush to correct the record [on domestic violence], some . . . spokesmen go overboard, presenting information that is frankly bogus."

The Problem of Domestic Violence Against Men Is Exaggerated

Ellis Cose

The 1994 murder of Nicole Brown, O.J. Simpson's former wife, raised the issue of domestic violence in the American media. Many critics subsequently argued that the media were exaggerating the incidence of domestic violence against women and claimed that women were as abusive as men in domestic conflicts. In the following viewpoint, Ellis Cose, a contributing editor for *Newsweek*, asserts that those who have argued that husbands are as abused as wives are misapplying the statistics on husband abuse to make it appear more frequent than it really is.

As you read, consider the following questions:

1. How have men's advocates responded to the O.J. Simpson case, according to Cose?
2. According to the author, what statistics have been exaggerated by men's advocates?
3. What does Cose suggest would be the best strategy for both men's and women's advocates to address domestic violence?

Though the O.J. Simpson case [in which Simpson was accused of murdering his former wife, Nicole Simpson] put marital violence on virtually every editor's agenda, the leaders of what is sometimes called the men's movement are not particularly happy with the result. Coverage has focused too much, they say, on evil male perpetrators and innocent female victims. To read the papers, Nicole Simpson is Everywoman, and O.J. Simpson is Everyman. So, taking a cue from women's rights groups, the men's advocates have taken the offensive, putting forth statistics and anecdotes to argue that for every victimized female there exists a suffering, battered male.

Mel Feit, director of the National Center for Men, contends that men have been too silent for too long. He believes battered men are treated with no more respect (by either the press or the public) than abused women were 15 or 20 years ago. One-sided coverage, he argues, only aggravates the problem it supposedly aspires to illuminate.

Bogus Information

Yet in their rush to correct the record, some of these spokesmen go overboard, presenting information that is frankly bogus. Many advocates insist, for instance, that women are as murderous as men—"half of spousal murders are committed by wives, a statistic that has been stable over time," declared a recent op-ed article in the *Los Angeles Times*. In fact, according to FBI statistics, the odds are nearly 2.4 times more likely that a husband will kill his wife than that she will kill him. In 1992, 1,432 women were killed by their "intimate" male partners; 623 men were killed by their female partners.

Men's activists are on firmer ground when they point to a 1985 study, funded by the National Institute of Mental Health, that found women to be as physically abusive as men. But even those results must be interpreted with care. That finding applies primarily, said one NIMH psychologist, to "moderate aggression" such as pushing and shoving. The "severe" aggression likely to land someone in a hospital is much more characteristic of men.

This does not mean that women are angels. David Gremillion, a University of North Carolina physician with a practice in Raleigh, North Carolina, says in most cases he sees "both partners are violent." In some instances (particularly involving elderly patients, or young men weakened by the AIDS virus), the female caretaker is the batterer. A new analysis by the Bureau of Justice Statistics found that, among blacks, wives and husbands did indeed kill each other at roughly equal rates. It also found that women were more prone than men to kill their offspring, and significantly more inclined to kill sons than daughters.

Nonetheless, the image of hordes of women wielding guns, knives, broomsticks or brass knuckles to terrorize their husbands is likely a fantasy. Certainly, some women resemble that description. Patricia Overberg, director of the Antelope Valley Domestic Violence Council in Lancaster, California, has counseled a few of them. And she runs the only shelter in America, she believes, that accepts abused men and women alike. Only five men have stayed there in the past three years. Fear of ridicule, she suspects, has kept the numbers down.

Twisting Statistics

The weeks following O.J. Simpson's arrest for murder in July 1994 witnessed an explosion of debate about domestic violence. . . . Sadly, much of the debate has been sullied by the willingness of the political right to engage in wild misrepresentations. Some of the people engaged in this process also bring their credibility as teachers and scholars to the exchange. To find academics presenting skewed information to the public casts doubt on the whole enterprise of scholarship, a doubt that will last long after the current debate is over. . . .

Regardless of one's politics, we must ask ourselves whether the truth of gender relations is so terrible that it must be concealed with a curtain of lies.

Linda Hirshman, *Los Angeles Times*, July 31, 1994.

George Gilliland is one man who refuses to be cowed by the prospect of mockery. In December 1993, in a three-story building in St. Paul, Minnesota, he opened the only battered men's shelter in the country. By his count, 54 men have already used the facility. It is worth noting, however, that Gilliland is not your typical saint. He's had his own domestic troubles: judges have issued orders of protection against him. A grown son told the *St. Paul Pioneer Press* that Gilliland beat him as a child. And he was convicted of disorderly conduct on the complaint of two female domestic-abuse workers who claim he threatened them.

Gilliland sees conspiracy in the criticisms. The current raft of charges, he says, come from enemies out to discredit him, an unethical press and a vengeful son. As for the orders of protection, he scoffs, "The last I knew I had about 13 of these things [filed against him]. . . . What the media doesn't say, though . . . is that I turned around and also filed for orders of protection. And those were also put into effect against the same people that applied for them against me."

Despite the controversy swirling around him, Gilliland does seem to have done some good. "Pascal" (who asked not to be identified) lived in the shelter for several weeks in 1994. He was desperate to escape a cocaine-abusing girlfriend who pummelled him without provocation, he said. He was grateful that Gilliland provided a sanctuary for him and his 3-year-old daughter. "It gave me a chance to ease my mind," he says.

Distortion Doesn't Help

Men's groups are on to something important when they argue for a broader dialogue on domestic abuse. As Judith Sherven, a psychologist in Los Angeles, observed, "We're talking about . . . dynamics that both people bring to the experience that results in violence." In such cases, simply branding the man a batterer solves nothing. The couple (or perhaps the entire family) needs help to climb out of a morass of mutually reinforcing pathologies. A dialogue that distorts the facts, on either side, however, is not likely to provide them with that help.

"We need to focus on real victims [of domestic violence], irrespective of gender."

Domestic Violence Affects Both Men and Women

Tish Durkin

In the following viewpoint, Tish Durkin contends that the media have perpetuated the myth that women are becoming increasingly violent toward men. Durkin contends that women actually suffer far more from domestic abuse than do men. But she also asserts that women's abuse of men is a legitimate problem that should be addressed seriously and not sensationalized by the media. Durkin is a contributing editor for *Mademoiselle*, a monthly magazine for women.

As you read, consider the following questions:

1. How does Durkin describe the mythical "violent femme"?
2. According to the author, how should Murray Straus's statistics on domestic violence be interpreted?
3. How do the rates of abuse perpetrated by women compare to those of abuse perpetrated by men, according to the U.S. Justice Department statistics cited by Durkin?

Tish Durkin, "The Myth of the Violent Femme," *Mademoiselle*, April 1994. Reprinted with permission.

A mousy housewife cuts off the penis of her sleeping husband, and the story makes headlines worldwide. Lorena Bobbitt of Manassas, Virginia, was acquitted of the charge of malicious wounding, but it is the act itself that no one can forget. No wonder men everywhere have been sitting with their knees together ever since.

Meanwhile, rumors flew about an alleged separation of Shannen Doherty and her husband, Ashley Hamilton, which they denied. With her history of being accused of assault, Doherty remains the national poster girl for female aggression: Men love her, leave her, and some take restraining orders out against her . . . or so we read in *People*.

Call it the year of the armed woman: In 1993, physically abusive female characters starred on television to great success. On one episode of the Emmy-award-winning series *Picket Fences*, a male calculus teacher was date-raped by a young woman wielding a hot iron. The CBS Tuesday Movie *Murder of Innocence* had a highly rated story line in which a wife guns down her husband. The huge audience response echoed similarly high sales of videos depicting violent women, from knife-wielding Glenn Close to ice pick–packing Sharon Stone.

What does it all mean?

The Violent Femme

She can be either fictitious or flesh and blood; she can use her fists, a gun or knife to maim or kill a man in a love- or sex-related situation. One thing is certain: At a time when crime and violence are among the top concerns of Americans, the Violent Femme is a compelling vision—one of tabloid television's favorite subjects and a bottomless source of material for jokes and chatter among the general public. She has become a national figure.

But is she real? More importantly, is she on the rise—or even a trend? With all the media and mass cultural attention, we might easily believe that—having spent human history tied down, boxed in and beaten up—women are turning the tables of abuse on men. We might start to think that violence, like distance running, has become an American sport in which men are soon to be outdone. We might even conclude that the numbers of men suffering from battered-boyfriend syndrome will soon eclipse the amount of domestic violence cases perpetrated by men against women.

If so, we'd be dead wrong.

"These cases exist—I represented a guy battered by a wife who was on serious drugs," says Sheila James Kuehl, counsel to the California Women's Law Center. Yes, violent tendencies are by no means the province of men alone. But as Kuehl points out, all reliable statistics point in the other direction: When it comes to serious physical abuse, women are still overwhelmingly on the receiving end. Case studies indicate that while psychological profiles of battered men are similar to those of battered women, there are key differences that modify the nature and severity of abuse. And though abused men do not have the emergency support services available to their female counterparts, this may be precisely because they need them less.

So, while images of abusive women hog the spotlight, a disproportionate number of numbing stories about abused women are relegated to the back pages of newspapers—and the back burner of mass consciousness. Somewhere along the line, we've sharpened our appetites for these Violent Femme tales and lost our taste for the all-too-true stories of flesh-and-blood women who suffer at the hands of violent men.

Up in Arms

First, a reality check: According to the National Crime Victimization Survey 1973–92, women are victims of family violence three times as often as men. Domestic violence affects a woman every 15 seconds and kills four women each day. Year after year, many more husbands and boyfriends kill wives and girlfriends than get killed by them.

That's not to say that women are all sweetness and light.

In 1975 and again in 1985, Murray Straus of the Family Research Institute at the University of New Hampshire conducted wide-ranging studies which found that wives assault their husbands as often as husbands assault their wives. In fact, Straus found, women were *more* likely than men to hit or threaten with a gun or knife, and as likely as men to use a weapon on their partner. Due to these findings, it became accurate to state that men fall victim to domestic violence as much as women do.

Angry men's magazines made new waves with these old numbers. "*We are the target*," bellowed a headline in the August 1993 *Penthouse* (emphasis theirs). "*Men are at least as likely to suffer domestic violence as women*," announced the text, taking Straus's message to the masses.

Given a closer look, the masses might not take this message too literally. Though Straus concludes that women are as likely to use a knife or gun against their partner, women don't seem to be shooting or stabbing as effectively as their mates: In 1992, when 383 wives killed their husbands, 913 husbands killed their wives. And since most men are bigger and stronger than most women, their fists, if so used, *are* weapons. Even if women strike men as often as men strike women, men hit harder. According to the U.S. Justice Department, women are the victims in roughly 95 percent of all types of domestic-violence cases. Allowing for conflicts between gay men, less than 5 percent of violence against another individual takes place at the hands of abusive women.

At the end of the *Penthouse* piece, an information box asked: "Have you been victimized?" followed by a 900 number. Months later, the magazine could identify no more than nine messages. Of course, this response occurred only within the scope of one magazine's circulation. According to the U.S. Justice Department, the number of reported cases of female violence in America amounts to fewer than 24,000 abused men. The 95 percent of cases in which women are assaulted by men adds up to—and this is a conservative estimate—*at least* 450,000 battered women.

It's not that many women don't hit men—Straus's study shows they do. But once the "violence equality" picture leaves the academic world or male-magazine pages, it looks different. Reality changes it. Even Straus himself agrees. "From a policy standpoint, the emphasis should be on battered women," he told the *New York Times* in 1992, "because women suffer by far the most injuries."

Suffering on Both Sides

Sad, but true: People of both genders do terrible things to the opposite sex. "I've interviewed men scalded by boiling water," says Dr. Malcolm George, a neurophysiologist at Queen Mary and Westfield College of the University of London and author of the study *Riding the Donkey Backwards: Men as the Unacceptable Victims of Marital Violence*. "One man's wife used to carry a hammer around in her handbag."

Such stories can ring a bell with anyone who knows a battered woman. "I have typed up temporary restraining orders for women who have had nails plunged up their vaginas," says Kathy Sallis, a legal advocate at Rainbow Services in San Pedro, California.

There are other areas, mostly psychological, where these stories are remarkably similar. The battered man endures the same torments—shock, rage, misplaced guilt—that the battered woman knows so well. He, like her, will agonize over whether to stay in the hostile situation or flee it. If he decides to stay, he often does for the same reason she does, be it worry about children or some form of dependence on his batterer. In short, abused men live much the same lives as abused women—until they start to deal with their problems. Then their paths diverge.

Men Don't Tell

For one thing, society discourages the male victim from coming forth. While in recent years a feminist climate has made it seem less difficult for women to speak up, men still have to deal with more ingrained sexual attitudes. "If a [battered] guy has the courage to dial 911," explains a male veteran who has been on both sides of domestic violence, "the cops see a guy and say,

'What's the matter, can't you handle the little woman?'"

The whole of Western culture stands behind that emasculating statement. While both men and women suffer shame in speaking up, victimized women aren't perceived as going against their gender identity. "Men are brought up to protect women, not to be beaten by them," points out Alvin Baraff, a clinical psychologist and founder of the Men-Center counseling service in Washington, D.C.

Equal Partners

As the problem of extreme violence in marriage has become more well known, many programs have been put in place to treat abusive men by explicitly focusing on their preoccupation with control. These programs attempt to change men's need for dominance into an appreciation that marriage is a partnership, not a dictatorship. These men must also learn that a woman who expresses unhappiness or irritation is issuing not a challenge but a plea for sympathy. Women in abusive relationships also need to own up to their feelings. It is easier for a woman to admit to fear than to anger, even when she has good reason to be angry. Too many women continue to believe that they have provoked their husbands' aggression, and that it is their duty to correct their behavior. Their restraint is read by their husbands as acquiescence to the abuse. Women who accept abuse as the price they must pay for marriage, who dismiss it as a temporary aberration, or blame it on alcohol unwittingly condone it and release their husbands from guilt.

At the other end of the spectrum, women who themselves use aggression not only increase the probability of becoming victims of their husbands' much more injurious violence but also provide them with a justification for it. Unless the causes of the stress are uncovered and solved, the pressure will build up until it explodes. It is possible in most marriages for women to talk about their frustrations without blaming the man. Simply announcing, "I need to talk some things out. Can you help me by listening? I feel like I'm bursting," can deflect a power struggle by making it clear that what follows is a plea for help. Men must learn to hear women as equals, and women must have an economically viable and physically safe way to make good on their promise to leave a violent home. It's a matter of life and death.

Anne Campbell, *Men, Women, and Aggression*, 1993.

When a man does speak up—and thus becomes a male oddity—he faces the prospect of being either gossipworthy or newsworthy. Note how the life of Dean Factor, ex-friend of Violent Femme Shannen Doherty, became the subject of a media frenzy, and how journalists gave almost daily updates on the prognosis of John Bobbitt's member.

Currently, few services address a battered man's emotional—or even physical—problems. "Many battered men end up in homeless shelters, but otherwise there isn't the support for men that there is for women," says Dr. George. But, evidently, there is less of a need among male abuse victims for such services. The only battered men's shelter that existed in Great Britain, begun in November 1992, closed soon after it opened. None has replaced it.

This may reflect battered men's reluctance to speak up, or society's reluctance to hear them. Yet it's hard to believe that there are enough physically endangered, socially silenced men out there to stack up against the numbers of abused women. Consider a single day's caseload at one Indianapolis battered women's shelter: Two fractured-rib cases, one woman with black eyes, one broken-nose case, one woman with both a broken leg and collarbone, a case in which the woman had bruises all over her body, two women with broken ankles—one of them with facial bruises as well. Add up the women across the country who take to shelters, emergency rooms and the streets because of intense and recurring physical violence, and you'll get a number close to 2.1 million women.

Of course, it shouldn't matter who gets hurt, as long as everybody who suffers gets help. Unfortunately, though, the amount of attention given to who gets hurt has a great deal to do with who gets helped. By focusing on the Violent Femme, and by implication the victimized male, our society threatens real women with real neglect. Because in order for budget dollars to keep flowing for female abuse victims, an awareness that there is a continual need for shelters must be maintained. "When men are battered at the same rate as women," says Carol Arthur, executive director of the Domestic Abuse Project in Minneapolis, Minnesota, "they can have an equal share of the [domestic violence funding] money."

Men Do Leave

After victims admit the fact of abuse and utilize the support services that are available, they must decide whether or not to leave their abusive partners and their families. When domestic violence is a question of life or death, who survives depends upon who can get out. It is unfair to assume that men have fewer qualms than women about abandoning their families. But it's an airtight fact that they have more money. according to U.S. Census Bureau figures for 1992, about 42,245,000 husbands had jobs, earning a median income of $30,028. Only 33,990,000 wives—well more than 8 million fewer—worked outside the home, with a median income of $15,252 per year. So the typical

American wife earns about half as much as her husband—if she earns anything at all. For the victim of domestic violence, the implication couldn't be clearer. "Men leave," says Kuehl of the California Women's Law Center, "and they *can* leave."

Just as money can free the battered man, the lack of it often traps the battered woman. Geneva Love, 29, is now serving a 17-years-to-life sentence in the Arkansas Women's Unit for the fatal shooting of her husband, Azell. Two days before the murder, when he finished beating her for the last of many times, all she asked him for was a bus ticket.

For women much more than men, the fact of fear is as cold as cash. There is no evidence that men's lives are commonly threatened by women they have left, but "seventy-five percent of the women killed by their mates are tracked down *after* they've left home," says Lee Rosen, chair of the American Bar Association's domestic violence council and a divorce lawyer in Raleigh, North Carolina. "The most dangerous times of their lives is when they come to see me."

"Goodness and badness don't come from sex," asserts Dr. George. "We need to focus on real victims, irrespective of gender." It seems silly to fight over who suffers most.

But when faced with an onslaught of mythic Violent Femmes, real women must fight back. With the 15 to 20 years it took to establish the fact that domestic violence against women exists, we can't grow immune to hearing about it. Just because the Violent Femme pushes the boundaries of testosterone-driven imaginations—and feeds female revenge fantasies—that's no reason to let her camouflage the needs of female abuse victims. Or let men highlight instances of their own suffering as a form of backlash against the growing power of women.

This doesn't give us the right to dismiss men in pain. Certainly, women's increasingly accepted tendency to ridicule wounded men would be wildly put down if the genders were reversed. "I don't know of a single man," Baraff muses over some women's it's-about-time take on John Bobbitt's maiming, "who would express delight at hearing that another man had cut off a woman's breast."

A good point, but the same week that Lorena Bobbitt drew her world-famous knife, 24-year-old Elizabeth Lezuma of Kerrville, Texas, was stabbed in her right breast by her live-in lover.

Jacqueline Schultz, 30, of Rockford, Minnesota, was stabbed 14 times during an argument with her husband.

Elizabeth Delgado, 19, of Springfield, Massachusetts, was shot in a friend's car by her ex-boyfriend, who had just served 60 days in jail for violating an order to stay away from her.

They all died.

Did you read about that?

"BWS expands the concept of legal self-defense."

Battered Woman Syndrome Is a Legitimate Defense

Ola W. Barnett and Alyce D. LaViolette

Some psychologists argue that many women who experience an extended pattern of spousal abuse suffer from "battered woman syndrome," which includes a well-founded fear that they will be killed if they try to leave their husbands. The battered woman defense has been used by women who have argued that their only means of escaping life-threatening abuse was to kill their husbands. In the following viewpoint, Ola W. Barnett and Alyce D. LaViolette maintain that when a woman who is suffering from battered woman syndrome kills her abuser, the killing should be considered self-defense. Barnett is a professor of psychology at Pepperdine University in Malibu, California. LaViolette has developed programs to stop domestic violence.

As you read, consider the following questions:

1. How do Barnett and LaViolette define battered woman syndrome?
2. In the study by E. Greene, A. Raitz, and H. Lindblad cited by the authors, what was the level of jurors' knowledge about the experiences of battered women?
3. According to studies cited by Barnett and LaViolette, why do men kill women? Why do women kill men?

While the law specifically, and society in general, have offered little help to the battered wife, and indeed may be partially responsible for the actions of those who strike back violently, many of these women now face homicide charges brought by the same society and its legal system.

Anonymous

Definition There has been confusion concerning the definition of the battered woman syndrome (BWS). Some authors use the abusive acts committed against the woman as the defining aspects of BWS (e.g., severity and frequency of assaults). Lenore A. Walker, in contrast, conceptualizes the syndrome as a severe stress reaction, a subcategory of post-traumatic stress disorder (PTSD). Basic personality components include fear, depression, guilt, passivity, and low self-esteem.

BWS as a Legal Defense

BWS expands the concept of legal self-defense. This defense holds that a battered woman is virtually held hostage in a violent household by a man who isolates and terrorizes her, convincing her that if she leaves he will track her down and kill her. A. DePaul describes the syndrome as "the situation of a long-time victim of physical, sexual, and psychological abuse who loses self-confidence, feels trapped, and eventually strikes back, assaulting or killing the abuser." Only six states currently have passed laws recognizing the battered woman syndrome.

The American Psychiatric Association conceptualizes BWS as the development of a set of personality attributes brought on by abuse that render the victim more able to survive in the relationship and less able to escape it. The battered woman's belief that escape is impossible and the depression that accompanies this belief lead to her entrapment in the relationship. The three components of the syndrome are as follows: (a) behaviors brought on by victimization, (b) learned helplessness behavior, and (c) self-destructive coping behaviors.

Although it is possible that battered women's behavioral repertoires included these elements before the battering, it is more likely that the fear engendered by the violence produced or exacerbated the conditions. E.M. Schneider fears, however, that use of BWS may reinforce the sentiment that women are helpless beings and may create a new category of mental incapacity. According to DePaul, "Without expert testimony to explain how women come to feel so dependent or fearful that they cannot leave an abusive relationship, juries often are left to wonder why the woman did not walk out long before she felt compelled to retaliate."

E. Greene, A. Raitz, and H. Lindblad studied the level of jurors' knowledge about the experiences of battered women.

Jurors were relatively informed about the findings of empirical research on a number of issues: violence escalates in a relationship; women are anxious, depressed, feel helpless, and suffer in many ways; battered women are afraid that their spouses might kill them; and leaving the batterer may lead to further harm. Jurors have much less information about other factors: Battered women blame themselves, feel dependent upon their husbands, accept their spouses' promises to change, can predict when the violence will occur, even occasionally provoke an assault to end the buildup of tension, and come to believe that they must use deadly force to stay alive.

The Impact of Violence

L.J. Veronen and H. Resnick point out that it is a mistake to focus on battered women's traits during the trial. Battered and nonbattered women are not significantly different. Instead, expert testimony should focus on the impact of violence and the woman's perception of threat. To accomplish this goal, expert testimony may need to include a description of the woman's conditioning history—for example, which cues have become classically conditioned to elicit fear. A woman whose husband informed her that after his nap he was going to torture her in his new underground torture chamber might think the time has come to prevent his ever waking up.

N.C. Jurik and R. Winn wanted to determine whether homicide by females has been affected by women's liberation and whether gender differences were still relevant. Their sample included 108 male-perpetrated homicides and 50 female-perpetrated homicides. Results indicated that, when women kill, they generally kill in their own homes during domestic conflict. They are prone to kill male partners, within a context of economic dependence, past attacks, and victim-initiated violence. In contrast, men are more likely to kill someone away from the home, and they usually initiate the violence when they kill.

Although in absolute numbers more men kill women than the reverse, L.A. Greenfeld and S. Minor-Harper documented that violent female offenders were more likely to have murdered a male (61.49%) than male offenders were to have murdered a female (52.70%). Women almost always kill a spouse or an intimate in an intimate setting.

In one study of more than 1,600 homicides, self-defense characterized almost all killings by females, but almost none by males. A number of other actions and motives typified male killers, but not females: (a) Men often hunt down and kill spouses who have left them; (b) men kill as part of a planned murder-suicide; (c) men kill in response to revelations of wifely infidelity, although men are generally more adulterous than

160

women; (d) men kill after subjecting their wives to lengthy periods of coercive abuse and assaults; and (e) men perpetrate family massacres.

Women Kill Their Abusers

The *Report of the Governor's Committee to Study Sentencing and Correctional Alternatives for Women Convicted of Crime, State of Maryland* established that 43% of the women in prisons and jails in Maryland had been physically abused and 33% had been sexually abused. According to Sheila Kuehl, who is working on the California Clemency Project for battered women who kill, 93% of the women imprisoned for homicide in California claim to have killed their batterers.

G.W. Barnard, H. Vera, M. Vera, and G. Newman, in a study of men and women in Florida prisons for spousal homicide, asserted that 73% of the women reported being physically abused by their husbands. For men, the precipitating event was usually some form of perceived rejection. Barnard and his colleagues called these murders of wives by husbands "sex-role threat homicides." In contrast, the women killed in response to what they saw as an attack or threat by their partners. Barnard and his colleagues cited the physical abuse of wives as the major factor in their lethal actions against their spouses. In reality, most battered women who kill are no threat to society. Nonetheless, few women are acquitted at trials; most (72%–80%) are convicted or accept a plea bargain, and many receive very long sentences.

The 1987 Committee on Domestic Violence and Incarcerated Women recognized that the criminal justice system does not act effectively to protect women from being beaten. A battered woman may not be able to obtain a restraining order or keep it in effect. She may be unable to obtain even temporary financial support for a 30-day period. The court will most likely allow her abuser visitation with the children. In the end, no one can guarantee her safety. The Committee determined that the criminal justice system's response was "inconsistent and inadequate," leaving some women with no option but to kill their abusers to end the violence.

A New York Committee on Domestic Violence has concluded that killing an assaultive male should not be the only option left to battered women. When leaving is more dangerous than staying, but staying amounts to living in daily terror, the battered woman's dilemma can reach its final, catastrophic climax. . . .

If a battered woman cannot stop the violence and perceives that she has no other options, a day may come when she makes a lethal choice: to kill herself or to kill her abuser.

"*Battered woman syndrome is simply a sign of the times. In a nation of victims, everything can be justified on the basis of abuse.*"

Battered Woman Syndrome Is Not a Legitimate Defense

Michael Fumento

Women who have killed their mates have begun using a new defense to avoid going to jail, asserts Michael Fumento in the following viewpoint. According to Fumento, this defense, called "battered woman syndrome," allows women to argue that they were forced to kill their abuser in order to escape the abuse because they were psychologically incapable of simply leaving. This defense, he argues, incorrectly absolves these women of the responsibility for killing their husbands and permits them to escape punishment for their crimes. Fumento is the Warren Brookes fellow at the Competitive Enterprise Institute, a Washington, D.C., organization.

As you read, consider the following questions:

1. How does Fumento describe the crimes of the women released by Florida governor Lawton Chiles?
2. What statistics from the Justice Department does Fumento cite to argue that the courts are more lenient toward women who kill their husbands than they are to men who kill their wives?
3. What are some of the cases the author describes in which women have received clemency in Maryland and Ohio?

Michael Fumento, "Are Women Getting Away with Murder?" *Insight*, February 6, 1995; ©1995 by The Washington Times Corporation. Reprinted with permission.

Lynn Herndon Kent was asleep in bed when her husband, Lamar, put a pistol to the back of her head and blew her brains out. Shortly before, he had taken out an insurance policy on her life. Now, with her blood soaking into the pillow, he called a friend to have him hide the gun, then called the police and explained tearfully that Lynn had been killed in a robbery. They didn't buy it, Kent confessed, and a judge sentenced him to 15 years in prison and 15 years on probation. But now Kent is free, because Florida governor Lawton Chiles has granted him clemency.

Are you outraged that such a thing could happen? Would you be less so were you to find out the names were switched, and that it was Lynn who did the killing? Yes, it was that which made the difference. Lynn Kent was released along with two other women: One had an argument with her live-in boyfriend, left the scene, returned and shot him dead; the other was an 18-year-old who killed her stepfather by shooting him in the back after luring him out in the country.

Clemency for Abused Women

A year before, Chiles—and a clemency board that he set up in 1993 exclusively to evaluate the cases of women who claimed abuse led them to murder—ordered two other releases. Assuming all these women had been physically abused—and for some there was corroborative evidence, while for others there was not—none of them were in immediate danger of life or limb; thus none could resort to the recognized legal protection of self-defense. Their crimes were premeditated—what used to be called "in cold blood." They are free today because they suffered from something called "battered woman syndrome."

Which is? "From everything I've read," says Cathy Young, vice president of the Women's Freedom Network in Washington, "it sounds more like an ideological concoction to justify acts that would not fall under the category of self-defense."

Couldn't these women have just walked away? Well, physically, yes. The theory holds that due to repeated battering, "the victim becomes completely passive," says Young. "It's an interesting sort of reasoning because it assumes the woman is so passive she can't leave a relationship, but she's not too passive to kill."

So battered woman syndrome equals insanity, right? Wrong. Insanity long has been recognized as a defense by courts. These women were sane. "Basically, it seems like a grab bag of justifications that can be used to justify just about anything," says Young.

A recent Justice Department analysis found that nearly 13 percent of wives accused of killing husbands were acquitted, compared with 1.4 percent of husbands accused of killing their wives. Of those convicted, 16 percent of the women received probation instead of prison, 10 times the rate for men. The average prison sentence for the homicidal wife was 6 years, compared with 17 for the husband.

The Law Is Clear

One way to beat a murder charge is to show that a homicide was an act of self-defense. In California the requirements of self-defense are strict: The defendant must prove she felt she was in imminent danger, that her feeling was reasonable and that killing her batterer was the only way to prevent that danger. . . .

[Some feminists] argue that courts should adopt a special understanding of self-defense for battered women who kill. These women, they say, suffer from "battered woman syndrome," a stress disorder that calls into question what they say is a male-oriented law of self-defense.

A woman who suffers from battered woman syndrome is said to have learned to be passive. So, if she returns again and again to a husband who abuses her, she is not to blame: The syndrome is at work. Assume she finally shoots him as he lies drunk and unconscious, since she fears for her life when he awakes, even though he presents no imminent danger to anyone else. She still ought to enjoy the protection of the law of self-defense, it is argued, because the syndrome has made her more sensitive to danger. . . .

But where do you draw the line? It's one thing to rely on the decent instincts of 12 randomly selected Americans to know when someone who has not strictly followed the rules of self-defense should nonetheless go free. It's quite another to swallow trendy legal theory undiluted.

David Frum, *Forbes*, January 18, 1993.

There also have been no mass pardons of wife killers as there have been of husband killers in both Ohio and Maryland. One of the Maryland women freed had hired a hit man and collected on her husband's insurance policy. The Columbus (Ohio) *Dispatch* reported that of the 25 women pardoned by outgoing governor Richard Celeste in 1990, 15 said they had not been physically abused. Six had discussed killing their husbands beforehand, and 2 had even tracked down their estranged spouses to kill them.

Battered woman syndrome is simply a sign of the times. In a nation of victims, everything can be justified on the basis of abuse of some sort. The Menendez brothers claim their parents abused them; instead of leaving home, they shot them to death. Lawyers for Colin Ferguson blame a racist American society for the shooting of whites and Asians on a Long Island commuter train. Texan Daimion Osby guns down two unarmed members of his own race. He couldn't help it, you see; he suffers from "urban survival syndrome."

Now we hear that a 350-pound woman shot her husband to death because he threatened to either leave her or put her in a nursing home unless she lost weight. Presumably, her lawyer will argue that she suffered a combination of mental battering and fat genes.

Yet there are those who have successively argued that what's good for the goose. . . . In March 1994, a Los Angeles jury found a man guilty of a charge less than murder because it bought his story that he bludgeoned his wife to death only after years of psychological abuse and only because his religion forbade leaving her. Says Deputy District Attorney Kathleen Cady, who prosecuted that case: "Every single murderer has a reason why they killed someone. I think it sends a very frightening message to the rest of society that all you have to do is come up with some kind of excuse when you commit a crime."

We got Chiles' message, loud and clear.

Periodical Bibliography

The following articles have been selected to supplement the diverse views presented in this chapter.

Carol J. Adams	"Help for the Battered," *Christian Century*, June 29–July 6, 1994.
Joseph R. Biden	"Domestic Violence: A Crime, Not a Quarrel," *Trial*, vol. 29, no. 6, Fall 1993. Available from the American Bar Association, 750 N. Lake Shore Dr., Chicago, IL 60611.
Susan Douglas	"Blame It on Battered Women," *Progressive*, August 1994.
Jean Bethke Elshtain	"Battered Reason," *New Republic*, October 5, 1992.
Jean Bethke Elshtain	"Women and the Ideology of Victimization," *World & I*, April 1993. Available from 2800 New York Ave. NE, Washington, DC 20002.
David Frum	"Women Who Kill," *Forbes*, January 18, 1993.
Nancy Gibbs	"'Til Death Do Us Part," *Time*, January 18, 1993.
Casey Gwinn	"Can We Stop Domestic Violence?" *American Jails*, March/April 1995. Available from 2053 Day Rd., Suite 100, Hagerstown, MD 21740-9795.
Patricia Horn	"Beating Back the Revolution: Domestic Violence's Toll on Women," *Dollars & Sense*, no. 182, December 1992.
Michele Ingrassia and Melinda Beck	"Patterns of Abuse," *Newsweek*, July 4, 1994.
Journal of Contemporary Criminal Justice	Special issue on domestic violence, vol. 10, no. 3, September 1994.
Wendy McElroy	"The Unfair Sex," *National Review*, May 1, 1995.
Ms.	Special section on domestic violence, September/October 1994.
Sara Paretsky	"The Hidden War at Home," *New York Times*, July 7, 1994.
Stanton Peele	"Making Excuses: Betrayed Men and Battered Women Get Away with Murder," *National Review*, November 21, 1994.

Elayne Rapping	"What Evil Lurks in the Hearts of Men?" *Progressive*, November 1994.
Donna Shalala	"Domestic Terrorism," *Vital Speeches of the Day*, May 15, 1994.
Jill Smolowe	"When Violence Hits Home," *Time*, July 4, 1994.
Mark Thompson	"The Living Room War," *Time*, May 23, 1994.

How Should Youth Violence Be Addressed?

Chapter Preface

In February 1995, a *U.S. News & World Report* story described how two boys—aged ten and eleven—dropped five-year-old Eric Morse from a fourteenth-story apartment window because he refused to steal candy for them. This account seemed to confirm the disturbing trends cited in the media about the perpetrators of youth violence—they are getting younger, are increasingly willing to resort to violence over trivial issues, and lack remorse.

While the Eric Morse tragedy does not prove that American children are becoming barbaric, statistics do reveal that the nation's youths are committing an increasing number of violent crimes. Between 1983 and 1992, according to the Federal Bureau of Investigation (FBI), juvenile arrest rates for violent crime increased 128 percent for murder and non-negligent manslaughter, 95 percent for aggravated assault, and 25 percent for rape.

While critics disagree over how to respond to this rise in youth violence, much of the debate centers on the juvenile justice system. The philosophy of that system is based on the belief that juvenile offenders are not fully responsible for their actions. Rather, it is held, they are children in the process of developing; with proper guidance and treatment, they can be rehabilitated into productive members of society. Critics argue that this philosophy originated at a time when juvenile crime consisted of relatively minor infractions such as truancy and joyriding, not violent transgressions like rape and murder committed by youths today. Consequently, some contend, today's violent juveniles should be transferred to the adult criminal justice system, in which they would be adequately punished.

Others are critical of the push to transfer juveniles into adult courts. For example, Alex Kotlowitz, the author of *There Are No Children Here: The Story of Two Boys Growing Up in the Other America*, argues that the juvenile justice system's emphasis on treatment and rehabilitation is the correct response to youth crime. "The debate . . . gets to the fundamental question of what it means to be a child, particularly in an increasingly violent world," he writes. "Children need help navigating through what can be a treacherous adolescent maze. That is why . . . society created juvenile courts."

Whether violent juvenile offenders are misguided children or dangerous criminals is at the heart of the debates in the following chapter on youth violence.

"The juvenile justice system must become a tough criminal justice system for young offenders."

The Juvenile Justice System Should Punish Violent Youths

Paul J. McNulty

In the following viewpoint, Paul J. McNulty predicts a surge in violent juvenile crime in the first decade of the twenty-first century. In order to head off this increase in violence, according to McNulty, the juvenile justice system must abandon its misguided efforts to rehabilitate wayward children and should instead punish youths who commit criminal acts. McNulty, who was director of policy and communications in the U.S. Department of Justice during the Bush administration, is president of the First Freedom Coalition, an anti-crime advocacy group in Washington, D.C.

As you read, consider the following questions:

1. What does the author say is the most reliable predictor of violent crime in a neighborhood?
2. According to McNulty, how do the views of liberals and conservatives differ concerning crime?
3. What three principles must guide reform of the juvenile justice system, according to the author?

Abridged from Paul J. McNulty, "Natural Born Killers?" *Policy Review*, #71, Winter 1995; ©1995 The Heritage Foundation. Reprinted with permission.

From 1985 to 1991, homicides committed by boys in the 15- to 19-year-old age group jumped 154 percent. From 1982 to 1991, the juvenile arrest rate for murder rose 93 percent, for aggravated assault 72 percent, and for forcible rape 24 percent.

If these statistics scare you, brace yourself. A breathtaking rise in juvenile crime is occurring even as the national rate of violent crime has leveled off, and the nation's population of juveniles has fallen. The greatest danger lies ahead. In the final years of the 1990s and throughout the next decade, America will experience an "echo boom"—a population surge made up of the teenage children of today's aging baby boomers. As today's five-year-old children become tomorrow's teenagers, America faces the most violent juvenile crime surge in its history.

The warnings of this coming storm are unmistakable. More violent crime is committed by older teenagers than by any other age group. Teenagers from fatherless homes commit more crime than teenagers from intact families. Put these two demographic facts together, and we are in for a catastrophe in the early 21st century.

Kids and Crime

Teenagers account for the largest portion of all violent crime in America. Offenders under the age of 21 commit more than one-fourth of all violent crime. Older teenagers (ages 17 to 19) are the most violent of all age groups: More murder and robbery is committed by 18-year-old males than any other group, and more than one-third of all murders are committed by offenders under the age of 21. No population poses a larger threat to public safety than juvenile and young adult criminals.

This violence is getting worse. While the teenage population in America declined between 1985 and 1995, violent crimes committed by juveniles rose sharply. According to the FBI, from 1988 to 1992 juvenile violent crime arrests increased by 47 percent. More juveniles were arrested for violent crime in 1991 and 1992 than in any other two-year period in U.S. history; the number of serious crime cases handled by juvenile courts rose nearly 70 percent between 1988 and 1992. Perhaps most disturbing, the number of 13- to 15-year-olds arrested for murder jumped from 390 in 1982 to 740 only 10 years later.

By the time the courts finally lock up an older teenager on a violent crime charge, the offender often has a long rap sheet with arrests starting in his early teens. And actual lock-ups are rare. Nowhere does the revolving door of justice spin faster than in the juvenile court system. Nearly one-quarter of all juvenile arrests are dismissed immediately, and only 10 percent result in detention of the offender. A 1987 justice department *Survey of Youth in Custody* reported that 43 percent of juveniles in state institutions had more than five prior arrests, and 20 percent had been arrested more than 10 times. Approximately four-fifths of these offenders had previously been on probation, and three-fifths had been committed to a correctional facility at least once in the past.

A large majority of teenage criminals are from broken and single-parent households; many teenage boys are growing up without fathers as moral guides and role models. The *Survey of Youth in Custody* reports that some 70 percent of offenders did not live with both parents while growing up, and more than half reported that a family member had served time in prison. Another study found that 75 percent of teenage criminals came from single-parent homes. These numbers are consistent with surveys of adult offenders in state prisons. Only 43 percent of these inmates grew up in homes with both parents.

The New Wave

The single most reliable predictor of violent crime in a neighborhood is its proportion of single-parent families, according to the *Journal of Research in Crime and Delinquency*. The last thing America needs is a population surge of teenage boys growing up in single-parent homes. Yet by the turn of the century, that is exactly what the country will face.

While the population of male teenagers actually decreased between 1985 and 1995, the number of crimes they commit skyrocketed. Soon the demographics will begin to change in favor of even more youth violence. In 1980, according to the U.S. Census Bureau, there were some 10.7 million males in the 15- to 19-year-old age group. By 1990 this population had declined by 15 percent to about 9.2 million. . . . But by the turn of the century, the population in this age cohort will have rebounded to more than 10 million, and by 2010, the number of 15- to 19-year-old males will be 11.5 million.

The young men who will comprise the crime-committing cohort by the middle of the next decade are now young boys in the critical stage of human moral development. But the moral training ground of these 10 million boys has changed dramatically over the past 30 years. Consider these grim statistics: Some 4 million babies were born in both 1961 and 1991, but in 1991 five times as many of them were born out of wedlock. Today, one out of every three children is born to a single parent, triple the rate of just 25 years ago. Nearly 70 percent of black children are born to unwed mothers. Over the same period, the divorce rate in the U.S. tripled, from 393,000 in 1960 to 1,175,000 in 1990. Today more than 25 percent of all children live with only one parent.

The combination of these population projections and the decline of the American family portends big trouble. At the beginning of the next century, the United States will have an extremely large number of young men under the age of 20. An unprecedented number in this group are today growing up in troubled family circumstances. Only by taking decisive action now, and most importantly by slowing the revolving door of juvenile justice, can America prevent this cohort from committing more violent crime than we have ever witnessed.

Catch and Convict

Nothing can be done to stop the 5- to 10-year-olds of today from becoming the 15- to 20-year-olds of tomorrow. Since repairing the home life in which these children are now being raised is, with few exceptions, one of the many tasks beyond the reach of government, America's future safety rests in its ability to discourage young trouble-makers from committing violent crimes when they reach their peak crime-committing years.

How this is best accomplished is where the debate begins, and largely the ground where the battle on the 1994 crime bill was fought. President Clinton wanted billions for so-called "crime prevention" programs, such as the now-famous midnight basketball program, but Republicans denounced this spending as a rehash of the Great Society programs that have already failed.

Villains

Tougher measures are long overdue for teen killers. The time has come to see them simply for what they are: villains. Many demonstrate no remorse, revealing an attitude of malignity and calculation—hallmarks of sinister premeditation. . . .

We must reform failing policies and forgo the belief that when it comes to youth violence, rehabilitation is the cornerstone of deterrence. It is not. Rehabilitation seeks to reform the wayward youth in custody; it does nothing to prevent others from charting the same course. We remain committed to a brand of social engineering that has extracted an enormous cost in lives as well as dollars.

Jeffrey Danzinger, *The Wall Street Journal*, April 7, 1993.

Indeed, the crime-bill dispute is the most recent example of a long-standing clash over the role of government in relation to crime prevention. Liberals argue that crime results from such things as inadequate education, economic deprivation, and low self-esteem. Consequently, they favor early intervention government programs aimed at preschoolers, government-initiated job opportunities, and treatment-oriented responses for young criminals.

Conservatives, on the other hand, argue that crime results from a lack of moral self-restraint. The absence of such restraint ordinarily follows from the absence of nurturing parental care, including consistent discipline. Families and government are not interchangeable in this regard; raising children is a task largely beyond the reach of government. Instead, government must focus on what it was created to do—catch and convict lawbreakers.

The challenge for conservatives now lies in suppressing juvenile crime at the first sign of trouble, often with young teenagers or even pre-teens, before these criminals become violent young men. Government's role is to enforce the law, and it should be vigorous and purposeful in the acceptance of that duty. When families fail to instill virtue in children, government must be prepared immediately to send a clear message to those children, and their parents, that lawbreaking will not be tolerated, and that the children will be held accountable. To do that will require a complete overhaul of the juvenile justice system. The first step in this effort is to understand the flawed nature of the current system.

Rehabilitation vs. Punishment

The failure of the juvenile justice system to stem the tide of youth crime is the result of a shift in philosophy. Punishment is now considered contrary to its intended mission.

The first juvenile court was established in 1899 in Cook County, Illinois; by 1925, there were juvenile courts in 46 states. Describing the hopes associated with this institution, Charles Silberman notes in *Criminal Violence, Criminal Justice:* "Juvenile courts have been monuments to American optimism. In their rhetoric, if not their actual operation, the courts represent expressions of faith in judges' capacity to change behavior and thereby turn wayward children into law-abiding citizens."

The goal of the juvenile justice system—rehabilitation—is a clear departure from the goals of the adult system—accountability and punishment. Because children are not fully developed, physically or mentally, it was argued that they could not be held accountable for wrongdoing. Criminality was not seen as the result of a decision by a morally responsible individual; rather, it was a type of youthful illness to be treated through the individualized attention of so-called experts. To ensure proper treatment, these experts—juvenile court judges, probation officers, reform school administrators, and parole board officials—were given broad discretion to develop and implement a rehabilitation program for each case.

The candid descriptions by juvenile judges of their role in relation to young criminals should shock and outrage inner-city residents held hostage by the rise in juvenile street violence. Judge Ben Lindsay, founder of the Denver Juvenile Court, has described his role within the court as "part educator, part artist, and part physician." He summarily declares: "[A] child's case is not a legal case." One of this century's most influential juvenile court judges, Harvey Baker of Boston, likened himself to a doctor in a dispensary, with there being no more formality in his courtroom than in a "physician's examination room."

In 1975, Justice William O. Douglas recounted a conversation he had with a juvenile court judge who, in the words of Douglas, "explained what I think was the original purpose of the juvenile delinquency acts of the various states. 'I, the judge,' he told me, 'and the bailiff and the other court attendants are like those on a hospital staff, dressed in white. We are doctors, nurses, orderlies. We are there not to administer a law in the normal meaning of criminal law. We are there to diagnose, investigate, counsel, and advise.'" More recently, Judge Walter Whitlack, now with the Cleveland Juvenile Court and a past president of the National Council of Juvenile Court Judges, stated, ". . . [A] child who has violated the law is not a criminal, but rather he is to be taken in hand by the state as protector and ultimate guardian rather than as his enemy."

Every step of today's juvenile justice system reflects its orientation toward treatment and rehabilitation and away from accountability and punishment. Those who commit crimes while under the age of 18 are not termed criminals, but are "delinquents." Juveniles are not arrested, they are "taken into custody." They are not jailed, they are "detained." And they are not charged with a crime, they are "referred" to the court. There, they are not tried; a "hearing" is held. A hearing cannot lead to a conviction and sentencing; it can only lead to a "finding of delinquency" and a "placement" in a "detention center" or "residential facility."

Toughen Up

The result of this confusion? The highest juvenile crime rates in American history. It is time to abandon this misguided philosophy. Government must affirm, through the consistent enforcement of law, the indispensable place of accountability in juvenile justice. Statistics previously cited unquestionably reveal that America has been heavily victimized by recidivistic teenage thugs who were quickly returned to the streets by idealistic judges.

The juvenile justice system must become a tough criminal justice system for young offenders. Three principles must guide its reform. First, the gap between lawbreaking and accountability must be significantly narrowed. Too many "minor" crimes by young offenders, such as truancy and vandalism, are tolerated by law enforcers, sending the message that there is no sanction for illegal behavior. Such wrongdoing left unaddressed may be a precursor to more serious crimes. Some jurisdictions are attempting to increase accountability in this regard. The "ASAP" initiative (Absent Students Assistance Program) in Houston, Texas, founded by Constable Victor Trevino, has had remarkable and cost-effective success through aggressive enforcement of truancy laws.

Second, violent crimes must be punished with appropriate penalties. Violent juveniles should receive substantial time in prison—with no early parole—as a matter of both justice and public safety. The offender's age may be taken into consideration at the time of sentencing.

Third, there must be a sanction for every crime. As noted criminologist James Q. Wilson observes, "There ought to be penalties from the earliest offense . . . so that juveniles are treated by the state the same way we treat our children. You don't ignore the fact that they're wrecking the house until they finally burn it down. You try to deal with it right away."

Every offender must pay for his criminal actions. While sanctions for less violent crimes will vary and may be creative, and in the majority of cases not involve incarceration, these punishments must nonetheless communicate the basic message that punishment will be imposed every time an offender is caught and convicted. Punishments should also range in severity, with offenders receiving more severe sanctions if they fail to complete their original sentences. . . .

Get Serious

Every night, Americans watch as the nightly news displays fresh pictures of teenage boys who are unafraid of the police and the criminal justice system. There are lots of smiles and taunts and confident glares, and virtually no worry or remorse. The stories are frequently the same: a teenager with multiple prior arrests now charged with a hideous violent crime.

Facing the largest potential crime wave in our history by the year 2000, America must start to deal swiftly and effectively with young law-breakers on the verge of becoming the violent teenagers on the evening news. Older siblings are telling them that the current system is a joke. The kindergarten boys of today will be tomorrow's violent thugs unless America gets serious about punishing juvenile criminals.

> "The emergence of a retribution . . . model for
> juveniles has gone hand in hand with a public
> and political unwillingness to allocate resources
> to children."

The Juvenile Justice System Should Rehabilitate Violent Youths

George M. Anderson

In the following viewpoint, George M. Anderson writes that in most states, the juvenile justice system confines youths to large institutions that are often violent, excessively punitive, and provide little or no treatment. He advocates the community-based programs being developed in a few states, including Massachusetts and Utah, which provide youths with education and therapy designed to prepare them for re-entry into their communities. Anderson is an associate editor for *America*, a weekly Catholic magazine.

As you read, consider the following questions:

1. What were the recidivism rates in California and Massachusetts, according to the National Council on Crime and Delinquency study cited by the author?
2. According to Jerome Miller, quoted by Anderson, why are officials reluctant to shut down institutions?
3. Why are minorities overrepresented in the juvenile justice system, according to the author?

George M. Anderson, "Punishing the Young: Juvenile Justice in the 1990s," *America*, February 29, 1992. Reprinted with permission.

The pattern emerging for juvenile offenders in many parts of the country is one that emphasizes punishment over rehabilitation. This pattern is not, however, new. It has been taking shape since the late 1970s, until there are now more juveniles confined than ever before, despite the fact that the juvenile population nationwide has dropped.

Crowding and state budget constraints, moreover, have meant that relatively little is made available for the kinds of intensive educational and therapeutic programs that advocates believe necessary to prepare youths in confinement for re-entry into the community. In a 1991 article in *Crime and Delinquency* entitled "The Punitive Juvenile Court and the Quality of Procedural Justice," Barry Feld, a professor of law at the University of Minnesota, wrote that the emergence of a retribution and just-deserts model for juveniles has gone hand in hand with a public and political unwillingness to allocate resources to children, particularly those who commit crimes.

The spirit of punitiveness toward youths adjudicated delinquent—the term used in the juvenile system for "found guilty"—prevails even though the actual number of serious offenders is small. Most juveniles in custody are there for non-violent or property offenses. But violent crimes highly publicized by the media have led state legislators to enact an array of mandatory and determinate sentencing laws that are packing juvenile detention centers and training schools around the country.

According to a report issued in 1991 by the Federal Office of Juvenile Justice and Delinquency Prevention (O.J.J.D.P), entitled "Children in Custody 1989," 8 out of 10 juvenile admissions are to institutional rather than non-incarcerative settings. Most of the youths are between the ages of 14 and 17. But in the large congregate care institutions that continue to be extensively used in states like California, New York and Florida, not only is it difficult to implement what rehabilitative programs do exist, there is also greater likelihood of physical violence, particularly as crowding intensifies. In addition, staff abuses in settings of this type, such as excessive isolation and physical restraints for punishment, have been frequently documented.

Punitive Policies

Crowding has become especially acute in the West. For years, the state with the highest per capita rate of incarcerated young offenders has been California. The attendant ills of the California approach are suggested in the title of a 1986 study of the state's Youth Authority by the Commonwealth Research Institute: "Bodily Harm: The Pattern of Fear and Violence at the California Youth Authority." David Lambert, a staff attorney with the National Center for Youth Law in San Francisco, spoke of the current situation during a telephone interview.

"California was once a progressive state, with an emphasis on treatment, but now," he said, "it's the opposite. Kids are spending longer and longer periods in closed facilities because the Youthful Offender Parole Board, which is made up of political appointees, isn't releasing them."

Mr. Lambert went on to say that what has been happening in regard to California's juvenile facilities is mirrored in its adult institutions, whose populations have doubled since the early 1980s. The same correspondence is true in other areas of the country too. In another 1991 article in *Crime and Delinquency*, Edmund McGarrell, a professor of criminal justice at the University of Indiana, observed that there is a definite relationship between increases in the two systems; states with the steepest increases in adult rates of incarceration tend to have equivalently greater increases in their juvenile rates. This relationship, he contends, has its source in what he terms "political choices of more punitive crime control policies."

A reflection of these more punitive crime control policies can be seen in the growing tendency to waive juvenile cases to the adult court when the offense is considered serious. California, Delaware, Florida, Vermont, Illinois, Montana, Georgia, Mississippi and Washington have all enacted waiver legislation of this sort. A dramatic illustration of the penalties it may entail can be seen in the Washington State case of Barry Massey. Convicted of murdering a marina owner during a 1987 robbery when he was 13, Massey was tried as an adult and received a sentence of life without parole.

Washington state, which, like California and other states, adopted a stringent just-deserts juvenile code in the late 1970's, is among those that rely heavily on large, secure institutions. "It has five," Mr. Lambert said, "with one of them, Green Hill, so old and decrepit that it's falling apart. It was slated to be closed, but because of a lot of opposition by the community and by state employees over job losses, state officials decided to keep it open and just fix it up."

Community-Based Sanctions

By way of contrast, Mr. Lambert went on to point out that Arkansas and Utah, which have small populations similar to Washington's, have taken a different route, away from reliance on the training school model toward a greater use of community-based sanctions. Utah in particular has made a commitment to what its Division of Youth Corrections calls in its mission statement the least restrictive setting for youthful offenders. Less than a fifth of those adjudicated delinquents are placed in secure institutions. During a telephone conversation with Dr. George

179

Kelner, superintendent of the youth detention center in Salt Lake City, Dr. Kelner pointed out that Utah's move toward community-based programs has meant that only a few small, secure facilities are in use for the more serious offenders. Even in these there is a heavy stress on treatment programs, education and social-skills development aimed at facilitating re-entry into the community.

"Big institutions make kids worse," Dr. Kelner said, "because they tend to be hostile, abusive and understaffed. Utah legislators have been sympathetic to the use of community-based alternatives, in part because kids are seen differently from adult offenders."

Re-emphasize Treatment

We must re-emphasize treatment [for juveniles]. Sure, some teenagers are psychopaths who cannot be rehabilitated. But most are still growing and capable of change under the right circumstances. How can we, as a society, just give up on a 13-year-old—even one who has committed the most heinous acts?

Victor Kamber, *USA Weekend*, May 13–15, 1994.

Utah's approach is largely based on that of Massachusetts, which generated wide attention for its radical departure from the institutional model in 1972. The then-commissioner of the Massachusetts Department of Youth Services, Jerome Miller, stunned the corrections establishment by closing all the state's training schools. In their place, he began to establish a network of alternative sanctions in community settings. He also involved the private sector as primary service providers. Almost all the programs—group homes, day treatment, outreach through "trackers"—are managed by contract with private providers, and even some of the secure programs are privately operated.

The new arrangement was not without its critics, who claimed that it was too lenient and compromised public safety. In 1989, however, the National Council on Crime and Delinquency—a non-profit research organization—conducted a comprehensive evaluation of the Massachusetts model and published its results in a report called "Unlocking Juvenile Corrections." Not only did the report conclude that there had been no compromise of public safety, it also found that juveniles committed to the state's Department of Youth Services—violent and non-violent offenders alike—had subsequently reduced both the severity and the frequency of their criminal activities. This finding, the report contends, suggests that the Massachusetts emphasis on rehabilitation was effective. The study included a comparison with recidivism rates in California: Youth released from California institutions had a reincarceration rate of 62 percent; Massachusetts' rate was 23 percent.

Other States

The Massachusetts model has been implemented to varying degrees by other states besides Utah. Maryland, for example, closed one of its two large training schools in 1987. In describing the process, the Center for Youth Policy at the University of Michigan pointed out in a study of its own that Maryland was careful to adhere to one of Miller's key concepts, namely, that the money that supported the institution must follow the youths back into the community to insure the availability of adequate resources for community alternatives.

In some jurisdictions, juvenile court judges have themselves been attracted to the least-restrictive-setting principle. Andrew Shookoff, a judge in the juvenile court of Davidson County, Tennessee, observed in another telephone interview: "There's a recognition that in the past too much reliance was placed on closed institutions, so now there's more of a commitment to emphasize sanctions in the community rather than in secure settings."

Judge Shookoff, a former law professor at Nashville's Vanderbilt University, went on to note that the Tennessee legislature, influenced by what Utah has done, has already shut down one new juvenile facility and reduced the bed space in others.

Despite the positive results of the Massachusetts model as reported in "Unlocking Juvenile Corrections," and its emulation by several other states, its originator, Jerome Miller, does not see immediate hope for improvement in the juvenile justice system as a whole. During a conversation at the Alexandria, Virginia, office of the National Center on Institutions and Alternatives, which he founded, Dr. Miller commented on the situation as he presently views it.

"Positive change might come about if there were a willingness among bureaucrats to challenge the law-and-order rhetoric that keeps state training schools going," he said, "but so far little substantive discussion of the issue is taking place, because shutting down institutions means touching state jobs and the profits of institutional vendors, and that represents a major political risk.". . .

Litigation

On the other hand, in some jurisdictions litigation initiated by advocacy groups has resulted in positive change. Mr. Lambert, whose office has filed class action suits in over 10 states, cited Oklahoma as an illustration.

"Oklahoma was sued in 1978 because kids who didn't need secure settings were being locked up in closed institutions under terrible conditions, so eventually state officials shut the institutions down. Now the state is redirecting resources in an appropriate way that utilizes community-based alternatives."

Other states, like South Carolina, have been more resistant in the face of lawsuits. "There," Mr. Lambert said, "the response hasn't been to close anything, but simply to get more money from the legislature to patch the institution up, as they did with Green Hill in Washington State, so that a Federal judge will let them pass muster."

The District of Columbia, which also relies on large institutional settings, is another jurisdiction that has resisted making improvements sought through a class action suit, in this instance brought by the local Public Defender Service in 1985. Despite a consent decree negotiated a year later, little has changed at the secure facilities the District operates in nearby Laurel, Maryland. Their bucolic names, Cedar Knoll and Oak Hill, belie the actual nature of the locked cottages, where isolation—a factor in the high suicide rate of children confined in large, closed facilities—continues to be used as a form of punishment. David Reiser, an attorney, noted in a conversation that children whom District judges themselves have said do not require secure confinement, are nevertheless sent to Cedar Knoll and Oak Hill because the District has not developed adequate space in group homes for those adjudicated delinquent for non-serious offenses.

Race and Poverty

Virtually all the youths at Cedar Knoll and Oak Hill are African-American, and one especially troubling aspect of the growing numbers of incarcerated juveniles there and elsewhere concerns race. With respect to their proportion in the population at large, minorities are vastly overrepresented. The "Children in Custody" survey found that nearly 60 percent of youths in public custody facilities are either black or Hispanic. Nor does this circumstance hold true only in states with large urban areas like Los Angeles, New York and Miami. In Utah, whose black population statewide is less than one percent, the Division of Youth Corrections has reported that blacks held in detention are represented eight times more frequently than would be expected from their proportion in the youth population at risk.

Ira Schwartz suggests in his 1989 book *[In] Justice for Juveniles*, that the imbalance lies in the fact that black and Hispanic juveniles are more likely to be arrested than white youths who commit similar crimes. Racial bias in arrest procedures has been pointed out by other commentators as well. Because of poverty, moreover, the families of minority youths are often unable to arrange for the kind of strong legal representation more generally possible for white families. Even when free legal counsel is available, it may be inadequate. Mary Broderick, defender-division director at the National Legal Aid and Defender Association, remarked in a conversation that juvenile court is frequently used as a training ground for prosecutors and public defenders, and, therefore, the most inexperienced attorneys may be assigned there, some of them just out of law school.

The imbalance is consequently not only between white and non-white, but also between rich and poor. Mr. Reiser contends that one reason white children seldom find themselves at Cedar Knoll or Oak Hill is that their parents usually possess the resources, through insurance, to have their delinquent children placed by the court in private psychiatric facilities. According to Dr. Miller, this phenomenon holds true around the country: "Most states have arrangements with expensive private hospitals where there's a disproportionate number of white juveniles," he said. "Few rich kids land in the criminal justice system at all."

Budgetary Constraints

As for the prevention of juvenile crime, budgetary constraints that have caused communities to make sharp curtailments in their most basic public services have long-range negative implications for youth at risk. . . .

Edward Loughran, the commissioner of the Massachusetts Department of Youth Services, whose programs underwent a $5 million cut in 1991, remarked that the sharply restricted funding for public services around the country is at least obliging some jurisdictions to look more closely at alternative treatment programs because they are far less costly than continued reliance on institutions. Promising programs exist in states as resistant to change as Washington. Washington, in fact, began one that has been adopted in other states: Homebuilders, which, as its name implies, tries to meet the needs of minors in trouble with the law by addressing the needs of the family as a whole.

But resistance on the part of state and local juvenile justice officials to experiment with such programs on a wide scale remains strong in regions with an entrenched reliance on the institutional model. If Jerome Miller is correct, solid changes are not yet to be expected because, as he put it, the will to do right for at-risk youth is not present at this moment in the nation's history.

> *"It seems reasonable . . . that juveniles who commit violent crimes be tried as adults."*

Violent Juveniles Should Be Tried as Adults

Suzanne Fields and Joseph Perkins

In Part I of the following two-part viewpoint, columnist Suzanne Fields argues that teenage boys who commit rape should be tried as adults, although it would be preferable to prevent such rapes from occurring by increasing adults' involvement in children's lives. In Part II, Joseph Perkins contends that because of the severe nature of the violent crime committed by youths today, the juvenile justice system should be reformed. He holds that violent juveniles should be tried as adults, and that the court proceedings and criminal records of violent juveniles should be open to the public. Perkins is a columnist for the *San Diego Union-Tribune*.

As you read, consider the following questions:

1. How are men different from women, according to John Updike, as quoted by Fields?
2. What percentage of the American public favors trying juveniles as adults, according to Perkins?
3. According to Perkins, why should the court proceedings of violent youths not be closed to the public?

Suzanne Fields, "Teenage Mischief Becomes Teenage Terror," *Conservative Chronicle*, November 17, 1993. Reprinted with permission. Joseph Perkins, "Crime, Age, and Punishment," *The Washington Times*, June 4, 1994. Reprinted by permission.

I

Teenage boys know how to push the boundaries. That's how they learn what they can get away with and what they can't. We see it around us, on the front pages and on the evening news.

That's also how they develop a sense of right and wrong. If they listen only to their hormones when engaging the girls, or limit their expression of the competitive spirit to displays of physical toughness with other boys, they can become sadistic young savages.

In the novel *Lord of the Flies*, several civilized English boys, shipwrecked on an island without adult supervision, descend into uncivilized behavior and ruthlessly indulge selfish and violent sexual gratifications.

A man of a certain age understands this scenario in both flesh and brains. John Updike, now 60, muses with eloquent sophistication on the physical drives of being a man:

"Any accounting of male-female differences must include the male's superior recklessness, a drive not, I think, toward death, as the darker feminist cosmogonies would have it, but to test the limits, to see what the traffic will bear."

The more permissive the cultural message, the greater the recklessness, the more violent the traffic jams among adolescent boys.

Many of them race into lawlessness because they never learn how to rein their appetites. Irreverence, rebelliousness, rudeness and disrespect easily decline into cruel, mean, vicious, indecent behavior that is literally and figuratively criminal.

Consequences

Criminal behavior has consequences. Many young men haven't learned that, either. We know how dangerous a young man with a gun can be, but many young men today use their bodies as weapons, too.

The consequences—they are a changin'.

When four young men, ages 15 to 19, were accused of gang rapes by two 14-year-old girls in Germantown, Maryland, a suburb of the nation's capital, they were charged with first-degree rape, a charge that can only be brought against adults—or children charged as adults, stripped of the protections available to juveniles—and carries the potential for life in prison.

"We woke up a lot of kids," said Maj. Carol Mehrling, chief of Montgomery County's investigative service. "No matter how old you are, there is right and wrong. Kids must not continue to think that nothing will happen to them if they commit serious crimes."

That's a start. Violent actions require uniform punishment no matter what the age. We used to say that if a boy is old enough to go to war, he's old enough to drink. If a boy is old enough to rape, he's old enough to do a man's time.

More troubling for society is how to reach young boys before they suffer the illusion that they are men. One of the boys charged with first-degree rape is the son of the superintendent of Montgomery County schools. Friends and neighbors, all middle class, are looking for scapegoats among the usual suspects—television, videos, movies, peer pressure.

They're also looking at themselves with greater scrutiny, wondering if they spend enough time with their children and if they bear any responsibility for the breakdown in moral behavior.

Gorrell/*Richmond Times-Dispatch*. Used by permission.

The changes in middle-class residential neighborhoods are part of the equation. Many are empty of adults during the day. Children who in another era would come home to Mom with milk and cookies now return to empty houses. Both parents are working, or divorce has created a single-parent home. (You don't have to wait for Halloween to find a haunted house.)

In 1990, the Search Institute, a nonprofit organization in Minnesota, studied more than 45,000 children, mostly white and Midwestern, and found that nearly half of the sixth graders and more than half of the 12th graders spent at least two hours a day at home alone without an adult.

Cultural critics often prefer to talk about the underclass than the middle class, but many middle-class children form only transient relationships with adults in their lives. Teachers and coaches have little time to give individual attention. The daily family dinner, where news of school, Granny and the hamster is exchanged, is a ritual as endangered as meat loaf and mashed potatoes made from scratch.

When adults are but distant figures it's easy to mock authority. Boys have the sexual capability to act like men, but without the emotional maturity and understanding to love, respect and protect the women they desire (with or without condoms).

We can and sometimes must punish them as adults, but we'd do better to get to know them when they're still children.

II

I read the news this week [May 29–June 4, 1994], oh boy. In Cleveland, Tennessee, 17-year-old Shannon Blaylock went on trial for the rape and robbery of his former foster mother. She was stripped, bound, burned with cigarettes, repeatedly raped and shot in the leg. In Griffin, Georgia, six boys, ages 11 to 14, appeared before a juvenile court judge on charges of raping a 9-year-old girl. She was picking berries when she was attacked.

In Murietta, California, two 19-year-olds, Khamchan Ketsouvannasane and Xou Yang, were named prime suspects in a brutal attack that left a German tourist dead and her husband seriously wounded.

Not an Aberration

It might be something of a comfort if these depraved acts were an aberration, if the juveniles involved were unusually bad seeds. But youth violence is occurring with increasing frequency throughout the country. America has an epidemic on its hands.

FBI statistics bear this out. Between 1987 and 1991, the number of juveniles arrested for such violent crimes as rape, robbery, aggravated assault and homicide increased 50 percent.

This ominous trend owes to a number of factors, the most significant of which are that more and more kids are packing firearms—viewing their weapons almost as fashion accessories—and more are involved with drugs. Indeed, between 1984 and 1994, the number of juveniles arrested for gun-related murder increased by 80 percent. The youth arrest rate for sale or use of such hard drugs as heroin and cocaine skyrocketed 700 percent.

Lawmakers in both Washington and state capitals have fallen all over themselves to pass legislation proving to voters that they are getting tougher on crime. But neither the 1994 federal crime bill nor the various "three strikes" and related bills that assorted state legislatures have ginned up will make a dent in juvenile crime.

That's because youthful offenders rarely pass through the adult criminal justice system. Most are tried in juvenile courts, which treat even the most hardened, unrepentant, inveterate young criminals as though they are reclamation projects for some latter-day Father Flanagan.

But that's old think. Juvenile delinquency today is not about fist fights or joy rides in stolen cars or vandalizing property. It's about drive-by shootings and carjackings and gang rapes and murdered tourists. The juvenile justice system has yet to evolve to reflect these changes in the severity of youth crimes.

About the only "get tough" measure federal and state lawmakers have taken to address youth crime is the creation of boot camps. If a kid is underage and maims or even kills someone, he's sentenced to push-ups at 5 o'clock in the morning. Sorry, but that hardly seems a deterrent to youth violence.

If lawmakers insist on throwing money at boot camps, they need to target the right juveniles. It does little good to send violent young offenders to a camp. They require stronger punishment.

But a month or two of boot camp could do some good for the kids who commit nonviolent offenses. It would be a happy medium between caning and the slap on the wrist that they now receive.

As to violent youth, laws need to be enacted that will make them think twice about preying on the innocent. It seems reasonable, for instance, that juveniles who commit violent crimes be tried as adults. Such a reform is favored by 73 percent of the American public.

As it is now, many young offenders are well aware they will receive lenient treatment in juvenile court no matter how loathsome their crime. They will be far more circumspect if they know that they will be tried and sentenced as an adult if they commit adult crimes.

In a similar vein, there is no reason that all juvenile court proceedings should remain closed to the public and the criminal records of all young offenders remain confidential. It may be reasonable to protect the privacy of juveniles who commit nonviolent acts. But if a youth is arrested for a violent crime, he deserves no special privacy.

Moreover, those who may come in contact with the violent youth—classmates, teachers, neighbors, employers—have a right to know about the youth's criminal background so that they can take proper precaution. America is plagued with youth violence because the juvenile justice system continues to treat young offenders with kid gloves.

We will continue to read weekly reports of underage rapes and robberies and assaults and murders until lawmakers finally get around to enacting some reforms.

"*Three different studies . . . show significantly higher recidivism rates for youths tried in adult courts compared to those tried in juvenile courts.*"

Violent Juveniles Should Not Be Tried as Adults

Jennifer Vogel

Politicians and the courts in various states are advocating harsh penalties for youthful offenders—including lowering the age at which violent juveniles can be tried as adults. In the following viewpoint, Jennifer Vogel argues that such efforts are overreactions to sensationalistic stories and inflated crime statistics reported by the media. She argues that placing juveniles in the adult criminal justice system puts youths at risk for abuse and fails to reduce crime. Vogel is an investigative reporter for *City Pages*, a weekly publication in Minneapolis–St. Paul, Minnesota.

As you read, consider the following questions:

1. According to Vogel, what rationale do pundits provide for the push for harsher penalties for youths?
2. What percentage of juvenile offenses are violent crimes, according to the author?
3. What alternatives to harsh penalties does the author describe?

Jennifer Vogel, "Throw Away the Key," *Utne Reader*, July/August 1994. Reprinted with permission.

Judged by any number of statistical yardsticks—infant mortality, child poverty, teen suicide and incarceration—America in the '90s is doing in kids at an alarming rate. It's estimated that every day, 2,700 babies are born into poverty, more than 2,000 students drop out of school, 250 kids are arrested for violent crimes, and 1,700 are abused by their parents. Youthful America's vision of its own future has never been more dire, particularly in the cities. As one 17-year-old African-American put it on his way into court: "I been dead since I was 12, so I'm not afraid of dying. I'm just waiting to get kicked into the grave."

Watching the courts and Congress, it's easy to conclude that the country is waging a battle against its children. While schools, jobs, and the social safety net continue to erode, more kids are finding themselves caught up in an ever-expanding criminal justice system. Politicians and the major media, having discovered a boom market in the public frenzy for bigger jails and longer sentences, have made juvenile offenders the Willie Hortons of the '90s. [Willie Horton is a black convict who became the symbol of crime in George Bush's 1988 presidential election campaign.]

"Over the 1980s, the United States achieved the highest rates of incarceration in the industrialized world, moving past South Africa and the former Soviet Union," notes a 1993 study by the Milton S. Eisenhower Foundation. "Because the inmates were disproportionately young, in many ways prison building became the American youth policy of choice. . . . By the 1992 elections, one in every four young African-American males was either in prison, on probation, or on parole."

Well-Founded Skepticism

These are uncommonly honest observations compared to the reams of recent studies and white papers on "the juvenile problem." Generally speaking, young people themselves are far more candid than politicians and pundits about what lies ahead. When a national study compared the worries of high school seniors in 1979 to those of 1991, it found less concern about nuclear war, more about hunger and poverty. The numbers bear out their skepticism:

• Unemployment among teens was 19 percent in 1993, up from 15.3 percent five years earlier—and for black youths, the figure was twice that high. For those who do find jobs, the average hourly wage has fallen nearly 10 percent since the mid-1980s.

• Since 1970, Aid to Families with Dependent Children benefits have declined an average of 45 percent in inflation-adjusted dollars, according to the Children's Defense Fund.

• In 1992, there were 14.6 million children living below the poverty line, the Children's Defense Fund says, about 5 million more than in 1973.

- In 1993, there were 3 million victims of child abuse, according to the National Committee for the Prevention of Child Abuse—a rate 50 percent higher than in 1985. Studies also indicate that the majority of prison inmates were abused as children.
- Teen suicide rates increased nearly 20 percent during the 1980s.

The Push for Harsher Penalties

But numbers like these are not the stuff of legislative debate, in Washington or in state legislatures around the country. Almost without exception, the trend among lawmakers is to use highly publicized incidents of brutal violence—often charged with racial stereotypes—to push for harsher penalties. In Minnesota in 1992, a 16-year-old black youth who broke into a suburban home and killed a white woman and her child became the poster child for juvenile justice reform. Neighbors actually circulated a petition to have him tried as an adult; 20,000 signed on. In Minnesota as elsewhere, legislators have decided to play to mob sentiments.

Of course this shift requires a rationale, and pundits have been quick to provide one. Juvenile justice laws weren't set up to deal with these new monsterlike children, they say, but to give kids stealing cookies from cookie jars a slap on the wrist. (The presumption here is that juvenile law just isn't tough enough; in fact, kids in some states tend to serve longer sentences in juvenile facilities than adults convicted of similar crimes.) While there already are numerous provisions for getting serious juvenile offenders into adult courts, the "reforms" sweeping the nation now seek to wipe out the protected status of juveniles as a class, making it easier to put young offenders on the road to lifelong incarceration by the age of 13 or 14.

News outlets play their part by routinely featuring images of vacant-eyed children carrying out acts of random violence. They happily parrot jacked-up statistics and stereotypes about teenagers, capping the information with headlines like "Killer Kids"—or this, from the *Los Angeles Times*: "Who are our children? One day, they are innocent. The next, they may try to blow your head off." One of the most prominent myths of the media is that kids are the biggest problem this country faces in its battle against crime, when in fact they make up only 16 to 17 percent of total arrests, according to one expert.

The percentage of kids arrested has remained fairly constant during the past 10 to 15 years. Though statistics is anything but an exact science, it appears that there's been a decline in juvenile property crimes such as theft, break-ins, and robberies, and an increase in murders, aggravated assaults, and other violent crimes. Even so, only a small percentage of juvenile offenses are violent crimes: about 5 percent in 1990.

Says Bob DeComo, senior program manager for the National Council on Crime and Delinquency: "I think the public perception is that [violent crime committed by juveniles] has increased much more dramatically than is really the case. It is a fact that violent crimes are up, but the extent is overstated in part because of attention to crime in general. It's still the case that the public is much more likely to be victimized by an adult."

A Futile Trend

State legislatures around the country have responded to concerns about the rising number of juvenile killings, often overreacting to certain highly publicized cases of brutal and senseless murder involving teens. In recent years, most states have made it easier—even automatic—to try juvenile killers as adults. Ignoring the immaturity of a 15- or 16-year-old, lawmakers have accepted the idea that murder is an adult crime and thus deserves an adult punishment. . . .

The national trend toward trying juveniles as adults in order to incarcerate them longer may address the need for justice and retribution, but it cannot be counted on for dissuading kids from the temptations and thrill of street crime and gang membership. No matter how punitive society becomes and what kind or how strong of a message is sent out to the street, teens who are attracted to crime always will turn a deaf ear to deterrence. Besides, by the time a juvenile offender has "graduated" to murder, it is likely too late to reach him.

Russell Eisenman, *USA Today*, January 1994.

Not that some of the numbers aren't troubling. In 1981, according to Federal Bureau of Justice statistics, youths were charged with 53,240 violent crimes; in 1992, the figure was 104,137. There's something about kids that clearly *isn't* the same as it was 20 years ago. "We're reaping the benefits of 12 years of lessening federal commitments," says Miriam Rollin, vice president for advocacy development for the National Association of Child Advocates:

I would think that if the concern was for the future, that would lead more clearly to the response that lets us invest in them. I think people are scared. I don't know that we've ever had the kind of desperation among young people, particularly in poverty, nor have we had the number of young people in poverty as we do today. I think people understand, to a certain extent, what that means. That you are potentially creating a very dysfunctional young person. There aren't enough jails and facilities to lock up all the poor kids in this country, but that's what they are on their way toward doing.

Deferring the Problem

Around the country, the most popular solutions include defining new classes of juvenile crime, making juvenile records public, creating boot camps for young offenders, tightening up curfew laws (in some cases fining parents who don't keep their kids in the house at night), and installing metal detectors in schools. One state proposed trying 12-year-olds as adults, and another has sought to eliminate age guidelines altogether.

But, like deficit spending, locking up youths may only be a way to defer the problem. In a speech before Congress in March 1994, Michael E. Saucier, national chair of the Coalition for Juvenile Justice, said the approach "looks tough but is short-sighted. It addresses the problem of serious juvenile crime by allowing youth to be dealt with in an adult setting, a setting that is almost completely bankrupt when it comes to crime prevention, rehabilitation, or reducing recidivism."

"Juveniles in adult institutions are five times more likely to be sexually assaulted, twice as likely to be beaten by staff, and 50 percent more likely to be attacked with a weapon than youths in a juvenile facility," Saucier continued. "The most revealing research is three different studies conducted over a ten-year period that show significantly higher recidivism rates for youths tried in adult courts compared to those tried in juvenile courts for the same offenses and with similar personal profiles."

It isn't that there are no workable alternatives—just that the very concept of rehabilitation has fallen out of favor. Every year the Office of Juvenile Justice and Delinquency Prevention gives awards to particularly effective programs around the country. Those honored in 1993 included a Nebraska program in which juvenile offenders are educated and taught independent living and family reconciliation strategies. It boasts a 50 percent reduction in recidivism. In New Hampshire, juvenile offenders are offered the chance to do community service work for local businesses or nonprofit agencies in lieu of going to jail, again resulting in very low recidivism rates.

The choice is clear, says Rollin: "Would you rather have them get out after they've had some sort of program or have them grow up in an adult facility and come out better criminals, having completed the ideal criminal mentoring program?"

"Schools have a responsibility to help students understand, avoid, and survive . . . not only infectious diseases, but . . . violence, as well."

Conflict Resolution Programs Can Prevent Youth Violence

Deborah Prothrow-Stith and Michaele Weissman

Many of the nation's schools have instituted conflict resolution programs designed to teach youths how to settle disputes nonviolently. In the following viewpoint, excerpted from their book *Deadly Consequences*, Deborah Prothrow-Stith and Michaele Weissman describe one such program that they say can prevent fighting among high school students. Prothrow-Stith is assistant dean at the Harvard School of Public Health in Cambridge, Massachusetts. Weissman is a freelance writer in Newton, Massachusetts.

As you read, consider the following questions:

1. What five ideas do all conflict resolution programs share, according to the authors?
2. What is good and bad about fighting, according to the students' list presented by Prothrow-Stith and Weissman?
3. What are some responses to insults that can prevent fights, according to the authors?

Public health has a long history of collaboration with public schools to safeguard the lives of children. At school, many young people are gathered together at one location; public health takes advantage of this "captive" audience to promote a health agenda. To protect children from measles, mumps, polio, and diphtheria, public health officials use the legal clout and administrative resources of schools to require that parents have their children inoculated. Public health clinicians screen children in school-based clinics for vision and hearing difficulties, for tuberculosis, for scoliosis, and for other remediable conditions. In the classroom, public health–sponsored health education is a staple. Children are taught about fitness, human reproduction, nutrition, substance abuse, and so forth. Education programs operate on the assumption that individuals who understand the health risks confronting them are more likely to make healthy decisions.

When I began to think about creating a behavior modification program that would teach adolescents how to avoid fighting, I did not doubt that this program belonged in the public schools. I believed then and I continue to believe that high schools have a responsibility to help students understand, avoid, and survive the lethal menaces of childhood and adolescence—not only infectious diseases, but drugs, AIDS, alcohol abuse, teenage pregnancy, suicide, and violence, as well. The violence prevention curriculum I created [*The Violence Prevention Curriculum for Adolescents*] was designed to fit within a tenth grade health course. I assumed that truthful information about the risks of fighting could and would change students' attitudes about fighting and, over time, their behavior. I was not aiming at miracles. I did not think that a single intervention would save the world. I saw the curriculum as a beginning, a first step, that would eventually be joined with other interventions inside and outside the schools. I kept the successful campaign to reduce smoking as my model: In 25 years, using an imaginative array of public health strategies, we had reduced the number of smokers in the United States by 30 percent. Health education in the schools had been an important component in the anti-smoking effort. I believed health education in the schools would play a similar role in the effort to reduce adolescent violence. . . .

Conflict Resolution

Programs in many schools all over the country have been designed to help school children with what one school teacher calls "the fourth R—Relationships." The goal of these "conflict resolution" programs is to teach children how to get along with one another peacefully. All of these programs share certain ideas:
- That conflict is a normal part of human interaction.
- That when people take the time to explore their prejudices,

they can learn how to get along with (and enjoy) people whose backgrounds are different.

- That most disputes do not have to have a winner or loser. Win/win is the ideal way to resolve most disputes.
- That children and adults who learn how to assert themselves non-violently can avoid becoming bullies or victims.
- That the self-esteem of children will be enhanced if they learn to build non-violent, non-hostile relationships with their peers. . . .

Alternatives to Fighting

"Conflict resolution" goes hand and hand with my violence prevention curriculum. . . . I think it is extremely important to help teenagers understand the risk of violence to their survival, to learn about their own anger, and to learn some practical skills for deflecting angry confrontations and fights. . . .

The point of the violence prevention course is to provide young people with alternatives to fighting. The first three lessons of the ten-session curriculum provide adolescents with information about violence and homicide. Urban teenagers are not surprised to learn that most homicides occur among people of the same race, people who know each other. This fact corresponds to their experience. They are surprised to find out that gangs and drugs do not cause 80 or 90 percent of all homicides. This misperception is as self-serving for them as it is for the rest of society. Like adults, young people would rather think that UZI-toting, crack-selling gang members are responsible for the violence. No one wants to face how ordinary most assaults and most homicides are. No one wants to admit that the mass of these crimes involves plain people; acquaintances, family members, who drink, who disagree, who have a gun.

Some of the most interesting classes occur in the next set of lessons. These deal with the nature of anger. The goal is to help students understand that anger is a normal emotion that they will not outgrow, an emotion that each of us must learn to handle without hurting ourselves or others. We start by having the students list all the things that make them angry. Many have never had a chance to reflect in this way before. A fast-writing teacher can travel around the room filling up blackboard after blackboard with things that students say make them angry. Among the approximately 100 entries compiled by one class of inner city youths were extremely serious items such as drugs, gangs, and teenage pregnancy, and items that were silly and "adolescent":

Someone dies . . . V.D. . . . ignorant people . . . drug addicts . . . police . . . teachers who accuse you of cheating . . . teachers who have favorites . . . girls who have short hair . . . girls who won't buy you anything . . . girls who try to get you to support a baby that's not yours . . . threat of nuclear war . . .

no money . . . parents who try to tell you what to do . . . gangs
. . . men who talk to young girls . . . people who don't wash
. . . dandruff . . . boys who are homosexuals . . . boys who
"stick and kick" (get a girl pregnant and then leave her) . . .
people who think school is a beauty parlor . . . smoking on the
bus . . . boys with pierced ears.

Creative Initiatives

It is a sad commentary that metal detectors, magnetic door locks,
X-ray machines and surveillance cameras are being installed in
schools across the country. But it is encouraging that school administrators, teachers, parents and students themselves are responding to the crisis of violence with an impressive variety of
creative, school-based initiatives. . . .

In Dayton, Ohio, the SPEIR program (Students Participating
Equally in Resolution) coaches youngsters in "anger management" and communication skills. In Cambridge, Massachusetts,
The Harvard Negotiation Project teaches high school students
how to calm emotional flare-ups and defuse conflicts nonviolently. More than 100 public schools in New York are offering a
course in "Resolving Conflict Creatively.". . .

These programs empower young people not only to cope with violence at school, but also to deal with aggression and conflicts they
will face for the rest of their lives. Such programs ought to be required for high school graduation in every school in the nation.

Coretta Scott King, *Liberal Opinion Week*, October 11, 1993.

The next lesson is designed to help teenagers think about the
way they deal with their own anger. Students list all the ways
they respond when angry and then rate them as healthy or unhealthy. Students tend to be quite imaginative in their healthy
strategies. Some of the healthy ways students report responding
to anger include:
Read a book . . . walk . . . Leave—walk away
(kids saw this as potentially healthy and potentially unhealthy)
. . . listen to music . . . have sex
(Young people tend to see sex as a "healthy" way to deal with
anger. Adults do not. The discussion that follows can be interesting.)
. . . lock yourself in your room . . . hang out . . . argue
(arguing they see as healthy or unhealthy depending on the circumstances)
. . . sleep . . . watch T.V. . . . slam doors . . . talk on phone . . .
bite nails . . . grit teeth . . . yell/scream . . . sing . . . eat . . .

> play ball . . . do homework . . . take a bath . . . count to ten
> . . . lift weights . . . talk it out . . . cry . . . meditate . . . throw
> things that can't be broken . . .

Their unhealthy list included:

> Take it out on someone else . . . drink alcohol . . . take drugs
> . . . fight/kill . . . attempt suicide . . . mark on walls . . . rob
> people. . . .

Fighting, of course, is always on the list. In the next lesson we
do a cost/benefit analysis of fighting. We have students create
two lists describing what is good and what is bad about fighting.
This leads students to the realization that they have more to lose
than to gain from fighting. This conclusion is drawn from the
students' list; it is not a teacher-imposed insight. Inevitably, the
list describing what is bad about fighting is longer and more impressive than the list telling what is good about fighting. There
really is much more to lose than to gain from fighting. Here is
the list created by one class:

What's Good and What's Bad About Fighting

Good	Bad
winning	kill someone
prove your point	get killed
get a reputation	might lose
get attention	get embarrassed
enjoyment	get suspended from school
relieves tension	get expelled
evens the score	lose a job
satisfaction	get a bad reputation and no one
earn money	wants to hang out with you
(become a pro)	because you're always fighting
	have an enemy coming after you
	revenge cycle begins
	get clothes dirty or torn
	get scarred for life
	may have to pay for broken things
	lose respect of friends
	parents responsible for medical bills
	get punished
	hurt innocent bystanders
	hurt person (then be sorry)

Looking at this list—their own list—students begin to think
about fighting. Many of the males have never before considered
not fighting. They begin to question their own values. They also
question mine. They want to know where I stand. "Does this
mean," they ask me, "that you would never fight?" I tell them
that I am not a pacifist, that I do think there are issues that are

worth fighting for and perhaps even dying for. I would fight to protect my husband and children if I believed that fighting was the only way to save them from imminent danger, I tell them, but I would not fight because someone called me, or my husband or my children, a name. Many of the students attribute my attitude about fighting to my sex. "What about your husband?" they want to know. One student asked me what I would expect Charles to do if he were walking down the street with our daughter and a man *on the other side of the street* started calling her names. For me, of course, the answer is easy. I would expect Charles to ignore the insults, explain to Mimi that they were not going to listen to such foolishness and then walk in the other direction as quickly as possible. The mere asking of this question is an important reflection of the level at which many adolescents think about these issues. The combination of their age-appropriate narcissism and the special emphasis that poor males put on respect hobbles their ability to make distinctions between real threats and trivial ones. The head of a mentoring program in Pittsburgh who was interviewed by Professor Ron Ferguson had an interesting comment that illuminates the issue of respect: *"One of the things that we observed,"* he told Professor Ferguson, *"was that the young men had a difficult time respecting one another: . . . They wanted to receive respect, but they didn't have proper training to respect one another. We had to work on this with them."* Many young black men seem to feel that showing respect for someone else is a form of toadying. The combination of their super-sensitivity to slights and their lack of sensitivity to the feelings of others sets the stage for fights and violence.

Making Students Think

Another question that students often ask is "What if someone calls your mother a bad name? Don't you *have* to fight then?" There is a certain sweetness and loyalty to their mothers inherent in this question that I find touching, but of course completely wrong-headed. "Look," I always answer, "so you get into a fight because someone calls your mother a bad name. You get your clothes torn, or you get thrown out of school for fighting, or maybe you get killed. Is that respectful of your mother? Don't you think your mother would rather that you come home alive, in one piece, that you stay in school and graduate? Isn't that the real way to show her respect?" "Yes," they say, "but . . . but . . . but. . . ." This way of thinking makes inner city young people uneasy. I have never had a student convert to non-violence right before my eyes, but I know they do think about what I am saying. In fact, you can see them thinking really hard, during the classroom discussion, and that is the whole point of the curriculum—to engage them, to make them think about their behavior, to make them understand the control they have over their behavior and to begin to question the inevitability of fighting.

A third question I am often asked by high school students is what I would do if someone just came up to me and hit me for no reason. Again, this question is interesting as it highlights the psychological concerns of young people, especially young males, and their sense of being perpetually vulnerable—not only to the potential assaults of known foes, but to the potential assaults of strangers. I usually answer this question by saying that I do not know what I would do if randomly assaulted, but I would hope, given how common gun-carrying has become, that I would be self-possessed enough to retreat. When facing any combatant in a fight, especially a stranger, one has no way of knowing if he or she is armed. The point to be remembered, I say, is that there is almost always more to be lost than gained from fighting, and the list of what you can lose is topped by your most precious possession—your life. Then I explain that fights almost always have a history. Rarely does a stranger smack a stranger. I tell them that I feel certain that no one in the classroom has ever been the victim of a completely random assault. The students usually assent to this point. We can then talk about the kinds of fights they have had, the facts of which generally corroborate the statistics relating that most fights occur between people who know each other, who argue.

Role Plays

This discussion is a good lead-in to the concluding set of lessons in which mock fights—"role plays"—are created, staged, videotaped, analyzed, discussed, and then re-worked with different endings. Students break down into small groups to create their skits and rehearse. Each group of "actors" is asked to decide:

- Who is going to fight?
- What will they fight about?
- Where will the fight take place?
- Who will be the friends, girlfriends/boyfriends and onlookers?

The sketches must describe real-life circumstances. Students are not allowed to create role plays about strangers and criminal violence. Nor do we allow profanity. Skits continue right up to the moment in which the first imaginary punch is thrown. At that moment the teacher shouts, "Cut" and the "role play" is over.

The goal of the "role plays" is to show kids—in reality to have kids show themselves

- that most fights are embedded in a series of relationships.
- that most fights have a history.
- that the best and safest time to intervene to stop a fight is

early in its genesis when the antagonists' animosity is just building.

- that there are techniques for preventing fights, once you recognize the patterns.

Each group of students presents their four or five minute playlets before the entire class. Videotaping, if the school owns the equipment, greatly improves the ability to analyze the "role plays." At the next class, if the role plays have been videotaped, . . . the teacher replays the tape and asks the class to decide where each fight could have been prevented.

Stopping Fights

Students pick out the spot where a friend instigates the dispute by shouting, "Are you going to let that jerk stomp on your shoes?" where he could just as easily have said one of these to his friend:

- "Hey man, a little dirt on your sneaker is not worth fighting about."
- "Hey man, take it easy, it was an accident."
- "Hey man, let's give this hothead some room to chill out."

Students learn the most when they come up with their own strategies for stopping fights, but often it takes a lot of adult prompting for a teenager to see that he or she does not have to rise to every insult. One of the most talented people teaching the violence prevention curriculum, Ann Bishop, from Cathedral High School, always tells her students that the best way to respond to insults is with a non-defensive question:

- "Why would you want to say that?"
- "Why would you want to tell me I am ugly (or dumb, or fat) and hurt my feelings?"

This response stops the insulter short. Suddenly he (or she) is on the defensive.

By talking about these issues in the classroom, students have a chance to think up non-violent strategies for getting out of hot spots, before they are in a crisis. Another one of my violence prevention colleagues, Peter Stringham, M.D., a family practitioner who works in a health center in a poor, white neighborhood with a great deal of violence talks to all his adolescent patients about fighting and tries to get his young patients to memorize a few stock answers that can help them avoid fights.

- "This isn't worth fighting about."
- "If you've got a problem with me, I'll talk, but I don't want to fight."
- "I have nothing against you and I don't want to fight."

Humor seems to be the best strategy for diffusing potentially violent situations. Some kids are absolute masters at using humor to lower the temperature of a tense interaction. They do it intuitively. During one role play about a fight between two young males who were rivals for the same girl's attention, I saw a young male, "who'd just been called a 'dumb, ugly blank-head,'" by his rival turn sweetly to his foe and say, "I know you couldn't be talking to me." Everyone broke up—the other "actor," the whole class, me. For the quick-witted, this tactic works wonderfully to halt heated exchanges. Laughter removes the desire to hit. Unfortunately, not all of us have the talent to think of the perfect rejoinder when we are in a high-pressure situation.

Many students have a difficult time when we get to the end of the curriculum. They want a perfect strategy for avoiding fights that won't cause them any embarrassment or loss of social standing. Unfortunately, there are no such strategies. Not for kids living in a society that largely condones violence. Children who choose not to fight are bucking the trend, or rather, they are beginning a new trend. It's not easy. Ann Bishop tells the story of one of her students who really connected with the curriculum. Sometime after he took the course, he got into a conflict with another kid in which he was expected to do battle. The student used the techniques he had learned to prevent the fight. He probably prevented an injury, or maybe even a death. When the incident was over, however, the young man's friends did not praise his efforts. They thought he was a coward and told him so. Even his parents did not approve of his peace-making. Afterward, the young man became depressed. He felt terrible. Part of him believed what the others were saying—that not fighting was unmanly. Ann had to work with him for many months before he could begin to feel good about what he had done.

Educating students about violence is not an easy process. Not in this society, but if we do not tell kids that it is alright not to fight, no one else will.

"There is no evidence that [conflict resolution] programs produce long-term changes in violent behavior."

Conflict Resolution Programs Are Ineffective

Daniel W. Webster

Conflict resolution programs, which have been implemented in many American schools, strive to teach youths how to settle disagreements without resorting to violence. In the following viewpoint, Daniel W. Webster opposes these programs for the following four reasons: There is no evidence that the programs are effective; similar programs addressing other health and social problems have failed; the underlying assumptions of the programs are questionable; and the programs enable politicians to ignore the social and economic conditions that cause youth violence. Webster is an instructor in the Injury Prevention Center at the Johns Hopkins School of Hygiene and Public Health in Baltimore, Maryland.

As you read, consider the following questions:

1. Why might the desire to be healthy and safe encourage high-risk behavior, according to Webster?
2. According to the author, why are youths not motivated to use social skills learned from conflict resolution programs?
3. Why are negotiation skills of little relevance for youths in low-income neighborhoods, according to Webster?

Excerpted from "The Unconvincing Case for School-Based Conflict Resolution Programs for Adolescents" by Daniel W. Webster, *Health Affairs*, vol. 12, no. 4, Winter 1993. Reprinted by permission.

Frustration with the limited ability of the criminal justice system to stem the tide of youth violence has created considerable political pressure on governments and public agencies to do something about the problem. Statements by President Clinton and his secretaries of education, justice, and health and human services, as well as the actions of state and local officials, suggest greater future priority on public health approaches to violence, with their emphasis on primary prevention.

School-Based Programs

While many interventions stress primary prevention, school-based conflict resolution programs for adolescents have been one of the most popular public health strategies to reduce violence. A major focus of these programs is to teach and encourage students to use nonviolent methods of resolving disputes. In addition, these programs often present information about risks of victimization and use various methods to challenge attitudes that support the use of violence.

Conflict resolution programs now exist in thousands of middle and high schools. Some states are considering making these programs mandatory in public schools. The Centers for Disease Control and Prevention (CDC) has promoted and funded school-based conflict resolution programs, especially within the context of broader community programs. In practice, however, most school-based conflict resolution programs are implemented with no significant complementary efforts to address aspects of youths' environment (family, peers, and community) that foster violent behavior.

As with many other health-related social problems that affect youth (for example, substance abuse, teen pregnancy, and sexually transmitted diseases), school-based programs that heighten awareness, discourage risky behavior, and teach relevant social skills are an intuitively appealing and politically expedient response. Because of this and the desperation of many schools and communities, these programs have been widely implemented without adequate scrutiny to determine the scientific rationale and evidence of efficacy.

Skepticism

I am skeptical that existing conflict resolution programs can reduce interpersonal violence, for the following reasons: (1) There is no evidence that such programs produce long-term changes in violent behavior or risk of victimization; (2) in the absence of other supporting interventions, classroom-based curricula generally have failed to produce sustainable behavior changes for other health and social problems among youth; (3) the assumptions regarding conflict resolution programs and violence are questionable; and (4) the programs provide political cover for politicians, bureaucrats, and school officials and distract the public from the structural determinants of youth violence.

Violence Prevention Curriculum for Adolescents

This ten-session curriculum developed by Deborah Prothrow-Stith is perhaps the most widely used conflict resolution program in the nation. It was designed to teach adolescents about their risks of being injured or killed by violence, how to recognize and cope with anger, and how negative consequences of fighting usually outweigh any positives. Students are encouraged to find ways to deal with their anger and interpersonal conflicts other than with physical violence and are provided opportunities to role-play hypothetical conflict situations.

The short-term effectiveness of this curriculum was evaluated in a study involving tenth-graders at six inner-city high schools around the country. A teacher from each of these schools attended a one-day training session on how to use the curriculum. These teachers assigned classes to either an intervention or a control group. Teachers also were responsible for administering pretests two weeks before implementing the curriculum and posttests one month after the curriculum was completed. Usable data were available for only four of the sites.

When data for these four schools were combined and pretest measures were accounted for in the statistical models, no significant differences were found in posttest scores on knowledge about violence, attitudes about ways to handle conflicts, acceptance of violence, violence locus of control, self-esteem, self-reported fighting, drug use, or weapon carrying. . . .

The evaluators gave two possible reasons for lack of program effect: poor implementation and targeting the program to the wrong age group. Implementation by classroom teachers is likely to be a problem for any packaged curriculum. One of the barriers to program success most commonly cited by youth violence prevention practitioners is that teachers are usually overburdened with other educational responsibilities, and some have not bought into the idea of conflict resolution. With regard to the appropriate age group, the evaluators suggested that the program would have been more effective with middle school students than with high school students. Considering the early onset and relative intractability of aggressive behavior patterns, such a program actually may be more appropriate for children under age ten. . . .

Effectiveness of Other Prevention Curricula

Although no long-term evaluation of conflict resolution curricula has been conducted, there is an adequate body of evaluation research on curricula directed toward preventing other high-risk behavior among adolescents. While these evaluation results are not directly generalizable to conflict resolution programs, they offer several relevant lessons.

Project ALERT, a brief school-based curriculum to prevent substance use, delivered in the seventh grade with booster sessions in the eighth grade, could be compared with some of the brief conflict resolution curricula in use today. The program addressed social skills and peer influences, which are relevant to violence as well as to substance abuse. Despite initial promising findings, a large-scale experiment found that once the lessons stopped, so did the program's effect on drug use.

Reprinted by permission of Doug Marlette and Creators Syndicate.

Joy Dryfoos reviewed a broad array of evaluations of prevention programs addressing delinquency, substance abuse, and teen pregnancy. In general, she found that curricula that simply provided information about risks and used scare tactics were ineffective at changing behavior. A similar conclusion was made by the House Select Committee on Children, Youth, and Families concerning adolescent curricula to prevent human immunodeficiency virus/acquired immunodeficiency disease syndrome (HIV/AIDS).

Evaluations of more intensive curricula to prevent substance use that involve training in a variety of social skills including resisting peer pressure show more promising results. Dryfoos found that social-skill training was often a component of successful programs to prevent high-risk behavior among adolescents when the programs were relatively intensive and included follow-up booster sessions. She concluded, however, that there was no good evidence that social skill–oriented programs can prevent delinquency and that substance abuse programs that rely on social-skill training are generally ineffective with high-risk youth.

In her synopsis of the effectiveness of adolescent health education curricula, Dryfoos concluded, "We cannot rely on brief classroom-based curricula to alter complex socially derived patterns of behavior." Well-designed curricula could, however, be useful components of more comprehensive communitywide strategies that involve parents, community leaders, mass media, advocacy, and law enforcement. In its analysis of the limitations of stand-alone HIV/AIDS prevention curricula, the Select Committee on Children, Youth, and Families added to the call for more comprehensive interventions the necessity of providing "assistance in escaping the social and economic conditions that foster risk-taking."

Violence and Health Behavior

Many adolescent conflict resolution curricula are based on the following premises, which lack empirical support.

(1) Violent behavior is similar to other health behavior, and models of individual health behavior change can be readily applied to the problem of violence. Clearly, the behavior of perpetrators and potential victims of violence has important health consequences. The extent to which this behavior fits models designed to predict and alter other health behavior, however, is much less clear. For example, it is commonly presumed that a person's desire to be healthy and safe will be a key motivator for reducing or avoiding high-risk behavior. These desires, and in some cases, instincts, could actually encourage high-risk behavior when it comes to violence. Many inner-city youths believe that to survive, one must be tough, be willing to fight, carry a gun, and be willing to shoot it. Convincing youths otherwise is extremely difficult when they feel that they cannot rely on the police or others to protect them.

Based on the assumption that an insufficient level of perceived risk often prevents persons from making health behavior changes, many health education efforts include efforts to increase individuals' levels of perceived risk. Paradoxically, this also may increase violent behavior. Not only does a heightened sense of risk often prompt gun acquisition and carrying, but it also may exacerbate feelings of hopelessness already pervasive in many poor inner-city areas. Some youths in these areas engage in high-risk activities partly because they believe their chances of living beyond age thirty are slim anyway.

More broadly, key determinants of interpersonal violence often differ from determinants of other health behavior in nature and intensity. In the vast majority of acts of interpersonal violence by youth, there is an explicit intention to harm another person. The motives for such acts vary—extreme anger, revenge, self-protection, greed, desire to control or dominate someone—but are largely unique to violence. These motives can be intense, particularly in the heat of the moment, when a person may be overwhelmed by anger or fear. Individual-focused health education models and methods, therefore, may be inadequate for altering or overcoming these motivations.

(2) The violence prevention training needs of each student are similar enough that all would benefit from participation in a standardized program. In the spirit of primary prevention, conflict resolution programs often are delivered in blanket fashion, rather than being targeted to high-risk groups. While this makes a program relatively easy to administer within schools and avoids stigmatizing persons deemed to be at high risk, it does not adequately address the widely different needs of students. . . .

Social Skills and Behavior

(3) Adolescents who engage in violent behavior do so because of deficiencies in social information processing or other skills needed to solve social conflicts nonviolently. . . . Evaluations indicate that improvements in social skills generally do not lead to behavioral changes outside of controlled settings. . . .

There are many plausible explanations for the difficulty in producing behavioral change despite having measurable improvements in social skills. . . . Some argue that most social behavior is largely unthinking in nature and is driven by overlearned social scripts, particularly in moments of crisis. It seems unrealistic to expect youths to use brainstorming techniques practiced a few times in school to come up with alternative ways of handling spontaneous social conflicts. It is much more plausible that they would rely instead on their well-learned scripts. . . .

Programs that focus primarily on social-skill deficits are likely to be futile if youths are not motivated to use the skills. There are many reasons why they would not be so motivated. Aggressive youths tend to believe that aggressive behavior increases status among their peers, particularly in the short term, and provides tangible rewards. Acting tough and maintaining a reputation as someone willing and able to commit serious acts of violence is considered a necessity within gangs and groups involved in drug trafficking. Even outside of delinquent groups, there is considerable social pressure for youths, particularly males in low-income communities, not to back down when provoked. Although attitudes about violence often are discussed in conflict resolution programs, brief adult-led curricula cannot be expected to produce sustainable attitude change, particularly because adolescents are in a developmental stage characterized by defiance of adults.

(4) The most important social skill needed to reduce the risk of violence is how to negotiate one's way through conflicts. The apparent reasoning behind this premise is that for a large proportion (30 percent) of homicides, the circumstance surrounding the incident is classified as an "argument." To my knowledge, no one has studied police report narratives in an attempt to refine the "argument" category for homicide circumstances, but it is likely to include a wide variety of circumstances surrounding hostile interpersonal interactions.

For most middle-class adults, arguments usually stem from disagreements and competing interests. These conflicts often can be solved through negotiation. Negotiation skills may be of little relevance in a wide variety of other situations that involve heated interpersonal exchanges, particularly for youths in low-income neighborhoods. In my observation of conflict resolution programs in crime-ridden neighborhoods, it is rare for students to bring up incidents that fit the negotiated solution model well. More often, students talk about taunts, put-downs, competition over girlfriends and boyfriends, shake-downs, gang retaliation, and attempts to assert dominance over adversaries. Fights between boys in their early and middle teens are usually about status and respect. This is not surprising when one considers the heightened concern for respect among young people living in ghetto areas who generally are disrespected by society and deprived of legitimate opportunities to acquire symbols of status.

Potential Dangers

Regardless of how one interprets the existing research relevant to adolescent conflict resolution programs, opportunity costs must be considered in decisions to promote these programs. It is difficult to determine the amount of resources being devoted to adolescent conflict resolution programs. These programs are inexpensive to implement compared with other interventions; that is a big part of their appeal. Nevertheless, they are very popular, and in the aggregate, they consume considerable resources. Private companies are scrambling to fill the market's need for curriculum development and delivery. Thousands of teachers, counselors, health educators, and volunteers are spending countless hours in financially strapped schools and communities delivering programs to captive audiences of students.

In the absence of convincing evidence that adolescent conflict resolution programs reduce violence, these efforts may be better used in ways that are more likely to prevent violence or that have other socially desirable payoffs. For example, individualized attention to enhance students' academic performance could reduce school failure—often a precursor to antisocial behavior and a contributor to economic conditions that spawn violence. While there are many reasons why our schools have failed our youth, the ever-growing (and unrealistic) demands upon schools and teachers to solve students' social problems undoubtedly interfere with the teaching of necessary academic and vocational skills. Inadequate parental supervision and attention is another strong risk factor for delinquency. Resources thus could be devoted to mentoring and supervised recreation. Alternatively, more resources could be devoted to comprehensive early interventions for high-risk children.

In addition, promoting conflict resolution programs may actually hinder violence prevention by diverting attention from social and economic conditions that engender violence, the failure of governments and other social institutions to improve these conditions, and politically contentious issues such as strict gun control. Taking on powerful interest groups is difficult. Promoting conflict resolution programs as the solution to youth violence lets politicians off the hook by giving them something to point to when they are asked about what they are doing to reduce violence.

"Schools must discipline."

Punishment Should Be Used to Reduce School Violence

John Hood

According to John Hood, attempts to reduce violence in America's public schools have been hampered by two forces: an anti-punishment philosophy within the education profession and legal restrictions on schools' ability to discipline unruly students. In the following viewpoint, Hood contends that in order to overcome these obstacles, the nation should "adopt a private model for education" in which students are effectively disciplined and educated. Hood is research director at the John Locke Foundation, a state policy think tank in Raleigh, North Carolina, and a contributing editor of *Reason*, a monthly libertarian magazine.

As you read, consider the following questions:

1. Why are suspension and expulsion especially valuable forms of discipline, according to the author?
2. How does Hood respond to the argument that violent students need more self-esteem?
3. How does the student-school relationship differ in private versus public schools, according to the author?

Excerpted from "School Violence" by John Hood, *The Freeman*, February 1994. Reprinted by permission.

When politicians talk about education issues, they often mention such topics as school spending, teacher quality, parental involvement, and the curriculum. But when *teachers* talk about education issues, they almost always zero in on the topic that most concerns them: school violence. In talking to teachers around my home state of North Carolina, I have found this to be universally true. Teachers bring it up—whether it's retelling a "horror story," complaining about school boards and lawyers protecting students from punishment, or simply observing that students "aren't what they used to be.". . .

And the evidence is that they aren't. Violence in schools is up. Discipline is less predictable and not uniformly enforced. Students are, according to most teachers, more difficult to keep quiet, harder to teach, and deficient in basic personal and behavioral skills. Yet educational activists tend to focus more on opposing discipline practices they abhor—such as corporal punishment and expulsion—than on addressing the problem. In fact, today's public educators are probably incapable of dealing effectively with school violence and discipline problems. To do so requires rethinking how education is organized and the proper relationship between pupil and teacher, and more generally, between pupil and school. . . .

Legal Restrictions on School Discipline

A range of school disciplinary measures, ranging from public embarrassment to expulsion, have been successfully challenged in court. In the 1975 case *Goss* v. *Lopez*, the U.S. Supreme Court decided that the due process clause of the Fourteenth Amendment gave students the right to receive oral or written notice of the charges against them and, if they deny the charges, an explanation of the evidence and a chance to tell their side of the story. While no formal hearing was required for short-term suspensions, the Court suggested that more formal procedures might be required to impose longer suspensions or expulsions. While suspension remains an important response to acts of violence by students, these procedural limitations have made administrators more hesitant to use them.

Restrictions on suspension and expulsion are especially troubling because of the great damage that violent and disruptive students can do to the educational process. These students not only disrupt the classroom, thus making it difficult for other students to learn, but also generally weaken the authority of teachers and administrators. "This type of student," writes education researcher Kurran Heston, "has a negative effect on everyone around him or her." It's in the interest of the majority of students that schools be able to quickly eject such students from class. "Eighty to ninety percent of the kids in a classroom are good kids," Oakland, California, schoolteacher Ruth Meltsner told *Policy Review*. "A small number are impossible and you spend all your time dealing with them."

Other decisions have further limited school disciplinary practices. Indeed, Heston notes that since 1950, "schools have been placed under the jurisdiction of the courts, whereas the court may decide it is necessary to step in regarding discipline." James S. Coleman, who has conducted landmark studies comparing public and private school students, argues that "the growth of student rights constitutes a fundamental change in the relation of the school to the student, which had been that of trustee for parental authority." This has been replaced, Coleman says, by a relation in which the student "is regarded as having full civil rights."

Extending civil-rights protection to unruly students has created an unworkable, and sometimes absurd, situation in public schools. "The due process system assumes bad faith on the part of teachers," says Bruce A. Miller, special counsel to the American Federation of Teachers, "but teachers aren't lawyers—they have to have some freedom of action." Sociologist Jackson Toby agrees, and observed that a generation ago it was possible for principals to rule schools autocratically, to suspend or expel students without much regard for procedure. While some injustices occurred, the administrators were able to avoid significant violence and discipline problems. "Student assaults on teachers were punished so swiftly that they were almost unthinkable," Toby wrote. . . .

The Establishment View of Discipline

Surveying the academic literature on school violence and discipline will leave the average person with an almost irresistible urge to alternately laugh and cry. When you see such article titles as "Should Students Be Punished?" and "Multicultural Classroom Management," you know you've entered a world of make-believe, divorced from the reality of dangerous classrooms and disruptive students. "The case against punishment has been steadily growing," wrote John Martin Rich, a professor of education at the University of Texas at Austin. "Critics claim that [even] nonphysical punishment can damage relationships, create resentment, and compel rather than encourage obedience. Moreover, punishment may promote school absenteeism, dropping out, school vandalism, and excessive anxiety." Education "experts" hated the film *Lean on Me* because they thought it sent an overly simplistic message about the efficacy of discipline and expulsion to reduce violence and increase student achievement. "Its popularity shows how badly the public can be deceived when offered easy solutions to its fears of teenagers, blacks,

Hispanics, drugs, and crime," wrote one particularly excitable professor in *Education Week*. "In fact, the public support [Joe] Clark has gained for his tough-guy antics may well demonstrate the fragility of democracy."

NEW VERSION OF DRIVE BY SHOOTING!

Gamble/*Florida Times-Union*. Used by permission.

The self-esteem craze is particularly amusing. Over the past couple of decades, programs to boost self-esteem among students have proliferated in many school systems. "The litany of statistics about self-destructive tendencies such as substance abuse, crime, and suicide must surely be seen as a signal from young people that many do not find much about themselves to like," wrote education professor James A. Beane in *Educational Leadership*, a prominent journal. Beane argues that enhancing self-esteem in school will, in addition to addressing behavioral and academic problems, "extend the idea of personal development beyond coping with problems and into personal efficacy or power, which, in turn, may lead toward action," thereby helping to "build the personal and collective efficacy that helps us out of the morass of inequity that plagues us."

Beane and others assume that a lack of self-esteem leads to crime and substance abuse. In fact, violent students are often fixated with themselves and quite comfortable with their actions—*and continue to commit crimes because they think they won't be punished.*

Other education "experts" contend that school violence stems from racial and cultural inequities and therefore cannot be effectively combatted by disciplinary efforts. Herbert Grossman, a teacher at San Jose State University, wrote in *Contemporary Education* that the population of the United States is rapidly becoming less "EuroAmerican." As a result, he says, fewer students respond positively to and profit from classroom management techniques "that have been designed with EuroAmerican middle-class students in mind." Grossman advocates "cultural sensitivity" when operating classrooms containing racial minorities. What about misbehavior and discipline? Grossman questions whether minority students can be expected to "sit in a quiet and controlled manner."

Education "experts" often argue that discipline is used in a discriminatory manner, and that attempts to combat school violence are merely smokescreens for punitive actions against minority students. Prejudice, Grossman writes, "drives many minority and working-class students to actively resist both their teachers and the system by purposefully misbehaving." Prejudice, he continues, "may also contribute to the unnecessary suspension of so many African-American, Hispanic, and working-class students." In conclusion, Grossman asserts that "the elimination of teacher prejudice is one of the most important steps educators can take to reduce disciplinary problems with minority students."

Both the self-esteem and multicultural fixations represent a fundamental challenge to the role of punishment and discipline in deterring school violence. Even more radical theorists enjoy some following in the education establishment, which has traditionally included radicals whose view of incorrigible students and nonconformists was more positive than negative. They're the kind of people who refer to the 1992 riots in Los Angeles as a "rebellion." In the school context, they view strong action against violent students as punishing society's victims, rather than addressing crime's so-called "root causes."

Public vs. Private

Radical theorists like these would present little threat to sound school administration if it were not for the current structure of American education. A system of publicly owned, controlled, and regulated schools, staffed by public employees and subject to the control of outside public authorities, is incapable of withstanding today's assault against punishment and common sense. Similarly, the legal restraints and requirements that have been placed on the administration of school discipline and security measures exist because of school's public nature.

In some districts, to be sure, violence has become so common that traditional obstacles to security measures have been over-come. A number of schools have banned gang clothing and in-signia, as well as opaque book bags. San Diego's school system got rid of lockers, which resulted in inconvenience for students but also reduced gun crimes, robberies, and graffiti. Programs to encourage positive behavior and involve parents are great, says San Diego school police chief Alex Rascon, but in the meantime "the answer is to lock the campuses down. Have everyone enter through one door, sign in, and have permission to see a teacher ahead of time." Good security, Rascon adds, is inconvenient "but we just cannot dilly-dally around with the way things are now." It's unfortunate, however, that conditions have to escalate to crisis level before school administrators are given leave to take basic steps to reduce the threat of violence.

Private schools, by comparison, often maintain strict and uni-form regulations that result in few incidents of violence or dis-ruption, even in inner cities or other areas where crime is an in-tegral part of the surrounding neighborhood. Private schools mete out not only more effective, but in many students' minds, fairer discipline, according to James Coleman: "This suggests that the legalistic approach to ensuring fairness in discipline may be less effective than other approaches . . . [and] may in-deed be counterproductive for effectiveness of discipline."

In a private school setting, the role of the student is not that of "citizen" (to use the Supreme Court's term) with constitutional rights. Rather, the relationship with teacher and administrator is an economic one; if school personnel no longer believe they can handle a violent student, they do not have to continue providing him with educational services. In addition, private schools are often smaller, less bureaucratic, and, frankly, better able to keep kids interested in learning—all of which contribute to a greater sense of safety and security.

Thus, to address the epidemic of school violence in America, we will have to reconsider the governance of schools them-selves. Any other measure—from peer counseling to handgun control—will ultimately fail without a fundamental change in the relationship between student and school. Schools must dis-cipline, but they will be free to do so only when released from the political constraints of the present system. At the same time, they must be held directly accountable to parents and students (their customers) if punishment becomes capricious or exces-sive. In short, we must adopt a private model for education. The intellectual and psychological development of all our chil-dren—and, in some cases, their lives—depend on it.

"The threat of suspension or expulsion . . . may not mean much to some children."

Punishment Will Not Reduce School Violence

Pedro Noguera

Pedro Noguera is president of the Berkeley school board and a professor in the School of Education at the University of California, Berkeley. In the following viewpoint, he argues that traditional disciplinary methods and increased security efforts will not be effective at reducing violence in America's schools. He argues that the presence of adults who are genuinely interested in students' welfare can do more than threats of punishment to encourage nonviolent behavior.

As you read, consider the following questions:

1. What is the difference between moral authority and institutional authority, according to Noguera?
2. According to the author, why should policies to deter violence not be aimed solely at individuals deemed likely to be violent?
3. What type of teacher do students consistently respect, according to Noguera?

Pedro Noguera, "Coming to Terms with Violence in Our Schools," *Rethinking Schools*, vol. 8, no. 1 (Autumn 1993). Reprinted by permission of *Rethinking Schools*, 1001 E. Keefe Ave., Milwaukee, WI 53212. Tel. 414-964-9646.

Violence in schools is not new. If one looks at the history of education in the United States, particularly of urban public schools, it is clear that problems of violence have been around almost as long as schools have been in existence. What is new, however, is the dramatic increase in school violence and the growing use of guns to resolve disputes.

As a first step in addressing this problem, we must recognize that in many ways our schools are safer than the communities where many children live. Many of the kids that I have worked with tell me they are more worried about violence in their neighborhood than they are about violence in school. At least in schools there are rules against violence and adults present who are supposed to enforce such rules. On the streets, in the playgrounds, and even at home, there is often no such protection.

Too often we unfairly place unreasonable expectations on our schools. We expect schools to be safe places, and of course they should be, but we ignore the fact that our society is increasingly unsafe. It is unrealistic to expect that our schools can escape the violence that pervades our society.

Combating violence is difficult because it is promoted and legitimized by the mass media and by political leaders. While it is difficult to determine to what extent the glorification of violence in movies and on television affects young people, psychological studies suggest that, at the minimum, such exposure has a numbing effect on viewers.

Children receive mixed messages when violence is construed as a legitimate way to achieve political and military objectives. The justification of the killings in Waco, Texas, by FBI agents in 1993; Clinton's rationalizing the deaths of Iraqi civilians during bombing raids by U.S. war planes as unfortunate "collateral damage"; the U.S. invasions of Panama in 1989 and of Grenada in 1983—all legitimized the use of deadly force against civilians.

Given the regularity with which violence is used for "legitimate" purposes, it is not surprising that children are confused about the appropriateness of responding violently to conflicts with others.

Problems Within Schools

There are also internal reasons, however, that schools are vulnerable to violence. Many teachers receive no training on how to deal with violence; it is rarely part of the curriculum in teacher training. Further, the individuals responsible for enforcing discipline often have no legitimacy or credibility in the eyes of students. There is an absence of moral authority—which is different from institutional authority or the authority derived from one's job title. Just being an adult or holding a certain title doesn't mean that kids will automatically accept your right to exercise authority over them.

I can think of several schools where you can find kids shooting dice in the hallways or engaging in some other blatantly inappropriate behavior, and teachers will pretend not to see it because they are afraid to tell the kids to stop. Yet in the same school there will be certain individuals who can stop them, not through force or intimidation, but because of the relationship they have developed with the kids. These are adults who can tell kids, "That's not allowed here. I expect better of you than that," and the kids respond.

When we don't have adults in schools who understand the experience of the kids, who can speak in a language they understand and communicate in ways that are meaningful to them, then it becomes almost impossible to develop a safe and respectful school environment.

In urban schools, most teachers do not live in the communities where they work. They have a limited knowledge of their students' lives outside of school. This physical and psychological detachment from the students' lives is often compounded by differences based on race and class. Together, these factors add considerably to the inability of teachers and school personnel to respond effectively to the causes of violence in schools.

In addition, schools typically rely on ineffective methods to deal with violence. The threat of suspension or expulsion—the ultimate punishment and the one that is often relied upon as the *only* way to deal with violence—may not mean much to some children, particularly to those who have already experienced failure in school or who may not attend school regularly.

Currently, the most fashionable response to school violence is the tendency toward making schools more like prisons. Many schools now have metal detectors stationed at the entry points. In the last few years, New York City has spent close to $28 million to install metal detectors. Other districts have hired armed security guards or installed sophisticated security systems, turning schools into lock-down facilities. It is ironic that we are using prisons as our models for safety and security, even though prisons are generally not safe places. Further, these measures are undertaken without sufficient thought to the social and psychological consequences that may result from changing the school environment in this way.

A Personal Perspective

When I look at this problem, I see it not only through the eyes of a researcher and policymaker, but through my own personal experience. As a former teacher of African Studies at a continuation high school, I have worked with many young men who have been incarcerated and who have lived within an environ-

219

ment filled with violence. As a school board member, I have presided over expulsion hearings for students who have committed acts of violence; I have also had to make decisions that profoundly affect the lives of students and the schools they attend. As an activist in my community, I also work closely with parents and teachers, trying to develop an effective response to the violence that consumes our youth.

I also remember what it was like for me growing up in New York. The threat and possibility of violence permeated my school and community, and most people I knew accepted it as an ugly but unavoidable part of life.

Far from Foolproof

Schools are cracking down. At least 45 urban systems now screen students with metal detectors. Even elementary schools are using them. . . . School officials also are removing student lockers and prohibiting the carrying of overcoats and large bags during school hours. In Concord, New Hampshire, police lectured junior high school teachers on guns and violence, telling them what to do if a student pulls a gun in class (don't make any fast moves and follow the student's orders).

But such steps are far from foolproof. Consider metal detectors. Most schools use hand-held "wands" rather than walk-through detectors because they are less expensive (on average, $115 versus $2,500). But they are also less effective. And because it would take hours to screen every student, many schools don't: In New York, only about 1 in 9 is checked. Ultimately, it is virtually impossible to secure a school: Large buildings have as many as 50 exits that must remain unlocked from the inside to allow for quick escape in case of fire.

Thomas Toch, *U.S. News & World Report*, November 8, 1993.

At an early age I learned that bullies often got their way; that the best way to avoid a fight was to show no fear; that you must always be willing and prepared to hurt someone if necessary. I learned that violence was an effective means to get status and respect. I learned that in order to survive, I would have to deal with violence. At 14 my cousin of the same age was stabbed to death for refusing to give up his leather jacket. The next year a kid I knew in school was arrested for the kidnap and rape of a female student. Luck, the fears of getting caught, of ruining my future and embarrassing my family, prevented me from falling victim to violence.

Still, my experience has influenced my understanding of how

kids view violence. At a gut level, I understand why kids fight or why they might react violently toward a teacher. I know why so many see violence as a legitimate way to resolve problems, because I once felt the same way.

In our society we often categorize individuals who commit violence as deviants and sociopaths. Many counselors and psychologists view violent behavior as a form of conduct disorder based on socially maladaptive tendencies. This type of labeling presumes that there are some individuals who are potentially violent and who should be kept away from the rest of the population, which is ostensibly made up of good, honest, law-abiding people. Labeling children in this way influences how we see them and contributes to self-fulfilling prophecies.

Such dichotomies prevent us from understanding an issue like violence because they set up artificial dividing lines that presume the existence of fundamental differences between people based on morals or social conduct. Moreover, such distinctions keep us from recognizing how difficult it is to predict who is potentially violent, and leave us dumbfounded when a young person with no past record of violent behavior suddenly "goes off" violently on someone else. While many children do need individual attention, and isolation may at times be the only way to respond, policies aimed at deterring violence should not be directed solely at those considered likely to engage in violence.

Dealing with Violence in Schools

As a starting point toward dealing with violence in schools, we must identify some of the factors that contribute to the problem. Some, such as the availability of guns and the promotion of violence in the media, may seem beyond the control of parents and school personnel. While we must devise strategies for addressing these issues, we may want to first focus on how to create a school environment that promotes respect, dignity, and non-violence.

For too many students, going to school is a violating and demeaning experience. The anonymity of large schools and the irrelevance of what is taught to the experience and aspiration of children cultivates indifference and disrespect toward school and the adults who work there. Feelings of hostility and resentment are exacerbated when adults arbitrarily enforce rules, forgetting that they are working with children. Further, some adults are just plain mean when they deal with kids.

I have found that children consistently respect those teachers that set high standards for behavior and academic performance, and who demonstrate a personal interest in their students. Most schools have at least one teacher that fits this description. But too often that person works in isolation rather than being used as a role model for effective teaching. One way to spread around the knowledge and experience of such teachers is to establish mentoring relationships and to encourage collaboration between teachers.

There are also ways to provide security that do not dehumanize the environment. At one junior high school in Oakland, California, an elderly woman serves as the campus security monitor, rather than an armed guard or large, intimidating man. This woman lives in the neighborhood surrounding the school and understands the kids' reality, culture, and needs. Without the threat of force this woman is able to break up fights, enforce basic school rules, and keep those who do not belong off the school campus. She can do this because she speaks in terms the children understand and, most of all, because the kids know that she truly cares about them. She has moral authority, derived not from her position, but from who she is and what she represents in their community.

In my conversations with students who attend schools with a reputation for violence, I am struck by their total dissatisfaction with the schools. Rather than appreciating the potential opportunities that might result from their education, they see attendance at school primarily as a way to meet and socialize with friends. These children have no respect for their schools or the adults who work there. School, like the park, the neighborhood block or hang-out spot, is seen as appropriate a place as any for carrying out reprisals against enemies or sorting out personal conflicts. School is not a special place where violence is deemed inappropriate. Further, their feelings about school may be so negative that the institution itself may become the object of their violence through vandalism or harassment of teachers and other adults.

Larger Issues

As we look at the problem of violence within schools, we must connect it to the larger issues confronting schools, particularly inner city schools. School violence is not strictly an urban phenomenon, nor is it limited to low-income communities. Increasingly, middle-class suburban schools, and even schools in affluent areas, have problems with violence. However, the problems of urban schools are particularly acute and are complicated by their connection to the prevalence of poverty, crime, and despair in our cities.

Urban schools must not only address the academic needs of their students, they must also find the resources to provide social and psychological support to students and their families. Yet many schools define their mission too narrowly. Problems like violence, drugs, and teen pregnancy are often seen as beyond the scope of what schools can or should address. Clearly, extra resources in both funding and skilled personnel are needed to expand the services that schools provide. Perhaps even more important, schools need a broadened vision of what they can do to respond more effectively to the needs of children.

Violence in our schools is only a symptom of a much larger problem facing schools and society generally. To treat the problem in isolation only perpetuates a reliance on failed methods. There are no easy answers. But at the minimum we have to find more ways to bring together, on a regular basis, students and those adults with whom they can identify. We must also work toward making our schools more humane and responsive to children's needs. This may not sound like much, especially when compared to the high-tech solutions promoted in most quarters. But in the long run it may have the greatest impact.

Periodical Bibliography

The following articles have been selected to supplement the diverse views presented in this chapter.

Anne Chase — "School Violence: Two Ways to Fight Back," *Governing*, March 1993. Available from 1414 22nd St. NW, Washington, DC 20037.

Mark Curriden — "Hard Times for Bad Kids," *ABA Journal*, February 1995. Available from 750 N. Lake Shore Dr., Chicago, IL 60611.

Jeffrey Danzinger — "Children Who Murder," *Wall Street Journal*, April 7, 1993.

Nick Gillespie — "Arrested Development," *Reason*, December 1994.

Daniel Goleman — "Hope Seen for Curbing Youth Violence," *New York Times*, August 11, 1993.

Ann Hartman — "Broken Homes, Mended Lives," *New York Times*, December 30, 1994.

David M. Kennedy — "Can We Keep Guns Away from Kids?" *American Prospect*, Summer 1994. Available from PO Box 383080, Cambridge, MA 02238.

Penelope Lemov — "The Assault on Juvenile Justice," *Governing*, December 1994.

Laura Mansnerus — "More Courts Are Treating Violent Youths as Adults," *New York Times*, December 3, 1993.

Adam Marcus — "How Liberals Put Teachers in the Line of Fire," *Washington Monthly*, June 1994.

New York Times — "What Can Be Done About the Scourge of Violence Among Juveniles? The Experts on Different Fronts of the Battlefield Discuss Strategies," December 30, 1994.

Jackson Toby — "The Politics of School Violence," *Public Interest*, Summer 1994.

Thomas Toch with Ted Gest and Monika Guttman — "Violence in Schools: When Killers Come to Class," *U.S. News & World Report*, November 8, 1993.

Joseph B. Treaster — "Hard Time for Hard Youths: A Battle Yields Few Winners," *New York Times*, December 28, 1994.

USA Today	"The Young Desperadoes," January 1994. Entire issue on youth violence.
Wall Street Journal	"The Young and the Violent," September 23, 1992.
James D. Wright, Joseph F. Sheley, and M. Dwayne Smith	"Kids, Guns, and Killing Fields," *Society*, November/December 1992.

What Policies Would Reduce Violence?

Chapter Preface

"Americans are preoccupied more than ever by violent crime," according to Stephen Braun and Judy Pasternak, staff writers for the *Los Angeles Times*. Braun and Pasternak contend that although violent crime has actually decreased slightly in recent years, a growing number of Americans "appear threatened by examples of mayhem they read about in their own communities" and are looking for solutions.

Some people argue that the most effective response to violent crime is increasing the incarceration of criminals. These critics maintain that the nation's criminal justice system has a "revolving door"—that many violent criminals spend little or no time in prison but are instead allowed back on the streets, where they commit more crimes. "We must build enough prison capacity to lock up every violent and repeat offender and to keep them, at least the most serious violent offenders, locked up for substantially more time," argue Michael K. Block, a professor of economics and law, and Steven J. Twist, the director of the National Rifle Association's Crime Strike Division. According to Block and Twist, statistics from the 1980s reveal that increases in prison populations translate directly into reduced rates of violent crime.

Others dispute the effectiveness of increased incarceration in curtailing violent crime. For example, in their report *Does Imprisonment Reduce Crime? A Critique of "Voodoo" Criminology*, James Austin and John Irwin analyze statistics from the 1960s through the early 1990s and conclude that "crime rates have not declined despite the massive increases in prison and jail populations." Patrick McCormick, writing in *U.S. Catholic* magazine, agrees:

> Since the early '80s we have nearly tripled our prison capacity and increased the Federal Bureau of Prisons' budget over 470 percent. . . . In the same period we have more than tripled our prison population. . . . And yet neither of these responses have had an appreciable effect on the rate of violent crime.

McCormick argues that America's growing prison system may in fact perpetuate violent crime by serving as a "breeding ground for violent felons."

Whether increased incarceration is an effective solution to violent crime in American society is one of the issues debated in the following chapter.

VIEWPOINT 1

"By mobilizing the broad array of existing resources in medicine . . . toward the prevention of . . . violence, considerable progress can be made."

A Public Health Approach to Violence Is Needed

Mark L. Rosenberg, Patrick W. O'Carroll, and Kenneth E. Powell

In the following viewpoint, Mark L. Rosenberg, Patrick W. O'Carroll, and Kenneth E. Powell argue that rather than the traditional approach of responding to violence after it occurs, the public health approach—which involves analyzing the problem and instituting appropriate interventions—should be used to prevent violence from happening. All three authors are with the Centers for Disease Control and Prevention (CDC) in Atlanta, Georgia, where Rosenberg is the director of the Division of Injury Prevention and Control, Powell is the associate director for science at the Division for Injury Prevention and Control, and O'Carroll is the deputy chief of the Public Health Information Systems Branch of the Information Resources Office.

As you read, consider the following questions:

1. How do the authors define violence?
2. What causes most violent injuries, according to the authors?
3. According to the authors, what social problems will impede the public health response to violence?

"Let's Be Clear: Violence Is a Public Health Problem" by Mark L. Rosenberg, Patrick W. O'Carroll, and Kenneth E. Powell, *JAMA*, June 10, 1992, vol. 267, no. 22, pp. 3071-72.

We have worked for more than 10 years in the US Public Health Service to clarify the patterns of violence through surveillance and research and to identify and evaluate interventions to prevent and reduce the impact of violence. It is time to be clear about what we mean by violence and why we believe that violence is a public health problem. Violence is the intentional use of physical force against another person or against oneself, which either results in or has a high likelihood of resulting in injury or death. Violence includes suicidal acts as well as interpersonal violence such as rape, assault, child abuse, or elder abuse. Fatal violence results in suicides and homicides.

The term *violence* has been used to connote both a subset of behaviors (which produce injuries) and outcomes (ie, the injuries themselves). We use *violence* to refer to a particular class of behaviors that cause injuries. By convention, the public health community refers to injuries from violence as "intentional injuries." Although this description is not entirely satisfactory, it is meant to distinguish injuries due to violence from injuries due to unintended motor vehicle crashes, falls, drownings, and burns.

Having clarified what we mean by the term violence, we must still explain why violence is a public health problem. Three hard questions need to be answered.

Criminal Justice Is Not Enough

Why should public health practitioners concern themselves with violence?

The health consequences of violence are tremendous, but traditionally our society has turned to the criminal justice sector to protect us from such violence. Why involve public health practitioners? Why not just beef up our efforts in criminal justice?

In answering this question, we must first recognize that criminal justice has been and will continue to be an important component of our efforts to curb violence. We must also admit that the application of criminal justice measures alone is not enough.

Indeed, the incidence of injuries and deaths from violence has continued to increase in the face of ever greater resources devoted to criminal justice. In fact, the level of violence is so high that by any traditional measure of public health importance, fatal and nonfatal injuries resulting from interpersonal violence have become one of the most important public health problems facing our country.

The criminal justice system relies on arrests and incarcerations to deter, incapacitate, and rehabilitate convicted offenders. Criminal justice professionals themselves have stated for years that much of the problem of violence is a "social problem," beyond the purview of the police and the criminal justice system.

For example, violence between family members and acquaintances accounts for more than half of all homicides. Most violent injuries do not stem immediately from criminal activities such as robbery. They occur as the result of violent arguments among people who know each other, and they generally do not occur in public.

Therefore, one reason that the public health community should become involved is that the problem is beyond the reach of the criminal justice system working alone. Another reason is that the public health community introduces a primary prevention focus to the problem of violence. The essence of public health is prevention, and it is that very essence that will enable the public health community to address the issues and problems in a manner that complements the efforts of the criminal justice system. By mobilizing the broad array of existing resources in medicine, mental health, social services, and substance abuse services toward the prevention of injuries and deaths from violence, considerable progress can be made.

A Time-Tested Approach

Do we in public health know how to prevent violence?

The short answer to that question is no. If we knew how to prevent violence, you would have heard about it before now. But a more accurate, complete answer to that question is no, we don't have the answers in hand, but we know how to get them! Public health brings to the table a time-tested, systematic approach to reducing the burden of illness, suffering, and premature death among human populations.

The public health approach consists of health-event surveillance, epidemiologic analysis, and intervention design and evaluation, focused unwaveringly on a single, clear outcome—the prevention of a particular illness or injury. This approach was originally developed to combat infectious diseases, when such diseases were the leading causes of death. It has been successfully applied, however, to many causes of premature death and preventable physical illness including lung cancer, coronary heart disease, and, more recently, motor vehicle crashes.

The public health approach to violence faces several daunting challenges. Not only is violence a multifaceted problem, with each face requiring a separate approach, but violence is intimately intertwined with a variety of major social problems for which no easy solutions are apparent. Poverty, unemployment, racism, and other injustices contribute in complex ways to violent behavior. These social problems deserve attention on their own, and it seems clear that their remediation would substantially reduce the incidence of violent injuries and deaths.

Public health action to reduce the incidence and health conse-

Rise High Projects

As a physician at Chicago's Cook County Jail clinic, John P. May, MD, bears daily witness to the toll violence exacts on patients, their families and communities.

But instead of becoming inured to its presence—or overcome by it—Dr. May has searched for a way to disrupt its relentless cycle. In 1993, the internist and several friends launched an anti-violence poster campaign aimed at young African-American males. The campaign, Rise High Projects, has since been adopted in several cities, including Chicago, Atlanta and Sacramento.

Dr. May is not alone: All across the country, doctors are coming to grips with the notion that violence is a major public health threat on a par with tuberculosis, tobacco and HIV/AIDS. . . .

Dr. May said he was inspired to action after realizing that violence largely was ignored in public health messages to inner-city youths. That omission didn't jibe with his experiences at the jail and, earlier, as a resident in the emergency department at Chicago's Cook County Hospital and as a soup-kitchen volunteer. In each of those environments, the specter of violence is omnipresent.

"I had been to schools and seen posters telling kids to brush their teeth and don't smoke and be careful of AIDS, and, yes, these things are important, but maybe not the *most* important," explained Dr. May, who says such messages are "inappropriate to the immediate needs" of many youths.

Hence, Rise High Projects, which uses dramatic, eye-catching posters to encourage adolescents to realize the consequences of violent behavior and to consider alternatives. The posters are displayed in schools and community centers, on buses and trains, at transit stops—anywhere youngsters are likely to frequent.

"We really need to look at the No. 1 killer of young people, and that's violence. How can we be effective in other health promotion strategies until we can empower them to overcome the risk and fear of violence?" Dr. May asked.

Wayne Hearn, *American Medical News*, March 21, 1994.

---

quences of violence faces other major impediments. Several distinctive characteristics of American society—characteristics highly valued by some—appear to be important determinants of violent behavior. The depiction of violence on television, in movies, and in other media, and ready access to firearms, are two examples. Exposure, especially of impressionable children and youths, to the creatively captivating scenes of aggression and violence depicted in the media fosters our acceptance and expectation of violence in America and probably contributes to the frequency of aggressive acts themselves. Firearms may or may not cause violent behavior, but there is increasingly compelling scientific evidence that they markedly elevate the severity of the health consequences of such behavior. The quarrelsome debate and the paralyzing ambivalence of American society about these issues has sometimes prevented, and still threatens to prevent, adequate research into the effect of media violence and access to firearms on violent behavior and associated injuries.

These social problems and issues are not synonymous with violence. However, they undoubtedly will continue to complicate and impede efforts by the public health community to reduce violent behavior and injuries. They will severely test the versatility of the public health model. We are just now beginning to apply public health methods to the prevention of injuries from violence. Will we be successful? Time alone will tell. But, given the track record of success for public health, we have every reason to be optimistic.

A High Priority

Is there a commitment from the public health sector to address this critical public health problem?

This question we can answer quite definitively yes. The Centers for Disease Control has made the prevention of violence one of its highest priorities, and we now have a variety of projects under way that pertain, either directly or indirectly, to reducing the health consequences of violence.

First, we are developing a comprehensive National Plan for Injury Control. Seven panels of experts were commissioned to develop recommendations for specific parts of the injury control field. One panel was commissioned to develop recommendations for the prevention of injuries from violence.

A major recommendation of this panel was to develop a national system or infrastructure for preventing violence. Such a system would provide surveillance, direct resources for prevention to those at highest risk, empower communities to address the problem of violence at the community level, evaluate intervention activities, and train workers in the skills needed to accomplish the task. Accomplishing these various tasks will require not only federal commitment but the commitment and coordinated efforts of state and local governments and a wide range of private-sector organizations. Encouraging such involvement and coordinating these efforts are two aspects of the work that the Centers for Disease Control does.

Another major recommendation of the violence panel is that firearm injuries should be prevented. There is much debate on how to do this, but there is a growing consensus that immediate access to highly lethal weapons is one of the most critical elements in the causation of many homicides. As health officials concerned with stopping the bloodshed, we cannot ignore this issue. Just as we were able to save countless lives from motor vehicle injuries without banning cars, we can save many lives from firearm injuries without a total ban on firearms. There is no controversy in the area of children's having unsupervised access to loaded guns. No one believes that children should have unsupervised access to guns, but few people are doing anything to prevent children from having such access. This, at least, is a place to start. Parents should be encouraged and assisted in every possible way to prevent their children from carrying guns or having unsupervised access to guns. Such efforts to empower families should begin now, while we in public health continue to explore the scientific issues associated with this question, through careful research and the evaluation of existing programs designed to reduce ready access to guns.

A Comprehensive View

We have to start thinking about violence as a public health crisis that requires public health solutions. That's how we thought of polio in the 1950s and how we think of AIDS today.

But let's not confuse the public health model with the medical model. The traditional medical model involves physicians curing sickness or treating injuries after they occur.

The public health model examines causes. It takes a comprehensive view. It seeks to involve everyone who can make a difference. And, it places a strong emphasis on preventing violence before it occurs.

Donna E. Shalala, *San Diego Union-Tribune*, December 13, 1993.

Second, we are developing guidelines for those who want to develop programs to prevent youth violence in their own communities. These guidelines are designed to prevent youth violence in general, but, in recognition of the disproportionate burden of violence borne by minority populations, we have sought extensive input on these guidelines from leaders of minority communities and those who have already implemented innovative programs in inner cities and urban centers.

Third, we will support the design, implementation, and evaluation of multifaceted community-based youth violence prevention programs. . . . Multifaceted programs are needed because of the complex web of factors that cause violence and violence-related injuries. Community-based programs are needed to assure involvement in, ownership of, and responsibility for the activities by community residents. Successful prevention activities need to be identified, documented, and shared without delay to facilitate the most rapid progress possible in reducing violent injuries and deaths.

Fourth, James O. Mason, MD, assistant secretary for health, Department of Health and Human Services, has asked the Centers for Disease Control to lead the development of a new Public Health Service–wide activity to identify, develop, and implement effective, community-based interventions for the prevention of youth violence.

In summary, violence is a major cause of injuries and deaths. The prevention of these injuries and deaths is an appropriate, and indeed a necessary, public health focus. The problem of violence probably has no simple solution, but the public health method of health-event surveillance, epidemiologic analysis, and intervention design and evaluation can undoubtedly make important contributions to the solution.

"Long-term prevention of urban violence is impossible *without changes in the underlying social and economic fabric."*

The Public Health Approach to Violence Is Misguided

Nathaniel Hupert

Many members of the medical profession have argued that the public health community can prevent violence by studying and intervening in its causes. In the following viewpoint, Nathaniel Hupert, a resident in the Primary Care Internal Medicine Program at the University of Pittsburgh Medical Center in Pennsylvania, contends that such an approach is inappropriate because it views violence as a result of individual irresponsibility and seeks to alter behavior accordingly. Hupert maintains that the true causes of violence are rooted in structural, socioeconomic factors such as poverty and racism, which he says are virtually ignored by the public health proponents.

As you read, consider the following questions:

1. How did the Centers for Disease Control (CDC) team try to intervene in Los Angeles emergency rooms, according to the author?
2. How does Hupert contrast the views of Antonia C. Novello with those of C. Everett Koop and George D. Lundberg?
3. How should the medical profession attempt to reduce inner-city violence, according to Hupert?

Excerpted from "Reducing Urban Violence: A Critique of the New Public Health Approach" by Nathaniel Hupert; ©1994 by Alpha Omega Alpha Medical Honor Society. Reprinted by permission from *The Pharos*, vol. 57, no. 1 (Winter 1994).

Several weeks after the 1992 Los Angeles riots, the Centers for Disease Control (CDC) flew a team of epidemiologists into Compton and South Central to implement two violence prevention programs. Their stated goal was to teach potentially violent Angelenos "ways to resolve disputes without violence," according to P. Cotton. Weeks later, upon leaving, the team admitted that their mission had met with little success—they said they had anticipated neither the complexity of the etiology of violence in the inner city nor the public outcry over their strictly educational approach. This outcome may have surprised the team, since the previous year one of them, Mark L. Rosenberg, had edited a book prescribing precisely this type of educational and behavioral intervention to remedy the problem of urban violent crime. Ultimately, however, the failure of the L.A. mission appears to have had little impact on the CDC's subsequent violence prevention plans. Scarcely two months after the riot, writing in the *Journal of the American Medical Association* (*JAMA*), members of the CDC's Division of Injury Control, which had organized the L.A. interventions, proposed a national public health campaign against violence modeled on the very behavioral strategies that were tried, resisted, and subsequently deemed a failure in L.A.

A Misguided Approach

This viewpoint is about what the CDC attempted to accomplish in L.A. and why it failed. I have chosen to explore this episode in detail because it provides a case study of the type of public health intervention that the CDC appears to be planning for the rest of the country in its blueprint for a national antiviolence campaign. To put it plainly, I believe the CDC's approach to medical professional intervention on the issue of urban violence is misguided. Its proposals rely on a reductionist etiological account of violence to justify intervention at the individual level and to minimize intervention at the structural or socioeconomic level. These proposals are incompatible with what community leaders have claimed to be the needs of inner-city residents, and therefore they risk casting the medical profession in a socially oppressive role. Nevertheless, the reductionist view of violent activity is popular among leaders of the medical profession. . . . Finally, I discuss an alternative approach that would allow the medical profession to address the problem of urban violence in a manner that might be more responsive to the stated needs of targeted urban communities, and therefore potentially more acceptable as a form of medical intervention on this issue.

Mark L. Rosenberg was in charge of the CDC team that went to L.A. after the riots. Its goal, he said upon arriving, was to "assess the injuries that occurred as a result of the disturbance and

. . . to work with the community to help them develop ways of starting and supporting long-term approaches to youth violence prevention." As director of the CDC's Injury Control Division since 1983, Dr. Rosenberg has played a central role in formulating antiviolence projects. "We've identified some programs we think will work," he said, "and want to share these with affected communities throughout the country." In the weeks after its arrival, the CDC team settled on implementing two programs that involved counseling the victims and "potential victims" of violence about nonviolent dispute resolution. One of them targeted emergency-room patients in the inner city. Rosenberg stated:

> If you can get to these people in the hospital when they have an injury, you may be able to teach them about the risks certain activities entail, about ways to resolve disputes without violence, or even *the wisdom of walking away from fights*. . . . The theory is compelling and we'd like to try it. (emphasis added)

A Tinderbox Situation

But the theory was not compelling to local medical leaders. Physicians who live and work in the districts hardest hit by the riots cautioned that by focusing solely on preventing the medical *effects* of violence in the inner city (namely on preventing injuries), the CDC's strategy tended toward a blatant disregard of its roots. This approach, they said, would not remedy the social conditions under which urban youth turn to violence. They saw tackling the underlying causes as the essential first step in violence prevention. Ron Guidry, a physician who was raised and was practicing in South Central Los Angeles, expressed his concern: "Those people [proposing solutions] have not sat down with the people on the street to reach a common ground. They just assume they know the problem." It would be "easier" he asserted, "to prevent things than to come in and try to get them cured." To sit a gang member down in an emergency room in South Central and tell him to walk away from violence would be to neglect a whole range of social and economic factors that first fed the social tensions that culminated in the riot and the quotidian violence of the L.A. ghettoes.

Reed Tuckson, president of the Charles R. Drew University of Medicine and Science, in the Watts district, argued that the violence endemic to urban inner cities is inextricably linked to socioeconomic conditions. The causes of this violence, he stated,

> relate very fundamentally to a community of people who absolutely feel hopeless and totally frustrated because of a history of insult, racism, disenfranchisement, and unfair financial practices of banks and other entrepreneurial institutions. They're frustrated simply trying to get through each day.

The result, Dr. Tuckson warned, was a tinderbox situation in the inner cities. "Tensions are so high," he concluded, "that the trigger is pulled by itself." Dr. Guidry agreed: "[If] we don't get any grassroots, from-the-bottom-up type structuring, the anger is going to boil up again." The proper method of prevention, he said, is "equal opportunity," economic programs to address the societal roots of violence, not initiatives designed simply to suppress violent acts without addressing their underlying causes.

The expedition had reached a standoff—while the CDC team tried to employ educational, behavior-modification techniques aimed at individuals "at risk" for violent activity, the community rebuffed them, calling their plans palliative remedies that avoided the type of socioeconomic intervention that would begin to address issues like unemployment and economic racism, which they claimed provided the setting for urban violence. The disagreement centered on where to assign causal priority when designing a plan for long-term violence prevention: to individual actions or to socioeconomic conditions (and their social and political sequelae). The CDC staffers reduced the issue of urban violence to the more clear-cut and manageable problem of *violent acts* by inner-city residents. Community leaders did not deny that violence is mediated by violent offenders, but they claimed that targeting intervention solely to the violent offender would *not* lead to reduction in violence so long as the urban structure remained unchanged. . . .

Violence, specifically urban and gun-related violence, was the subject of the June 10, 1992, issue of the *Journal of the American Medical Association*. Besides a commentary by Rosenberg and his colleagues at the CDC, this issue included an editorial by Past-Surgeon General C. Everett Koop and *JAMA* Editor-in-Chief George D. Lundberg, a statement by then Surgeon General Antonia C. Novello and colleagues, and comment by then Assistant Secretary for Health James Mason and coauthor. All supported the notion of a national "public health approach" to urban violence, but each held widely varying opinions about what such an approach would entail.

Diametrically Opposed Views

Before considering the CDC proposal for a national antiviolence campaign, I shall briefly review the proposals by Dr. Novello and Drs. Koop and Lundberg. Their writings represent two diametrically opposed views within the medical leadership concerning the origins of urban violence and its proper prevention.

Novello characterized violence as "a problem of epidemic proportion in our society," describing it further as "a multifaceted problem that results from many social and economic factors: poverty, racism, disregard for human life, family and community disintegration, denial of educational opportunity, peer pressure, and absence of positive values." To counter these forces,

Novello called for social and economic interventions:

> If we are to succeed in stemming the epidemic of violence, we must first address the social, economic, and behavioral causes of violence. We must try to improve living conditions for millions of Americans. We must try to provide the economic and educational opportunities for our youth that racism and poverty destroy.

To accomplish this, she called on physicians to engage in changing these social and economic issues in a profession-wide campaign:

> Just as we health professionals have done for other health problems, we have a clear duty to take a leadership role in the antiviolence movement. . . .
>
> . . . [T]he prevention of violence by using public health methods is as much our responsibility as is the treatment of its victims.

So, for Novello, the "public health approach" to violence prevention explicitly included social activism on the part of physicians to improve socioeconomic conditions in the inner cities. Her proposal, therefore, would address the community needs discussed by Guidry and Tuckson. Additionally, empirical research on the relationship of violent activity to relative economic privation and social class supports her etiologic claims.

Koop and Lundberg took the opposite tack. While they acknowledged that violence was now "a public health emergency," they wrote, "Regarding violence in our society as purely a sociologic matter, or one of law enforcement, has led to unmitigated failure." Rather, they advocated "additional major research on the causes, prevention, and cures of violence," which might lead to new "medical/public health interventions." By rejecting the possibility that social change could affect the rate of urban violence, these writers implied that it might be adequately addressed as a "medical/public health issue." True to Guidry's prediction, Koop and Lundberg held out the promise of a medical "cure." But, in fact, their beliefs about the failure of sociologic interventions are not totally well founded. Concerted efforts to alter violent criminal activity by changing socioeconomic conditions in the inner city have indeed been found effective in the few instances in which they have been tried. A more accurate statement for Koop and Lundberg to have made would have been that socioeconomic improvements have been shown to decrease rates of urban violent crime, but that such improvements have not been widely achieved or sustained in this country.

A Middle Ground?

Rosenberg and his colleagues at the CDC appear at first glance to have found a middle ground between these two proposals. While their stated etiological account of urban violence looks similar to Novello's, their proposed interventions include only

239

traditional medical or public health techniques, just as Koop and Lundberg recommended. A close examination of their plan, however, reveals that their proposals are motivated not by a structural account of the causes of urban violence, but rather by more subtle reductionist assumptions about the nature of violent activity.

A Structural Crisis

Our nation is experiencing a prolonged, deep-going structural and systemic crisis of its capitalist system. This is the main sickness which must be addressed if crime and violence are to be seriously reduced. . . .

The crisis is particularly sharp for African American and Latino youth who are confined to the hard life in the cities—a life of drugs, bad housing, underfunded schools, few recreation facilities and no jobs. These are youth whose unemployment rates range from 60 to 80 percent. Many have never worked, and if there is no basic change in the economy and the political situation, most have no future.

Jarvis Tyner, *Political Affairs*, January 1994.

At various points in their proposal, Rosenberg and his colleagues acknowledged the structural roots of urban violence. They stated, for example, that "violence is intimately intertwined with a variety of major social problems for which no easy solutions are apparent." These include "poverty, unemployment, racism, and other injustices." These comments accord with the statements of both Novello and the community leaders in L.A. Additionally, the CDC staffers stressed the need to "empower communities to address the problem of violence at the community level." "Community-based programs are needed," they maintained, "to assure involvement in, ownership of, and responsibility for the activities by community residents." Again, these comments suggest that the interventions proposed by CDC would be similar to the socioeconomic and political ones advocated by Novello, Guidry, and Tuckson.

But when describing their intervention plans, Rosenberg and his staff switched gears. First, they indicated that their proposed interventions would *not* directly address structural concerns: They said, "These social problems deserve attention on their own, and it seems clear that their remediation would substantially reduce the incidence of violent injuries and death." Then, they indicated that the target of their proposed "public health" campaign against urban violence would be violent behavior and *not* social conditions. Noting two such conditions—the media depiction of violence and the ready availability of firearms—Rosenberg and his colleagues said:

> These social problems and issues are not synonymous with violence. However, they will continue to complicate and impede efforts by the public health community *to reduce violent behavior* and injuries. They will severely test the versatility of the public health model. (emphasis added)

Thus, the CDC's locus of intervention remains fixed on violent behavior to the exclusion of structural, socioeconomic conditions of the inner city. In fact, those structural conditions are considered "impediments" to the public health campaign, rather than appropriate targets of intervention, as Novello, Guidry, and Tuckson suggested. The CDC staffers' description of the resources to be utilized in the new campaign further confirms the conservative nature of their proposal: "By mobilizing the broad array of existing resources in medicine, mental health, social services, and substance abuse services . . . considerable progress can be made." The final result is a justification for a medically oriented public health intervention in the problem of urban violence, one that lends itself easily to the type of emergency-room-education programs that provoked community disapproval and failed to achieve tangible results in L.A.

A Reductionist View

Given that they admitted a socioeconomic basis for urban violence, what kept the CDC staffers from advocating structural interventions? I believe their reticence stemmed at least in part from a reductionist view of human action that places primary importance on character and individual responsibility in considerations of health-related behavior. This stance, which has become pervasive among medical professionals, uncritically assumes that personal decisions in health affairs are unfettered by socioeconomic constraints, and that responsibility for human status lies primarily in the hands of the individual. Medical issues become personal issues; healthy living is seen as a reflection of good character. This view has significant repercussions for the consideration of violence as a threat to public health. Recall that Rosenberg, despite having admitted that social factors conspire in complex ways to influence violent behavior, suggested that inner-city youth should simply "walk away" from violence (without acknowledging, for example, the possibility that inner-city youth might not have anywhere else to *go*). Similarly, in their proposal for a national plan, he and his colleagues suggested not only that violence *can* be prevented without direct attention paid to socioeconomic factors, but moreover that such an acontextual approach *constitutes* the public health approach to violence. . . .

The writings of . . . Koop, Lundberg, and Rosenberg and colleagues contain significant parallels. . . . All of these physicians considered urban violence to be isolable from its socioeconomic context, fruitfully discussable as an issue of character, personal choice, and individual responsibility, and finally preventable by educational interventions. . . . Despite the protestations of community leaders such as Guidry and Tuckson, and even fellow medical/public health professionals such as Novello—people who claim that long-term prevention of urban violence is *impossible* without changes in the underlying social and economic fabric of the inner cities—the main architects of the coming national public health campaign against violence appear to want to bracket those concerns while once again targeting the violent individual as the proper locus of intervention.

In closing, I want to draw attention to a medical movement that may provide a model for the type of explicitly political activism advocated by Novello on this issue. International Physicians for the Prevention of Nuclear War (IPPNW) is an organization dedicated to mobilizing medical resistance to the production and use of weapons of mass destruction. For its political campaign against the vested powers of the military-industrial complex, IPPNW was awarded the Nobel Peace Prize in 1985. One of the founders of the movement, Bernard Lown, explained the physician's role in meeting the threat of nuclear holocaust in these terms:

> [T]he public can trust the physician in expressing an opposition to the nuclear arms race that derives from a deep commitment to preserving human life. The objective of the physicians' movement is to compel society to confront the essential fact that nuclear weapons and human beings cannot coexist long on this small planet.

If leaders of the medical profession hope to reduce the incidence of violence in our inner cities while respecting the views of people who live and work in those communities they should pattern their efforts in part after those of Dr. Lown. Imposing strictly behavioral interventions to teach violence-reduction strategies constitutes an inappropriate use of the medical profession's political power, because the structural injustices in the inner cities clearly *do* exist and *do* contribute to violent activity in complex ways. Without political activism by physicians to move society to "confront the facts" of these socioeconomic injustices, strictly behavioral interventions will remain politically oppressive to inner-city residents. If the profession seeks to address this topic, it must respond to the needs of urban communities, not the dictates of its own etiological assumptions about the origins of violence. The sooner organized medicine undertakes this explicitly political task, the better its chances are of having a positive impact on violence in our cities.

"We must ensure tough, cost-effective punishment for all offenders; [and] we must put more police on our streets."

Anti-Crime Measures Will Reduce Violence

Joseph R. Biden Jr.

Joseph R. Biden Jr., the Democratic senator from Delaware, is chairman of the Senate Judiciary Committee. In the following viewpoint, excerpted from a speech to the Wilmington Rotary Club in Wilmington, Delaware, Biden argues that violence is one of the most important issues facing America. He advocates a major crime bill (which was subsequently signed into law in September 1994) designed to reduce violent crime by mandating imprisonment for violent offenders, increasing the number of police officers nationwide, and reducing the number of guns on the streets.

As you read, consider the following questions:

1. How has the character of violence changed since the early 1980s, according to the author?
2. What four factors does Biden cite as contributors to violence?
3. Why is community policing preferable to current police practices, according to the author?

Excerpted from Joseph R. Biden Jr., "Combatting Violence in America," a speech delivered to the Wilmington, Delaware, Rotary Club, December 16, 1993 (*Vital Speeches of the Day*, March 15, 1994).

I have long believed that the single most important issue facing America, notwithstanding the economy, notwithstanding foreign policy, notwithstanding unemployment, notwithstanding NAFTA [North American Free Trade Agreement], is violence.

Violence in our nation has reached epidemic proportions, requiring all of us to fundamentally change the way we run our lives, because we now feel insecure about our physical safety and the well-being of our families. In the late 1970s, there weren't many places I feared to go; today, I doubt whether any one of you in this room would be willing to go to half a dozen places I could name in our own community.

Violence today has had a leveling effect—those of us who used to think we could take care of ourselves know we are defenseless when faced with a nine-millimeter semi-automatic pistol loaded with 22 rounds. Those of us who live in suburban neighborhoods used to feel we were immune from crime. Today, there is no immunity; shopping centers . . . are now robbed in broad daylight. Violence exacts a terrible price—on individual victims who suffer physical wounds and bear long-term emotional scars; and on our communities and society at large who suffer a loss of security and peace of mind.

The facts bear out our fears—the United States of America is the most dangerous country in the world. No country in the world has a higher per capita murder rate than the United States of America—there were 23,760 murders in 1992. No country in the world matches the rate at which women in the United States are raped—here, a woman is raped every 47 seconds. That is nearly four times higher than in Germany, 13 times higher than in Great Britain, and more than 20 times higher than in Japan. These rates have risen dramatically over the last several decades. Since the early 1980s, the murder rate has increased 23 percent and the rate of violent crimes has increased 41 percent. More than five and a half million felonies were committed in 1992.

Violent Kids

Even more troubling is that the character of the violence is changing—first, younger and younger kids are committing violent crimes. Since 1983, the number of juveniles arrested for murder increased 142 percent! In 1992, in the United States of America, more than 4,500 murders were attributed to killers under the age of twenty. Second, teen-age criminals commit crimes that are more impulsive and irrational. The randomness of crime—the chance of being victimized for being in "the wrong place at the wrong time"—has increased. Finally, the wide and easy availability of guns with frightening firepower multiplies the destruction caused by each act of violence.

More than 15,000 of the nearly 24,000 murders in 1992 resulted from gun wounds. Guns are the preferred weapon of those intent on violence. And, as doctors across the country have told me, the kind of guns preferred today wreak unparalleled havoc with the human body. One doctor explained how advances in emergency medicine mean trauma units can save almost everyone with a single .22-caliber wound—even to the head or the chest. But today the victims of violence come to hospitals not with single wounds, but with multiple gunshot wounds from the head to the neck; not with a .22-caliber bullet lodged in the chest, but with the lungs literally blown out of the body by a .45-caliber slug.

We have all read the stories and seen the news coverage of stories illustrating each of these characteristics: kids as young as 13 stalking and shooting tourists on the highways of Florida; the robber in Washington, D.C., who turned around on his way out of a jewelry store, and went back to lean over the counter and gratuitously shoot the owner with his semi automatic pistol!

This is a society out of sync: this is a society in trouble. The problem of violence is so big and so multifaceted that it can seem intractable. For years, we have debated the "conservative" and "liberal" answers to crime and violence—painting tougher punishment or educational and social programs as stark "either/or" choices—and then concluding that nothing has worked. But is this criticism fair? I think not. Have we really made sure violent criminals know that punishment will be severe and certain? No—in states across the nation violent offenders serve on average only 40 percent of their sentences. Have we really succeeded in providing at-risk youths with the education and job opportunities necessary to offset the lure of crime? No. Student drop-out rates and teen unemployment—particularly for minorities—remain high, the minimum wage continues to lag behind inflation. When I look at our response to violence, I am reminded of what G. K. Chesterton said about Christianity: it is not that it has been tried and found wanting, but, rather, that is had been found difficult and left untried.

Causes of Violence

As we pursue solutions, we must re-frame the debate not in terms of what sounds tough, but in terms of what works; we must face the fact that answers to the problems of violence and crime are not easy—they will take our most determined commitment of energy and time. We must begin to isolate the factors we know are contributing to the violence; we must be willing to confront the causes of violence no matter how difficult or unpopular.

Let me just mention four such factors—factors which often work in conjunction with each other: first, much has been written about the fact that violent adults were often the victims of abuse as children. Violence is learned behavior. The "cycle of violence" begins as children suffer violence at home themselves or see their mothers or other family members suffer abuse.

Second, we know that the lack of a male role model in the home is related to criminal behavior. More than 40 percent of the state prison population nationwide grew up without fathers in their homes. More than 70 percent of all juveniles in long-term state correctional institutions come from homes without a father present. Even after controlling the income, boys from fatherless homes are significantly more likely to commit crimes and to wind up in the criminal justice system. This effect is exacerbated by the fact that children in single-parent homes are six times as likely to be poor, and are at greater risk for abuse, as compared to children from intact families.

Third, the link between violent crime and illegal drugs is unquestioned. Drug-related murders have risen 118 percent since 1985 alone. The violent competition among traffickers for markets has turned some of our neighborhoods into war zones. Criminals and innocent bystanders alike are killed at ever increasing rates. Don't forget, though, that most drug-related crime is committed by drug buyers, not sellers. Addicts who have no jobs or whose jobs cannot support a drug habit snatch purses, mug pedestrians, and rob cars and houses to support their habits.

Fourth, the availability of guns means that crime is increasingly lethal. Yet we continue to permit the legal purchase of weapons of such ferocity that our police forces are routinely outgunned, that our citizens can be mowed down by those with guns that fire 15 or more rounds in mere seconds.

Anti-Crime Measures

What can we do to combat these factors? One thing we must not do is throw up our hands and declare defeat. Instead, we must commit ourselves to finding solutions, and I believe we must do so through a two-step strategy.

First, we must take immediate steps to address those who are now in the crime stream, committing violent acts and menacing others. The crime bill passed by the Senate in November 1993 contains provisions that will help with the first level of response. [The crime bill was signed into law in September 1994.] In particular, we must ensure tough, cost-effective punishment for all offenders; we must put more police on our streets; we must permit fewer guns in the hands of criminals; and we must begin intensive efforts to reach those who are at risk and deter them from crime.

Let me take these one at a time.

First, our ability to reduce crime in a cost-effective manner depends directly on our ability to target offenders with the appropriate type of sentence. This means, first and foremost, that we must identify violent offenders and make sure they go to prison. By the end of 1992, state prisons were housing 840,000 inmates—and local jails held an additional 450,000 persons. The price tag for this incarceration is steep: state spending on prisons doubled between 1986 and 1992, and there is no end in sight unless we become smarter in using our resources. We must have adequate prison space to get violent people off the streets. The Senate's crime bill contains $3 billion in grants to states for building and/or operating prisons for violent offenders.

Today's Conflagration

What do we do on the law enforcement side to suppress violent crime? How do we actually make reductions in violent crime? In my view, the evidence is absolutely clear that the vast bulk of violent crime is committed by a very small group of chronic offenders. . . .

And I think that in combatting violent crime, we in the criminal justice system must make it our primary goal to identify, to target, and to incarcerate this hard-core element of chronic offenders. They should be incapacitated in custody for the time dictated by the public's safety, and not by other artificial restraints like prison space. I think this is the only approach in law enforcement that has any prospect for reducing levels of violent crime. No matter how well we tinker with and perfect our social rehabilitation programs, they are not going to take hold for decades and decades. We have crime on the streets right now. We have to put out the fire today. Yes, we can redesign houses so they are more fireproof in the future, but right now we have a conflagration and we have to deal with it.

William P. Barr, *The Heritage Lectures*, July 29, 1992.

In addition, to encourage states to identify nonviolent offenders and offer them alternative, more cost-effective programs, the states can use the money to run military-style boot camps. These camps provide a regimented program of work and activities for nonviolent offenders under 25 years old; they must be combined with job training and supervision on release to ensure low recidivism rates. Running boot camps costs about one-third what a prison costs on a per inmate basis, so moving nonviolent offenders into boot camps is a cost-effective response to the prison space shortage.

Finally, both the federal and state systems suffer from the same key shortcoming: the lack of drug treatment. Drug treatment, as former Drug Director Bill Bennett acknowledged, cuts recidivism rates in half, and it is cost effective: for every 1 dollar we spend treating drug offenders, we save 3 dollars later—in reduced crime and in the other high social costs of addiction. The need is great. . . .

Police Efforts

The second key approach taken in the crime bill is an effort to deter crime before it occurs by putting more police on our streets. As simple as this sounds, the need is acute: In 1950, America had more than three police officers for every violent crime; today there are three violent crimes for every police officer. Trying to fight a "war on crime" without more police is like trying to fight a military conflict without an army. The crime bill passed by the Senate promises to put 100,000 more police officers on our streets by 1997.

And these police will engage in what is known as "community policing." Today, a typical urban police department assigns officers to large precincts; they ride in cruisers and respond to radio calls from any and all parts of the oversized "beat." This system isolates police officers; they are strangers in the very communities they are trying to protect. As a result, they are always behind the curve—responding after the fact to a crime's occurrence, picking up the pieces after the violence is already done.

Community policing is designed to integrate police officers back into the life of the community, so they can help prevent crime from occurring in the first place and be better positioned to respond when it does occur. It takes police out of their cars to walk smaller "beats" of five or ten block areas. It allows them to learn who is in the community—so they know the trouble spots, the trouble makers, the at-risk juveniles. They work cooperatively with community leaders, school officials, family workers, and others to tailor preventative programs to best fit the community. Where it has been put in effect, in four major metropolitan areas, the crime rates have dropped from 18 percent to 23 percent.

The third step we must take is to get deadly weapons off our streets. Banning assault weapons would at least make our streets less lethal, if not less violent. The Senate's crime bill contains a ban on the manufacture, sale and possession of military-style assault weapons—guns with no sporting purpose, useful for one thing only—killing people.

Finally, in 1993, the Congress acted to limit the availability of handguns, passing the Brady Bill to provide for a five-day waiting period and background check for handgun purchases while an instant-check system is put in place. This modest step toward controlling guns must be a first step only—we must impose a rational system of managing all guns if we are to end the senseless killings like those that occurred on the New York commuter train in December 1993.

Other First Steps

The Senate's crime bill takes other first steps. It contains up to $2 billion for states to initiate education, training and prevention programs to steer at-risk youth away from teenage gangs and criminal careers. Larger scale, intensive intervention programs for all those at risk—and beginning at the earliest ages—are the long-term answer. Although we have resisted such efforts because of the expense, we must remember that the cost of inaction is staggeringly high. And until we decide to undertake such a massive effort, we should remember that smaller versions of these ideas can work, too. These smaller steps are what the Senate's bill contains. The money provided through the bill can be used for programs like boys and girls clubs in public housing projects. Projects that have such clubs report teen crime rates lower than those without such facilities. We should not stop until there is a club in every housing project in the country.

We must also start the long fight to stop family and child abuse. I believe the ultimate "cure" to this violence is to fundamentally change our attitudes about it. Somehow, we seem to forget that society suffers what it tolerates. If we remain indifferent to the fact that crime is rising fastest against women and children, we must expect this violence to grow even worse. As a society, we remain largely indifferent to the violence flowing from one generation to the next; we must declare the cycle of violence against women and children intolerable. That's why I drafted legislation designed to educate the public, the courts and law enforcement about violence against women.

Now part of the Senate's crime bill, this legislation combines practical programs such as education for prosecutors and judges as well as the public and funding for battered women's shelters and family violence hotlines, with the creation of a civil rights remedy for victims of violence motivated by gender bias. This last provision will have a real impact, but, even more importantly in my view, it will signal our clear and unambiguous disapproval of violence against women. Again, this is a first step toward ending the cycle of abuse that trains far too many children in the ways of violence.

The crime bill is, by anyone's standard, the most significant attempt in years to deal with violent crime in America, but it pales in comparison to what could happen in this society if we were better able to educate our children, if they had both fathers and mothers in their households, and if there were some credible notion of economic opportunity ahead of those Americans who struggle with poverty.

If the nation is to make lasting progress in the fight against violent crime, we must undertake a second phase of more fundamental change—change that can happen only over the long term. Over the long term, we must find ways to ensure that all children grow up in homes with two parents to provide the care and the guidance children need. We must make sure that all children have enough to eat, so they can concentrate on learning at school. In the end, all these things—and much more—must be done to stem the rising tide of violence that is gripping our country.

Violence is a social problem, and like all the other difficult problems (poverty, racism, homelessness), it feeds dual temptations: on the one hand, we try to ignore it as long as it doesn't immediately affect us; on the other hand, we are overwhelmed and see it as inevitable and intractable. We must resist both temptations. Today, crime affects all of us—maybe not as immediate victims but as ultimate victims, robbed of our sense of security and our peace of mind.

Nor can we afford not to respond. We must not give in to the violence in our streets. Because if we do, our children will reap the whirlwind of chaos. No society can endure, politically or economically, where violence is the rule rather than the exception.

> "Not a single one of those 412 pages [of the crime bill] would have protected me . . . from [my] assailant."

Anti-Crime Measures Will Not Reduce Violence

Bruce Shapiro

In November 1993, Congress passed a major crime bill that established stiffer penalties for violent criminals, allocated more funding for prisons, and increased the number of police officers nationwide. Relating his experience as the victim of a violent attack, Bruce Shapiro argues in the following viewpoint that this and other measures designed to clamp down on crime and cut social services will not prevent violence. Rather, he says, they will sustain the conditions that encourage violence—the decay of human connections and societal supports. Shapiro is an associate editor of the *Nation*, a liberal weekly magazine of political commentary.

As you read, consider the following questions:

1. According to Shapiro, what might have prevented his assailant's attack?
2. What delusion frames the crime debate, according to Shapiro?
3. According to Judith Herman, quoted by the author, what protects survivors of extreme violence against post-traumatic stress disorder?

From Bruce Shapiro, "One Violent Crime," *The Nation*, April 3, 1995. Reprinted by permission of *The Nation* magazine; ©The Nation Company, L.P.

Alone in my home I am staring at the television screen and shouting. On the evening local news I have unexpectedly encountered video footage, several months old, of myself writhing on an ambulance gurney, bright green shirt open and drenched with blood, skin pale, knee raised, trying desperately and with utter futility to find relief from pain.

On the evening of August 7, 1994, I was among seven people stabbed and seriously wounded in a coffee bar a few blocks from my house. Any televised recollection of this incident would be upsetting. But the anger that has me shouting tonight is quite specific, and political, in origin: My picture is being shown on the news to illustrate why Connecticut's legislature plans to lock up more criminals for a longer time. A picture of my body, contorted and bleeding, has become a propaganda image in the crime war.

I had not planned to write about this assault. But for months now the politics of the nation have in large part been the politics of crime, from 1994's federal crime bill through the fall 1994 elections [from which the Republican Party emerged with a majority in Congress] through the Contract With America proposals [the new Republican majority's blueprint for their first 100 days, which included welfare reform and anti-crime measures]. Among a welter of reactions to the attack, one feeling is clear: I am unwilling to be a silent poster child in this debate.

Chaos

The physical and political truth about violence and crime lie in their specificity, so here is what happened: I had gone out for after-dinner coffee that evening with two friends and New Haven neighbors, Martin and Anna Broell Bresnick. At 9:45 we arrived at a recently opened coffeehouse on Audubon Street, a block occupied by an arts high school where Anna teaches, other community arts institutions, a few pleasant shops and upscale condos. Entering, we said hello to another friend, a former student of Anna's named Cristina Koning, who the day before had started working behind the counter. We sat at a small table near the front of the cafe; about fifteen people were scattered around the room. Just before 10, the owner announced closing time. Martin stood up and walked a few yards to the counter for a final refill.

Suddenly there was chaos—as if a mortar shell had landed. I looked up, heard Martin call Anna's name, saw his arm raised and a flash of metal and people leaping away from a thin bearded man with a ponytail. Tables and chairs toppled. Without thinking I shouted to Anna, "Get down!" and pulled her to the floor, between our table and the cafe's outer wall. She clung to my shirt, I to her shoulders, and, crouching, we pulled each other toward the door.

What actually happened I was only able to tentatively recon-
struct many weeks later. Apparently, as Martin headed toward
the counter the thin bearded man, whose name we later learned
was Daniel Silva, asked the time from a young man named
Richard Colberg, who answered and turned to leave.

Without any warning, Silva pulled out a hunting knife with a
six-inch blade and stabbed in the lower back a woman leaving
with Colberg, a medical technician named Kerstin Braig. Then he
stabbed Colberg, severing an artery in his thigh. Silva was a slight
man but he moved with demonic speed and force around the
cafe's counter. He struck Martin in the thigh and in the arm he
raised to protect his face. Our friend Cris Koning had in a moment's time pushed out the screen in a window and helped the
wounded Kerstin Braig through it to safety. Cris was talking on
the phone with the police when Silva lunged over the counter
and stabbed her in the chest and abdomen. He stabbed Anna in
the side as she and I pulled each other along the wall. He stabbed
Emily Bernard, a graduate student who had been sitting quietly
reading a book, in the abdomen as she tried to flee through the
cafe's back door. All of this happened in about the time it has
taken you to read this paragraph.

The Glittering Blade

Meanwhile, I had made it out the cafe's front door onto the
brick sidewalk with Anna, neither of us realizing yet that she
was wounded. Seeing Martin through the window, I returned inside and we came out together. Somehow we separated, fleeing
opposite ways down the street. I had gone no more than a few
steps when I felt a hard punch in my back followed instantly by
the unforgettable sensation of skin and muscle tissue parting.
Silva had stabbed me about six inches above my waist, just beneath my rib cage. (That single deep stroke cut my diaphragm
and sliced my spleen in half.) Without thinking, I clapped my left
hand over the wound even before the knife was out and its blade
caught my hand, leaving a slice across my palm and two fingers.

"Why are you doing this?" I cried out to Silva in the moment
after feeling his knife punch in and yank out. As I fell to the
street he leaned over my face; I vividly remember the knife's
immense and glittering blade. He directed the point through my
shirt into the flesh of my chest, beneath my left shoulder. I remember his brown beard, his clear blue-gray eyes looking directly into mine, the round globe of a street lamp like a halo
above his head. Although I was just a few feet from a cafe full of
people and although Martin and Anna were only yards away,
the street, the city, the world felt utterly empty except for me
and this thin bearded stranger with clear eyes and a bowie
knife. The space around us—well-lit, familiar Audubon Street,

where for six years I had taken a child to music lessons—seemed literally to have expanded into a vast and dark canyon.

"You killed my mother," he answered. My own desperate response: "Please don't." Silva pulled the knifepoint out of my chest and disappeared. A moment later I saw him flying down the street on a battered, ungainly bicycle, back straight, vest flapping and ponytail flying.

Aftermath

After my assailant had gone I lay on the sidewalk, hand still over the wound on my back, screaming. Pain ran over me like an express train; it felt as though every muscle in my back was locked and contorted; breathing was excruciating. A security guard appeared across the street from me; I called out to him but he stood there frozen, or so it seemed. (A few minutes later, he would help police chase Silva down.) I shouted to Anna, who was hiding behind a car down the street. Still in shock and unaware of her own injury, she ran for help, eventually collapsing on the stairs of a nearby brownstone where a prayer group that was meeting upstairs answered her desperate ringing of the doorbell. From where I was lying, I saw a second-floor light in the condo complex across the way. A woman's head appeared in the window. "Please help me," I implored. "He's gone. Please help me." She shouted back that she had called the police, but she did not come to the street. I was suddenly aware of a blond woman—Kerstin Braig, though I did not know her name then—in a white-and-gray plaid dress, sitting on the curb. I asked her for help. "I'm sorry, I've done all I can," she muttered. She raised her hand, like a medieval icon; it was covered with blood. So was her dress. She sank into a kind of stupor. Up the street I saw a police car's flashing blue lights, then another's, then I saw an officer with a concerned face and a crackling radio crouched beside me. I stayed conscious as the medics arrived and I was loaded into an ambulance—being filmed for television, as it turns out, though I have no memory of the crew's presence.

Being a victim is a hard idea to accept, even while lying in a hospital bed with tubes in veins, chest, penis and abdomen. The spirit rebels against the idea of oneself as fundamentally powerless. So I didn't think much for the first few days about the meaning of being a victim; I saw no political dimension to my experience.

As I learned in more detail what had happened I thought, in my jumbled-up, anesthetized state, about my injured friends—although everyone survived, their wounds ranged from quite serious to critical—and about my wounds and surgery. I also thought about my assailant. A few facts about him are worth repeating. Until August 7 Daniel Silva was a self-employed junk dealer and a homeowner. He was white. He lived with his mother and several dogs. He had no arrest record. A New Haven police detective who was hospitalized across the hall from me recalled Silva as a socially marginal neighborhood character. He was not, apparently, a drug user. He had told neighbors about much violence in his family—indeed not long before August 7 he showed one neighbor a scar on his thigh he said was from a stab wound.

Conditions Unrelieved

It has become unfashionable to suggest that social conditions can be criminogenic. Because for so long political leadership has neglected basic universal services: health, education, employment, housing, while at the same time periodically declaring various wars on various criminal enemies, the tendency is to believe that we've tried and failed to reduce crime, and now draconian measures must be "reluctantly" embraced. The fact is that our political and social system has never sought to relieve the conditions which breed most crime.

Van Zwisohn, *Socialist*, March/April 1994.

A week earlier, Silva's 79-year-old mother had been hospitalized for diabetes. After a few days the hospital moved her to a new room; when Silva saw his mother's empty bed he panicked, but nurses swiftly took him to her new location. Still, something seemed to have snapped. Earlier on the day of the stabbings, police say, Silva released his beloved dogs, set fire to his house, and rode away on his bicycle as it burned. He arrived on Audubon Street with a single dog on a leash, evidently convinced his mother was dead. (She actually did die a few weeks after Silva was jailed.)

No Protection

While I lay in the hospital, the big story on CNN was the federal crime bill then being debated in Congress. Even fogged by morphine I was aware of the irony. I was flat on my back, the result of a particularly violent assault, while Congress eventually passed the anti-crime package I had editorialized against in the *Nation* just a few weeks earlier. Night after night in the hospital, unable to sleep, I watched the crime bill debate replayed and heard Republicans and Democrats (who had sponsored the bill in the first place) fall over each other to prove who could be the toughest on crime.

The bill passed on August 21, a few days after I returned

home. In early autumn I actually read the entire text of the crime bill—all 412 pages. What I found was perhaps obvious, yet under the circumstances compelling: Not a single one of those 412 pages would have protected me or Anna or Martin or any of the others from our assailant. Not the enhanced prison terms, not the forty-four new death penalty offenses, not the three-strikes-you're-out requirements, not the summary deportations of criminal aliens. And the new tougher-than-tough anti-crime provisions of the Contract With America, like the proposed abolition of the Fourth Amendment's search and seizure protections, offer no more practical protection.

On the other hand, the mental-health and social-welfare safety net shredded by Reaganomics and conservatives of both parties might have made a difference in the life of someone like my assailant—and thus in the life of someone like me. My assailant's growing distress in the days before August 7 was obvious to his neighbors. He had muttered darkly about relatives planning to burn down his house. A better-funded, more comprehensive safety net might just have saved me and six others from untold pain and trouble.

From my perspective—the perspective of a crime victim—the Contract With America and its conservative Democratic analogs are really blueprints for making the streets even less safe. Want to take away that socialistic income subsidy called welfare? Fine. Connecticut Governor John Rowland proposes cutting off all benefits after eighteen months. So more people in New Haven and other cities will turn to the violence-breeding economy of crack, or emotionally implode from sheer desperation. Cut funding for those soft-headed social workers? Fine; let more children be beaten without the prospect of outside intervention, more Daniel Silvas carrying their own traumatic scars into violent adulthood. Get rid of the few amenities prisoners enjoy, like sports equipment, musical instruments and the right to get college degrees, as proposed by the Congressional right? Fine; we'll make sure that those inmates are released to their own neighborhoods tormented with unchanneled rage.

City-Hating

One thing I could not properly appreciate in the hospital was how deeply many friends, neighbors and acquaintances were shaken by the coffeehouse stabbings, let alone strangers who took the time to write. The reaction of most was a combination of decent horrified empathy and a clear sense that their own presumption of safety was undermined.

But some people who didn't bother to acquaint themselves with the facts used the stabbings as a sort of Rorschach test on which they projected their own preconceptions about crime, violence and New Haven. Some present and former Yale students, for instance, were desperate to see in my stabbing evidence of the great dangers of New Haven's inner city. One student newspaper wrote about "New Haven's image as a dangerous town fraught with violence." A student reporter from another Yale paper asked if I didn't think the attack proved New Haven needs better police protection. Given the random nature of this assault—it could as easily have happened in wealthy, suburban Greenwich, where a friend of mine was held up at an ATM at the point of an assault rifle—it's tempting to dismiss such sentiments as typical products of an insular urban campus. But city-hating is central to today's political culture. Newt Gingrich [the Republican speaker of the House] excoriates cities as hopelessly pestilential, crime-ridden and corrupt. Fear of urban crime and of the dark-skinned people who live in cities is the right's basic text, and defunding cities a central agenda item for the Congressional majority.

Yet in no small measure it was the institutions of an urban community that saved my life on August 7. That concerned police officer who found me and Kerstin Braig on the street was joined in a moment by enough emergency workers to handle the carnage in and around the coffeehouse, and his backups arrived quickly enough to chase down my assailant three blocks away. In minutes I was taken to Yale–New Haven hospital less than a mile away—built in part with the kind of public funding so hated by the right. As I was wheeled into the E.R., several dozen doctors and nurses descended to handle all the wounded.

By then my abdomen had swelled from internal bleeding. Dr. Gerard Burns, a trauma surgeon, told me a few weeks later that I arrived on his operating table white as a ghost; my prospects, he said, would have been poor had I not been delivered so quickly, and to an E.R. with the kind of trauma team available only at a large metropolitan hospital. In other words, if my stabbing had taken place in the suburbs I would have bled to death.

The Schwarzenegger Delusion

"Why didn't anyone try to stop him?" That question was even more common than the reflexive city-bashing. I can't even begin to guess the number of times I had to answer it. Each time, I repeated that Silva moved too fast, that it was simply too confusing. And each time, I found the question not just foolish but offensive.

"Why didn't anyone stop him?" To understand that question is to understand, in some measure, why crime is such a potent political issue. To begin with, the question carries not empathy but an implicit burden of blame; it really asks "Why didn't *you* stop him?" It is asked because no one likes to imagine oneself a victim. It's far easier to graft onto oneself the aggressive power of the attacker, to embrace the delusion of oneself as Arnold Schwarzenegger defeating a multitude single-handedly. *If I am tough enough and strong enough I can take out the bad guys.*

The country is at present suffering from a huge version of this same delusion. This myth is buried deep in the political culture, nurtured in the historical tales of frontier violence and vigilantism and by the action-hero fantasies of film and television. Now, bolstered by the social Darwinists of the right, who see society as an unfettered marketplace in which the strongest individuals flourish, this delusion frames the crime debate.

I also felt that the question "Why didn't anybody stop him?" implied only two choices: Rambo-like heroism or abject victimhood. To put it another way, it suggests that the only possible responses to danger are the individual biological imperatives of fight or flight. And people don't want to think of themselves as on the side of flight. This is a notion whose political moment has arrived. In the debate over the crime bill, conservatives successfully portrayed themselves as those who would stand and fight; liberals were portrayed as ineffectual cowards.

Human Connection

"Why didn't anyone stop him?" That question and its underlying implications see both heroes and victims as lone individuals. But on the receiving end of a violent attack, the fight-or-flight dichotomy didn't apply. Nor did that radically individualized notion of survival. At the coffeehouse that night, at the moments of greatest threat, there were no Schwarzeneggers, no stand-alone heroes. (In fact I doubt anyone could have "taken out" Silva; as with most crimes, his attack came too suddenly.) But neither were there abject victims. Instead, in the confusion and panic of life-threatening attack, *people reached out to one another.* This sounds simple; yet it suggests there is an instinct for mutual aid that poses a profound challenge to the atomized individualism of the right. Cristina Koning helped the wounded Kerstin Braig to escape, and Kerstin in turn tried to bring Cristina along. Anna and I, and then Martin and I, clung to each other, pulling one another toward the door. And just as Kerstin found me on the sidewalk rather than wait for help alone, so Richard and Emily, who had never met before, together sought a hiding place around the corner. Three of us even spoke with Silva either the moment before or the instant after being stabbed. My plea to Silva may or may not have been what kept him from pushing his knife all the way through my chest and into my heart; it's impossible to know what was going through his mind. But this impulse to communicate, to establish human contact across a gulf of terror and insanity, is deeper and more subtle than the simple formulation of fight or flight, courage or cowardice, would allow.

I have never been in a war, but I now think I understand a little the intense bond among war veterans who have survived awful carnage. It is not simply the common fact of survival but the way in which the presence of these others seemed to make survival itself possible. There's evidence, too, that those who try to go it alone suffer more. In her insightful study *Trauma and Recovery*, Judith Herman, a psychiatrist, writes about rape victims, Vietnam War veterans, political prisoners and other survivors of extreme violence. "The capacity to preserve social connection . . ." she concludes, "even in the face of extremity, seems to protect people to some degree against the later development of post-traumatic syndromes. For example, among survivors of a disaster at sea, the men who had managed to escape by cooperating with others showed relatively little evidence of post-traumatic stress afterward." On the other hand, she reports that the "highly symptomatic" ones among those survivors were "'Rambos,' men who had plunged into impulsive, isolated action and not affiliated with others."

The political point here is that the Rambo justice system proposed by the right is rooted in that dangerous myth of the individual fighting against a hostile world. . . . But the myth has nothing to do with the reality of violent crime, the ways to prevent it or the needs of survivors. . . .

I do not know what made my assailant act as he did. Nor do I think crime and violence can be reduced to simple political categories. I do know that the answers will not be found in social Darwinism and atomized individualism, in racism, in dismantling cities and increasing the destitution of the poor. To the contrary: Every fragment of my experience suggests that the best protections from crime and the best aid to victims are the very social institutions most derided by the right. As crime victim and citizen what I want is the reality of a safe community—not a politician's fantasyland of restitution and revenge. That is my testimony.

"Additional measures should be taken at the federal level if we are to succeed in restricting the availability of firearms."

Increased Gun Control Is Needed to Reduce Violence

Karl P. Adler et al. (The signatories are appended at the end of the viewpoint.)

The following viewpoint is signed by nineteen members of the medical profession in and around New York City, including the deans of several medical schools, the presidents of various hospitals, and Margaret Hamburg, the commissioner of the New York City Department of Health. The signatories contend that more stringent federal gun-control measures are needed to combat firearm violence in America, which they characterize as "a public health emergency" of "epidemic proportions." Among other actions, they call for a national licensing system for gun ownership, increased taxes on the sale of firearms, and tighter regulation of gun dealers.

As you read, consider the following questions:

1. What are some of the components of the national licensing system described by the authors?
2. According to the authors, what two purposes would be served by an increased tax on the sale of firearms and ammunition?
3. How should gun dealers' licenses be more tightly regulated, according to the authors?

Karl P. Adler et al., "Firearm Violence and Public Health: Limiting the Availability of Guns," *JAMA*, April 27, 1994, vol. 271, no. 16, pp. 1281-82; ©1994, American Medical Association. Reprinted with permission.

Firearm violence has reached epidemic proportions in this country and is now a public health emergency, accounting for one fifth of all injury deaths in the United States and second only to motor vehicles as a cause of fatal injury. In addition, for every fatal injury, an estimated seven nonfatal injuries occur. Further, firearm-related injuries imposed an estimated $19 billion economic burden on the United States in 1990 in addition to the direct health care costs. If firearm violence continues to increase, it is expected that by the year 2003, the number of deaths from firearms will surpass the number of deaths caused by motor vehicles, and firearms will become this country's leading cause of injury-related death.

The burden of firearm violence is borne to a considerable degree by our country's most vulnerable population—its young people. Homicide is the leading cause of death for young black men aged 15 to 34 years and the second overall leading cause of death nationwide for individuals aged 15 to 24 years. Suicide rates for both children and adolescents have more than doubled in the past 30 years, due primarily to the increased use of firearms. For many adolescents, guns have become a part of life, with surveys reporting that many high school students either carry guns or have easy access to them. Still another consequence of firearm violence is its impact on children who witness it. Recent preliminary research has found an association between children's witnessing community violence and subsequent development of emotional disturbances.

Little Purpose

Handguns and assault weapons in the hands of the civilian population serve little purpose. The sheer volume of handguns, rifles, and assault weapons now available, estimated at approximately 200 million firearms, could arm almost every individual in America. Studies clearly show that firearms are more likely to kill or injure a member of the owner's household than they are to successfully protect that household, and in addition they raise the risk severalfold for a suicide in that household. Over half of all suicides (59%) are caused by firearms.

By law, people with criminal records or a history of mental illness cannot purchase guns, but without an adequate background check of potential purchasers, a gun dealer cannot obtain this information. The Brady Handgun Violence Prevention Act, passed by Congress in November 1993 and signed into law by the president, mandates a 5-day waiting period with incentives for police to conduct background checks before a gun may be purchased. It also contains a provision for the development of a national instant criminal background check system. This is a useful provision but is only a first step; it will prevent some guns from falling into the hands of criminals and others who are legally prohibited from owning guns. Far more stringent steps must be taken. Ideally, handguns, which account for more than half of all homicides in the United States, should be banned completely, but we recognize that this strategy is not currently politically feasible.

Restricting the Availability of Firearms

Tougher gun control laws are being passed in some states, but considerable variation exists in gun control legislation across the country. Since guns are carried across state lines, additional measures should be taken at the federal level if we are to succeed in restricting the availability of firearms. Such measures should include the following:

Implementing a National Licensure System for Firearms Possession.

A national firearms control program should be implemented to focus on restricting firearm ownership through limitation of licensing to those who can rigorously justify a purpose for owning a gun. The licensing procedure should be designed to mandate a review of the individual's request for a firearm and to ensure that a minimal standard of safety and proficiency training has been received. The procedure should include verification of lack of criminal record through national and state databases as well as corroborative support of the applicant's specifically stated purpose for firearm ownership. For example, if weapons are purchased for hunting, a valid hunting license should be presented along with an explanation of why the specific firearm is necessary and how, when, and where it will be used. Comments from any professional organizations in which the applicant will participate and indication of the intent of the applicant should also be solicited. In addition, those applying for a license to possess firearms should be fingerprinted, provide proof of address, and have nationally recognized and documented training in the use, safe storage, and handling of firearms. The control of firearms through registration and licensing of their operation has clear precedent, eg, in licensing for motor vehicle operation.

Limiting the manufacture, sale, and distribution of military-style assault weapons.

A federal ban currently exists on the importation of certain military-style assault weapons, but this ban should be expanded to domestic manufacture and sales. Many weapons that are equipped to accept magazines with a large ammunition capacity are designed for short-range quick firing without the need for skilled marksmanship. Many are specifically designed to kill human beings at close range. Although these weapons account for only a small percentage of firearms deaths, there is no reason for anyone to own a weapon the only purpose of which is to kill humans. The sheer destructive power of such weapons justifies federal legislation to ban civilian access to them.

Increasing Tax on Firearms and Ammunition.

An increased tax on the sale of firearms and ammunition for civilian use would serve two purposes. First, the added tax might discourage some sales, thus decreasing availability. Second, the moneys collected through the tax could be used to facilitate better education and training for, and control of gun distribution to, potential purchasers and owners. The moneys could also be used to implement a firearm fatality and injury reporting system.

Reprinted by special permission of North America Syndicate.

Tightening Federal Licensing Requirements for Gun Dealers.

Over 270,000 individuals own licenses to sell guns. This license, easily acquired for a minimal fee by anyone not in a prohibited category (convicted felon, illegal alien, and so forth), should be more tightly regulated. Individuals who apply for a dealer's license should be more closely scrutinized than those who apply for a license to own a gun. Measures such as the increase in dealer licensing fees as proposed in legislation introduced by Senator Paul Simon should be implemented. In addition, Treasury Secretary Lloyd Bentsen has announced plans to unveil a proposal that will substantially increase dealers' license fees and impose other controls on licensed firearm dealers. Such a proposal should be supported as well.

Limiting the Number of Guns an Individual Can Buy.

Most states have few restrictions on the number of guns individuals are allowed to purchase at any one time, but some are proposing to impose such limits. To address the problem of interstate gunrunning, Virginia has enacted a law that limits to one a month the number of handguns a person may buy. National legislation such as that proposed by Representative Robert Torricelli and Senator Frank Lautenberg to limit the number of handguns a person may buy to one a month would be a modest step in the right direction in decreasing the availability of guns and providing consistency across state lines.

Implementing a Gun Return Program.

A well-publicized gun return program with incentives for turning guns in to local police authorities should be implemented to reduce the number of guns now in circulation. A 1989 Gallup poll showed that almost half of the families in the United States possess firearms and half of these possess handguns. Gun return programs would help in reducing the number of these guns. These programs have been instituted with some success in New York City and other cities.

Implementing a Firearm Fatality and Injury Reporting System.

Data on firearm injuries and death are limited; additional information is needed. A national firearm fatality and injury reporting system would provide information on the type of weapon used and the circumstances under which the injury or death occurred. A system such as that described in a bill introduced in 1993 by Representative Patricia Schroeder would provide vital information in regard to fatal shootings, but it should be expanded to include information on nonfatal firearm injuries as well. The system could be modeled on the federal Accident Reporting System, which collects a wide variety of information about motor vehicle fatalities and has led to major improvements in motor vehicle safety and a decrease in the associated fatality rate.

Education and Publicity

Educating the Public About the Dangers of Guns and the Need for National Regulation.

The key element of these interventions and of any new national firearms control program depends on the successful education of American society about the dangers of guns and the need to regulate the ways in which they are bought, sold, and used. Other forms of education, such as conflict resolution and peer counseling programs, would offer adolescents and other individuals alternatives to violence. These programs should be started as early as possible in the elementary schools. National publicity campaigns, especially those that use popular role models, should be used to urge against violence and violent behavior. Violence in the media has desensitized the public, especially the youth of this country, to the horrors of real-life violence; this issue should be directly and vigorously addressed. In addition, a campaign to raise the consciousness of health care providers concerning violence control and prevention might aid in mobilizing and focusing public opinion. The public health community should be encouraged to seek innovative formulations and programs focused on defining more clearly the elements of the epidemic.

The root causes of violence, especially poverty, substance abuse, and unemployment, must be addressed over the long term to deal adequately with violence in our society. An ongoing, multifaceted approach is clearly required.

Karl P. Adler, MD
Dean, New York Medical College
Valhalla, NY

Jeremiah A. Barondess, MD
President, The New York Academy of Medicine

Jordan J. Cohen, MD
Dean, College of Medicine, State University of New York (SUNY) Health
   Sciences Center at Stony Brook

Saul J. Farber, MD
Dean, New York University School of Medicine
Chairman, Board of Trustees, The New York Academy of Medicine

Spencer Foreman, MD
President, Montefiore Medical Center
Bronx, NY

Gary Gambuti
President, St Lukes-Roosevelt Hospital Center
New York, NY

Margaret Hamburg, MD
Commissioner, New York City Department of Health

Nathan G. Kase, MD
Dean, Mount Sinai School of Medicine, City University of New York

Jacqueline Messite, MD
Executive Director, Office of Public Health, The New York Academy of Medicine

Robert Michels, MD
Dean, Cornell University Medical School
New York, NY

Robert G. Newman, MD
President, Beth Israel Medical Center
New York, NY

Herbert Pardes, MD
Dean, Columbia University College of Physicians and Surgeons
New York, NY

Dominick P. Purpura, MD
Dean, Albert Einstein College of Medicine
Bronx, NY

"*Guns don't increase national rates of crime and violence—but the continued proliferation of gun-control laws almost certainly does.*"

Gun Control Does Not Prevent Violence

Daniel D. Polsby

Advocates of gun control argue that violence and crime increase in proportion to the number of guns circulating through society. In the following viewpoint, Daniel D. Polsby rejects this theory. He contends that the presence of large numbers of guns in the possession of citizens deters criminals from committing violent crime. According to Polsby, by reducing the number of guns in the hands of noncriminals, gun-control measures likely encourage violent criminals to commit crimes. Polsby is the Kirkland & Ellis Professor of Law at Northwestern University Law School in Chicago, Illinois, and an affiliated scholar at the Heartland Institute, a public policy research institute in Palatine, Illinois.

As you read, consider the following questions:

1. According to Polsby, what are the two types of gun-control laws in the United States?
2. On what basis does the author criticize Arthur Kellerman's study on the risks of handgun ownership?
3. How is the theory that gun ownership causes violence disproved by the cases of Switzerland, New Zealand, and Israel, according to Polsby?

Excerpted from "The False Promise of Gun Control" by Daniel D. Polsby, *The Atlantic Monthly*, March 1994. Reprinted with permission.

During the 1960s and 1970s the robbery rate in the United States increased sixfold, and the murder rate doubled; the rate of handgun ownership nearly doubled in that period as well. Handguns and criminal violence grew together apace, and national opinion leaders did not fail to remark on the coincidence.

It has become a bipartisan article of faith that more handguns cause more violence. Such was the unequivocal conclusion of the National Commission on the Causes and Prevention of Violence in 1969, and such is now the editorial opinion of virtually every influential newspaper and magazine, from the *Washington Post* to the *Economist* to the *Chicago Tribune*. Members of the House and Senate who have not dared to confront the gun lobby concede the connection privately. Even if the National Rifle Association can produce blizzards of angry calls and letters to the Capitol virtually overnight, House members one by one have been going public, often after some new firearms atrocity at a fast-food restaurant or the like. And in November 1993 they passed the Brady bill.

Alas, however well accepted, the conventional wisdom about guns and violence is mistaken. Guns don't increase national rates of crime and violence—but the continued proliferation of gun-control laws almost certainly does. Current rates of crime and violence are a bit below the peaks of the late 1970s, but because of a slight oncoming bulge in the at-risk population of males aged fifteen to thirty-four, the crime rate will soon worsen. The rising generation of criminals will have no more difficulty than their elders did in obtaining the tools of their trade. Growing violence will lead to calls for laws still more severe. Each fresh round of legislation will be followed by renewed frustration.

Perverse Laws

Gun-control laws don't work. What is worse, they act perversely. While legitimate users of firearms encounter intense regulation, scrutiny, and bureaucratic control, illicit markets easily adapt to whatever difficulties a free society throws in their way. Also, efforts to curtail the supply of firearms inflict collateral damage on freedom and privacy interests that have long been considered central to American public life. Thanks to the seemingly never-ending war on drugs and long experience attempting to suppress prostitution and pornography, we know a great deal about how illicit markets function and how costly to the public attempts to control them can be. It is essential that we make use of this experience in coming to grips with gun control.

The thousands of gun-control laws in the United States are of two general types. The older kind sought to regulate how, where, and by whom firearms could be carried. More recent laws have sought to make it more costly to buy, sell, or use firearms (or certain classes of firearms, such as assault rifles, Saturday-night specials, and so on) by imposing fees, special taxes, or surtaxes on them. The Brady bill is of both types: it has a background-check provision, and its five-day waiting period amounts to a "time tax" on acquiring handguns. All such laws can be called scarcity-inducing, because they seek to raise the cost of buying firearms, as figured in terms of money, time, nuisance, or stigmatization.

Despite the mounting number of scarcity-inducing laws, no one is very satisfied with them. Hobbyists want to get rid of them, and gun-control proponents don't think they go nearly far enough. Everyone seems to agree that gun-control laws have some effect on the distribution of firearms. But it has not been the dramatic and measurable effect their proponents desired.

Opponents of gun control have traditionally wrapped their arguments in the Second Amendment to the Constitution. Indeed, most modern scholarship affirms that so far as the drafters of the Bill of Rights were concerned, the right to bear arms was to be enjoyed by everyone, not just a militia, and that one of the principal justifications for an armed populace was to secure the tranquillity and good order of the community. But most people are not dedicated antiquitarians, and would not be impressed by the argument "I admit that my behavior is very dangerous to public safety, but the Second Amendment says I have a right to do it anyway." That would be a case for repealing the Second Amendment, not respecting it.

Fighting the Demand Curve

Everyone knows that possessing a handgun makes it easier to intimidate, wound, or kill someone. But the implication of this point for social policy has not been so well understood. It is easy to count the bodies of those who have been killed or wounded with guns, but not easy to count the people who have avoided harm because they had access to weapons. Think about uniformed police officers, who carry handguns in plain view not in order to kill people but simply to daunt potential attackers. And it works. Criminals generally do not single out police officers for opportunistic attack. Though officers can expect to draw their guns from time to time, few even in big-city departments will actually fire a shot (except in target practice) in the course of a year. This observation points to an important truth: people who are armed make comparatively unattractive victims. A criminal might not know if any one civilian is armed, but if it becomes known that a large number of civilians do carry weapons, criminals will become warier.

Which weapons laws are the right kinds can be decided only after considering two related questions. First, what is the connection between civilian possession of firearms and social violence? Second, how can we expect gun-control laws to alter people's behavior? Most recent scholarship raises serious questions about the "weapons increase violence" hypothesis. The second question is emphasized here, because it is routinely overlooked and often mocked when noticed; yet it is crucial. Rational gun control requires understanding not only the relationship between weapons and violence but also the relationship between laws and people's behavior. Some things are very hard to accomplish with laws. The purpose of a law and its likely effects are not always the same thing. Many statutes are notorious for the way in which their unintended effects have swamped their intended ones.

A General Deterrent to Crime

If a significant number of law-abiding people made a habit of carrying guns in public, they could create a general deterrent to crime. In *Armed and Considered Dangerous: A Survey of Felons and Their Firearms*, sociologists James D. Wright and Peter H. Rossi report that most felons worry more about encountering armed victims than about getting arrested. This fear has a real impact on criminal behavior.

Jacob Sullum, *Reason*, March 1994.

In order to predict who will comply with gun-control laws, we should remember that guns are economic goods that are traded in markets. Consumers' interest in them varies. For religious, moral, aesthetic, or practical reasons, some people would refuse to buy firearms at any price. Other people willingly pay very high prices for them.

Handguns, so often the subject of gun-control laws, are desirable for one purpose—to allow a person tactically to dominate a hostile transaction with another person. The value of a weapon to a given person is a function of two factors: how much he or she wants to dominate a confrontation if one occurs, and how likely it is that he or she will actually be in a situation calling for a gun.

Dominating a transaction simply means getting what one wants without being hurt. Where people differ is in how likely it is that they will be involved in a situation in which a gun will be valuable. Someone who *intends* to engage in a transaction involving a gun—a criminal, for example—is obviously in the best possible position to predict that likelihood. Criminals should therefore be willing to pay more for a weapon than most other people would. Professors, politicians, and newspaper editors are, as a group, at very low risk of being involved in such transactions, and they thus systematically underrate the value of defensive handguns. (Correlative, perhaps, is their uncritical readiness to accept studies that debunk the utility of firearms for self-defense.) The class of people we wish to deprive of guns, then, is the very class with the most inelastic demand for them—criminals—whereas the people most likely to comply with gun-control laws don't value guns in the first place.

Do Guns Drive Up Crime Rates?

Which premise is true—that guns increase crime or that the fear of crime causes people to obtain guns? Most of the country's major newspapers apparently take this problem to have been solved by an article published by Arthur Kellermann and several associates in the October 7, 1993, *New England Journal of Medicine*. Kellermann is an emergency-room physician who has published a number of influential papers that he believes discredit the thesis that private ownership of firearms is a useful means of self-protection. (An indication of his wide influence is that within two months the study received almost 100 mentions in publications and broadcast transcripts indexed in the Nexis data base.) For this study Kellermann and his associates identified fifteen behavioral and fifteen environmental variables that applied to a 388-member set of homicide victims, found a "matching" control group of 388 non–homicide victims, and then ascertained how the two groups differed in gun ownership. In interviews Kellermann made clear his belief that owning a handgun markedly increases a person's risk of being murdered.

But the study does not prove that point at all. Indeed, as Kellermann explicitly conceded in the text of the article, the causal arrow may very well point in the other direction: the threat of being killed may make people more likely to arm themselves. Many people at risk of being killed, especially people involved in the drug trade or other illegal ventures, might well rationally buy a gun as a precaution, and be willing to pay a price driven up by gun-control laws. Crime, after all, is a dangerous business. Peter Reuter and Mark Kleiman, drug-policy researchers, calculated in 1987 that the average crack dealer's risk of being killed was far greater than his risk of being sent to prison. (Their data cannot, however, support the implication that ownership of a firearm causes or exacerbates the risk of being killed.)

Defending the validity of his work, Kellermann has emphasized that the link between lung cancer and smoking was initially established by studies methodologically no different from his. Gary Kleck, a criminology professor at Florida State University, has pointed out the flaw in this comparison. No one ever thought that lung cancer causes smoking, so when the association between the two was established the direction of the causal arrow was not in doubt. Kleck wrote that it is as though Kellermann, trying to discover how diabetics differ from other people, found that they are much more likely to possess insulin than nondiabetics, and concluded that insulin is a risk factor for diabetes.

The New York Times, the *Los Angeles Times*, *The Washington Post*, *The Boston Globe*, and the *Chicago Tribune* all gave prominent coverage to Kellermann's study as soon as it appeared, but none saw fit to discuss the study's limitations. A few, in order to introduce a hint of balance, mentioned that the NRA, or some member of its staff, disagreed with the study. But readers had no way of knowing that Kellermann himself had registered a disclaimer in his text. "It is possible," he conceded, "that reverse causation accounted for some of the association we observed between gun ownership and homicide." Indeed, the point is stronger than that: "reverse causation" may account for *most* of the association between gun ownership and homicide. Kellermann's data simply do not allow one to draw any conclusion.

More Guns, Less Violence

If firearms increased violence and crime, then rates of spousal homicide would have skyrocketed, because the stock of privately owned handguns has increased rapidly since the mid-1960s. But according to an authoritative study of spousal homicide in the *American Journal of Public Health*, by James Mercy and Linda Saltzman, rates of spousal homicide in the years 1976 to 1985 fell. If firearms increased violence and crime, the crime rate should have increased throughout the 1980s, while the national stock of privately owned handguns increased by more than a million units in every year of the decade. It did not. Nor should the rates of violence and crime in Switzerland, New Zealand, and Israel be as low as they are, since the number of firearms per civilian household is comparable to that in the United States. Conversely, gun-controlled Mexico and South Africa should be islands of peace instead of having murder rates more than twice as high as those here. The determinants of crime and law-abidingness are, of course, complex matters, which are not fully understood and certainly not explicable in terms of a country's laws. But gun-control enthusiasts, who have made capital out of the low murder rate in England, which is largely disarmed, simply ignore the counterexamples that don't fit their theory.

If firearms increased violence and crime, Florida's murder rate should not have been falling since the introduction, in 1987, of a law that makes it easier for ordinary citizens to get permits to carry concealed handguns. Yet the murder rate has remained the same or fallen every year since the law was enacted, and it is now lower than the national murder rate (which has been rising). As of November 1993, 183,561 permits had been issued, and only 17 of the permits had been revoked because the holder was involved in a firearms offense. It would be precipitate to claim that the new law has "caused" the murder rate to subside. Yet here is a situation that doesn't fit the hypothesis that weapons increase violence.

The Futility Theorem

If firearms increased violence and crime, programs of induced scarcity would suppress violence and crime. But—another anomaly—they don't. Why not? A theorem, which we could call the futility theorem, explains why gun-control laws must either be ineffectual or in the long term actually provoke more violence and crime. Any theorem depends on both observable fact and assumption. An assumption that can be made with confidence is that the higher the number of victims a criminal assumes to be armed, the higher will be the risk—the price—of assaulting them. By definition, gun-control laws should make weapons scarcer and thus more expensive. By our prior reasoning about demand among various types of consumers, after the laws are enacted criminals should be better armed, compared with noncriminals, than they were before. Of course, plenty of noncriminals will remain armed. But even if many noncriminals will pay as high a price as criminals will to obtain firearms, a larger number will not.

Criminals will thus still take the same gamble they already take in assaulting a victim who might or might not be armed. But they may appreciate that the laws have given them a freer field, and that crime still pays—pays even better, in fact, than before. What will happen to the rate of violence? Only a relatively few gun-mediated transactions—currently, five percent of armed robberies committed with firearms—result in someone's actually being shot (the statistics are not broken down into encounters between armed assailants and unarmed victims, and encounters in which both parties are armed). It seems reasonable to fear that if the number of such transactions were to increase because criminals thought they faced fewer deterrents, there would be a corresponding increase in shootings. Conversely, if gun-mediated transactions declined—if criminals initiated fewer of them because they feared encountering an armed victim or an armed good Samaritan—the number of shootings would go down. The magnitude of these effects is, admittedly, uncertain. Yet it is hard to doubt the general tendency of a change in the law that imposes legal burdens on buying guns. The futility theorem suggests that gun-control laws, if effective at all, would unfavorably affect the rate of violent crime.

"Every violent criminal who is in prison is a criminal who is not committing other violent crimes."

Increased Incarceration Reduces Violent Crime

U.S. Department of Justice

The Department of Justice (DOJ) is the executive department of the U.S. government responsible for enforcing federal laws. In the following viewpoint, the DOJ argues that the incarceration of criminals is the solution to violent crime in America. To support its argument, the department cites statistics reporting that in the 1960s, when incarceration rates were low, crime rates increased rapidly. By contrast, according to the DOJ, in the 1980s and early 1990s, when incarceration rates were high, rates of reported crimes increased much more slowly and estimates of total crime decreased.

As you read, consider the following questions:

1. Why did the incarceration rate drop in the 1960s, according to the DOJ?
2. How did increased incarceration rates reflect the change of direction in criminal justice during the 1970s and 1980s, according to the authors?
3. According to the National Crime Victimization Survey, cited by the DOJ, by what percentage did the estimated number of aggravated assaults decrease between 1973 and 1980 and between 1980 and 1990?

Excerpted from *The Case for More Incarceration* (NCJ-139583, 1992), U.S. Department of Justice, Office of Policy and Communications, Washington, D.C.

Ask many politicians, newspaper editors, or criminal justice "experts" about our prisons, and you will hear that our problem is that we put too many people in prison. The truth, however, is to the contrary; we are incarcerating too *few* criminals, and the public is suffering as a result.

Every violent criminal who is in prison is a criminal who is not committing other violent crimes. Too many violent criminals are sentenced to probation with minimal supervision. Too many violent criminals are sentenced to prison but are released early on parole or simply to relieve the pressure of prison crowding. None of us is naive enough to think that these criminals will suddenly become upstanding, law-abiding citizens upon release. And indeed they do not. Much violent crime is directly attributable to our failure to sentence violent criminals to prison and our failure to keep them in prison beyond a fraction of their sentence.

Yes, we would have to build more prisons to implement a policy of more incarceration. Yes, this would cost money. But it would plainly reduce crime and help to protect the public—which is the first responsibility of any government. State and local governments are spending a growing but still modest portion of their budgets on corrections, and it is time to consider our priorities. . . .

Prisons Work

How do we know that prisons work? To begin with, historical figures show that after incarceration rates have increased, crime rates have moderated. In addition, when convicted offenders have been placed on probation or released early from prison, many of them have committed new crimes. One can legitimately debate whether prisons rehabilitate offenders; one can even debate whether, and how much, prisons deter offenders from committing crimes. But there is no debate that prisons incapacitate offenders. Unlike probation and parole, incarceration makes it physically impossible for offenders to victimize the public with new crimes for as long as they are locked up.

In the 1960's violent crimes reported to police more than doubled, but the nation's prison population declined by almost 8% from about 213,000 to under 197,000 in 1970. If the prison population had simply kept pace with the crime rate during this period, the population would have been over 495,000 by 1970—about 2½ times the actual figure. How can it be that so few persons were in prison during a period of soaring crime rates? The answer is that the chances of imprisonment for serious crimes fell dramatically. At the beginning of the decade, for every 1,000 adults arrested for a violent crime or burglary, criminal courts committed 299 offenders to a state prison; by 1970, the rate had dropped to 170.

This drop in the incarceration rate was no accident. The prevailing attitude among policy-makers at the time was that social spending and not imprisonment was the answer to crime. By the 1970's, it had become painfully apparent that the anti-punishment policies of the 1960's had failed. There was a change of direction in criminal justice toward tough law enforcement—arrest, prosecution, *and incarceration*—a change that continued through the 1980's and continues today.

Table 1

National Crime Victimization Survey
Crime Victimization Rates
(per 100,000 persons age 12 or older)

	1973	1980	1990
Rape	94.7	94.3 (−0.5%)	64.0 (−32%)
Robbery	674.0	656.0 (−3%)	565.7 (−14%)
Aggravated assault	1006.8	926.0 (−8%)	787.6 (−15%)
TOTALS	**1775.5**	**1676.3 (−6%)**	**1417.3 (−15%)**

NOTE: Figures include estimates of reported—and unreported—crimes, based upon interviews of a sampling of households nationwide. In 1990, approximately 95,000 people in 47,000 households were interviewed. Murders are not included. Survey began in 1973.

Source: Department of Justice.

This change was reflected in two different ways. First, there were more inmates sentenced to prison (traditionally measured by the rate per 100,000 population). In 1960, the rate of imprisonment (state *and* federal) per 100,000 was 117. This rate fell during the 1960's, and by 1970 it was 96 per 100,000. As a result of the new direction in criminal justice during the 1970's and 1980's, the imprisonment rate rose to 134 per 100,000 in 1980 and to 282 per 100,000 in 1990.

Second, the changed attitude toward incarceration was reflected in an increase in the chance of incarceration after arrest. In an article in *Science* magazine, a scholarly journal published by the American Association for the Advancement of Science, Patrick A. Langan, a Bureau of Justice Statistics statistician, has shown that the most important factor in the increased prison population between 1974 and 1986 was the greater likelihood that an arrest would result in a conviction and a sentence to prison. This factor was far more important than any increases in crime-prone populations, increases in reported crime and arrest rates, or increases in drug arrest and imprisonment rates.

Incarceration Affects Crime Rates

The increase in incarceration has been accompanied by a significant slowing of the increase in reported crime and by a decrease in estimates of total crime (reported and unreported crime combined). Using rates of crime *reported to police*, measured by the Federal Bureau of Investigation's Uniform Crime Reports, we see that from 1960 to 1970, the murder rate per 100,000 Americans rose by 55%, and from 1970 to 1980 it rose by 29%. From 1980 to 1990, however, it dropped by 8%. From 1960 to 1970, the number of rapes reported to police per 100,000 Americans increased by 96%, and by 97% from 1970 to 1980. From 1980 to 1990, the increase was only 12%. The same pattern can be shown for rates of reported robbery, which increased by 186% from 1960 to 1970 and increased by only 2% from 1980 to 1990. The FBI's "crime index" offense rate, which includes not only violent crimes but also burglary, larceny-theft, and motor vehicle theft, has seen an even more pronounced trend. From 1960 to 1970, the crime index rate more than doubled, increasing by 111%; from 1970 to 1980, it rose by 49%; but from 1980 to 1990, it actually *declined* by 2%.

The National Crime Victimization Survey, sponsored by the Bureau of Justice Statistics, estimates total crime against persons age 12 and above—both reported and unreported—based on interviews with a representative sampling of households. In 1973, the first year in which the survey was taken, there were an estimated 94.7 rapes per 100,000 population. This rate remained virtually unchanged in 1980 but had dropped by 32% by 1990. Similarly, there were an estimated 674 robberies per 100,000 population in 1973. By 1980, that rate had dropped by 3% and by 1990 it had dropped by another 14%. Aggravated assaults, which occurred with an estimated frequency of 1006.8 per 100,000 population in 1973, occurred at an 8% lower rate in 1980. By 1990, the rate had decreased by another 15% (Table 1).

The Effect on Individual States

Imprisonment and prison-construction policies have had a demonstrable effect in individual states. In the early 1980's, the Texas legislature adopted an approach that reduced the time that prisoners served, in an effort to open up space for the next class of felons. Between 1980 and 1989, the average prison term served fell from about 55% of the sentence to about 15% of the sentence, and by 1989 the parole population grew to more than 5 times its 1980 level. The "expected punishment"—average time served, reduced by the probabilities of arrest, prosecution, conviction, and sentence to prison—for serious crimes (murder, rape, robbery, aggravated assault, burglary, theft) fell 43% in Texas during the 1980's while it was increasing by about 35% in the nation as a whole, and the rate of these serious crimes reported in Texas rose by about 29%, while national rates fell by almost 4%.8

In Michigan, when funding for prison construction dried up in the early 1980's, the state instituted an early-release program and became one of only two states whose prison population declined from 1981 to 1984. Between 1981 and 1986, the rate of violent crimes reported to police in Michigan rose by 25% at the same time national crime rates were declining. In 1986, however, when Michigan embarked on a major prison-building effort, the state's violent-crime rate began to fall, and by 1989 it had dropped by 12%.

It strains credulity to believe that the lowered crime rates have been unrelated to the unprecedented increases in the nation's incarceration rates, even if there may have been other causes as well. As Langan put it in his *Science* article:

> Whatever the causes, in 1989 there were an estimated 66,000 fewer rapes, 323,000 fewer robberies, 380,000 fewer assaults, and 3.3 million fewer burglaries attributable to the difference between the crime rates of 1973 versus those of 1989 [*i.e.*, applying 1973 crime rates to 1989 population]. If only one-half or even one-fourth of the reductions were the result of rising incarceration rates, that would still leave prisons responsible for sizable reductions in crime.

"The great increases in the use of incarceration have not had any significant impact on crime rates."

Increased Incarceration Does Not Reduce Violent Crime

James Austin and John Irwin

James Austin is the executive vice president of the National Council on Crime and Delinquency, an organization that advocates prevention programs rather than incarceration as a solution to crime in American society. In the following viewpoint, he and coauthor John Irwin dispute the contention that increased incarceration of criminals reduces the incidence of violent crime. They argue that a careful evaluation of the evidence reveals that despite the increase of imprisonment that began in the 1970s violent crime has increased dramatically.

As you read, consider the following questions:

1. According to the Uniform Crime Reports (UCR) cited by the authors, by what percentage did violent crime increase between 1960 and 1991?
2. According to Austin and Irwin, the idea that increased incarceration will reduce crime is based on a "fallacious theory of criminal behavior." What is that theory?

Excerpted from James Austin and John Irwin, *Does Imprisonment Reduce Crime? A Critique of "Voodoo" Criminology* (San Francisco: National Council on Crime and Delinquency, 1993). Reprinted with permission.

During the 1980s, the United States engaged in an unprecedented imprisonment binge. Between 1980 and 1990 the prison population more than doubled, from 329,821 to 771,243—an increase of 134 percent. By 1990, the number of citizens incarcerated exceeded the population of six states and was larger than some major cities including San Francisco, Boston, and Washington, D.C. The incarceration rate (number of persons in prison on any given day per 100,000 U.S. population) increased during the same time period from 138 to 293. By way of historical comparison, the incarceration rate in 1850 was only 26 per 100,000. We now imprison at a higher rate than any nation in the world. . . .

Despite these historic increases, there is little evidence that America's imprisonment binge will end soon. . . . As of 1991, 42 states reported that they were planning to build over 100,000 prison beds at a cost of over $5 billion. This massive construction program represents a futile effort to catch up with the increasing prison populations. . . .

Given these recent trends, it seems fair to ask what is being accomplished by the massive expansion of imprisonment. . . . Those who are largely responsible for the expansion—elected officials who have harangued on the street crime issue and passed laws resulting in more punitive sentencing policies, judges who deliver more and longer prison terms, and government criminal justice functionaries who have supported the punitive trend in criminal justice policies—promised that the great expansion of prison populations would reduce crime in our society. For example, in 1991 a key U.S. Department of Justice official, Steven D. Dillingham, summarized the government's scientific basis for supporting incarceration as the best means for reducing crime: "Statisticians and criminal justice researchers have consistently found that falling crime rates are associated with rising imprisonment rates, and rising crime rates are associated with falling imprisonment rates."

Former Attorney General William Barr more recently restated this position, arguing that the country had a "clear choice" of either building more prisons or tolerating higher violent crime rates. This view implies that increasing the government's capacity to imprison is the single most effective strategy for reducing crime. But what is the scientific basis for supporting such a public policy?

Measuring Crime

To evaluate the "imprisonment reduces crime" argument, one must first understand the two methods by which crime rates are measured. One method involves the Census Bureau's annual surveys of persons living in households to determine how many households have been victimized each year by one of seven crimes—rape, robbery, assault, personal theft, household theft, burglary, and motor vehicle theft. This crime reporting system, known as the National Crime Victimization Survey (NCVS), began in 1973. The NCVS does not include crimes against businesses (shoplifting, commercial burglaries, etc.), drug crimes, homicides, or crimes against children under the age of 12. Furthermore, the NCVS tends to record a large number of trivial crimes which ordinarily are not reported to the police.

The second measure of crime is the Uniform Crime Reports (UCR) which includes crimes reported to the police and tabulated by the FBI. The UCR has been used since 1920 and like the NCVS, only captures a limited number of crimes (homicide, rape, aggravated assault, robbery, burglary, larceny theft, and motor vehicle theft). But unlike the NCVS, it does include homicides, crimes committed against businesses or commercial properties, and crimes committed against children under the age of 12 and those not living in households.

To support the proposition that increases in incarceration reduces crime, senior U.S. Department of Justice officials have compared UCR violent crime rates (homicides, robbery, assault, rape, and kidnapping) with imprisonment rates between 1960 and 1990 in ten year increments.

By selectively using these ten year increments, the Justice Department shows that, during the 1960s, imprisonment rates dropped by 19 percent while reported violent crime rates increased 104 percent. During the 1970s, violent crime rates continued to increase again, but by only 47 percent, while imprisonment rates increased by 39 percent. And, in the 1980s, as imprisonment rates increased by 99 percent, violent crime rates again increased, but by only 11 percent.

In other words, although violent crime rates have steadily increased over the past three decades, the rates of increase were lowest during the 1980s when imprisonment rates were at their highest levels. These data have led the Department of Justice to claim that violent crime will decline even more, if more persons are imprisoned. Dillingham writes,

> No one knows for sure what the 1990s will bring. But my guess, based on the lessons learned over the past three decades, is this: If imprisonment rates continue to rise, overall violent crime rates will not increase and could actually fall in the 1990s. A big "if", of course, is whether imprisonment rates will continue their steady upward climb.

Proponents of the viewpoint that incarceration reduces crime base their conclusion on two assumptions. The first is that criminals will "think twice" and will be deterred when faced with the likely prospect of stiff prison sentences. The second is that, by removing high rate offenders from society for extended periods of time, substantial reductions in crime rates will be realized. This claim was first advanced by the RAND Corporation, which claimed it had discovered new scientific methods for identifying the so-called "career criminal." Based on self-report interviews with inmates, the RAND researchers found that a small percentage of the interviewed inmates claimed to have committed an inordinate number of crimes while on the streets. If these criminals were telling the truth to the researchers, then one could argue that by sentencing them to long prison terms, they would be "incapacitated" and crime rates would decline dramatically. Based on these findings, Peter Greenwood of the RAND Corporation advocated that by selectively incapacitating these "high rate" offenders for lengthy periods of imprisonment, crime rates would drop.

A study conducted by Edwin Zedlewski and widely disseminated by the U.S. Department of Justice estimated that for each person incarcerated, nearly 200 crimes would be prevented each year and "society" would save $2,300 per crime. Both studies have been uncritically embraced by law enforcement officials as proof that greater use of imprisonment lowers crime rates.

A Careful Examination of the Evidence

A more careful examination of all the available information on crime and incarceration suggests that the great increases in the use of incarceration have not had any significant impact on crime rates. In the first place, crime rates have not declined despite the massive increases in prison and jail populations. Between 1960 and 1991, despite unstable fluctuations in crime rates, the fact remains that in the face of a 165 percent increase in imprisonment rates, the overall UCR crime rate increased by over 200 percent, property crimes by nearly 200 percent, and violent crime by over 370 percent.

Returning to the argument set forth by the U.S. Department of Justice that crime rate increases were lowest in the decade of the 1980s and highest in the 1960s, a more careful year-by-year analysis of the same UCR data cited by the U.S. Department of Justice shows that the nation's overall crime rates have had relative periods of stabilization in all three decades (1960–1962; 1970–1973; 1975–1978; and 1980–1984) only to be followed by crime rate increases despite increases in the use of imprisonment. For the imprisonment theory to be valid, these countervailing trends should not have occurred or should somehow be explained by the imprisonment theory. If there were a direct causal relationship between imprisonment and crime rates, stabilization in crime rates during theses time periods should not occur.

Imprisonment advocates also claim that crime has been reduced since 1973 by over 25 percent with most of the decline

Figure 1
Comparisons of Prison, UCR, and NCVS Trends
1973–1991

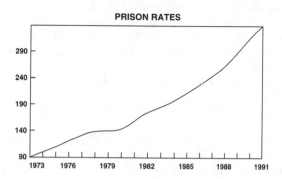

PRISON RATES

per 100,000 total population

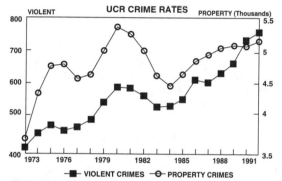

UCR CRIME RATES

per 100,000 total population

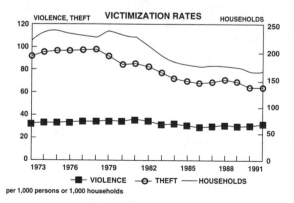

VICTIMIZATION RATES

per 1,000 persons or 1,000 households

Source: James Austin and John Irwin, *Does Imprisonment Reduce Crime? A Critique of Voodoo Criminology*, February 1993.

occurring since 1980. They have based their case exclusively on the 1973–1991 NCVS household surveys. Figure 1 summarizes the UCR, NCVS, and imprisonment rates between 1973 and 1991—the time period for which all three measures have been recorded by the U.S. Department of Justice.

During this same time period, imprisonment rates more than tripled from 98 to 310 per 100,000. Despite this increase, both UCR property and violent crime rates actually increased by 82 percent and 38 percent, respectively. There was a decline in UCR rates between 1980 and 1984 but only to be followed by a steady increase thereafter. Similar to the UCR rates, the NCVS data also show a decline in household reported crime beginning in 1980.

Imprisonment advocates initially heralded the 1980–1984 decrease in both the UCR and NCVS crime rates as imprisonment rates grew from 138 to 179 per 100,000 as proof that imprisonment reduces crime.

But beginning in 1985, the UCR crime rate began to increase despite the fact that the imprisonment rate continued to escalate. Only the NCVS overall rates continued to decline through 1991. However, even for the NCVS data, there has been virtually no decline in violent crime rates. In fact, since 1986, the NCVS violent crime rate has increased 11 percent from 28.1 to 31.3 per 1,000 persons. Only property theft and household burglary as reported by the NCVS have shown declines. . . .

Voodoo Criminology

The failure of the massive expansion of prison populations to accomplish its most important objective—the reduction of crime—should come as no surprise because the idea that increased penalties will reduce crime is based on a simplistic and fallacious theory of criminal behavior. It starts with the idea that every person is an isolated, willful actor who makes completely rational decisions to maximize his or her pleasure and to minimize his or her pain. Consequently, individuals only commit crimes when they believe it will lead to more pleasure, gain, or satisfaction and with minimal risk of pain or punishment. If penalties for being caught are small or non-existent, then many persons who are not restrained by other factors (e.g., strong conventional morals or the disapproval of close friends or family) will commit crimes—indeed a lot of crimes. Only by increasing the certainty and severity of punishment will people "think twice" and be deterred.

The punishment/incapacitation/deterrence theory assumes that all individuals have access to the same conventional lifestyles for living out a law-abiding life. This is not true for most of the individuals who are caught up in our criminal justice system. For many, particularly young members of the inner-city underclass, the choice is not between conventional and illegal paths to the good life, but illegal and risky paths or no satisfaction at all. They are faced with a very limited and depressing choice between a menial, dull, impoverished, and undignified life at the bottom of the conventional heap or a life with some excitement, some monetary return, and a slim chance of larger financial rewards, albeit with great risks of being imprisoned, maimed, or even killed. Consequently, many "choose" crime, despite the threat of imprisonment.

For many young males, especially African Americans and Hispanics, the threat of going to prison or jail is no threat at all but rather an expected or accepted part of one's life. Most minority males will be punished by the criminal justice system during their lifetime. Deterrence and punishment are effective only when the act of punishment will actually worsen your lifestyle. For millions of males, imprisonment poses no such threat.

Periodical Bibliography

The following articles have been selected to supplement the diverse views presented in this chapter.

George M. Anderson — "Gun Control: New Approaches," *America*, March 11, 1995.

Michael K. Block and Steven J. Twist — "Lessons from the Eighties: Incarceration Works," *Commonsense*, Spring 1994. Available from 229½ Pennsylvania Ave. SE, Washington, DC 20003.

Richard Blow — "A Social Disease," *Mother Jones*, May/June 1993.

Bill Bradley — "America's Efforts to Curb Violence: The Anti-Crime Bill Is Not Enough," *USA Today*, November 1994.

Christian Social Action — Special issue on violence, May 1994. Available from 100 Maryland Ave. NE, Washington, DC 20002.

John J. DiIulio Jr. — "Let 'em Rot," *Wall Street Journal*, January 26, 1994.

Catherine Farmer — "Self-Control, Not Gun Control," *Freeman*, February 1995. Available form the Foundation for Economic Education, Irvington-on-Hudson, NY 10533.

Health Affairs — "Special Issue: Violence and the Public's Health," Winter 1993. Available from 7500 Old Georgetown Rd., Suite 600, Bethesda, MD 20814.

Patrick McCormick — "Crime in America: Just the Facts, Ma'am," *U.S. Catholic*, March 1995.

Political Affairs — Entire issue on crime and violence, January 1994. Available from 235 W. 23rd St., New York, NY 10011.

Daniel D. Polsby — "Equal Protection," *Reason*, October 1993.

Jane Ellen Stevens — "Treating Violence as an Epidemic," *Technology Review*, August/September 1994.

Josh Sugarmann — "Reverse Fire," *Mother Jones*, January/February 1994.

Andres Tapia — "Healing Our Mean Streets," *Christianity Today*, July 18, 1994.

Ernest van den Haag   "How to Cut Crime," *National Review*, May
30, 1994.

Carol Cavness Walker   "To Limit Handgun Availability," *Christian
Social Action*, September 1993.

Ben Wattenberg   "Crime Solution—Lock 'em Up," *Wall Street
Journal*, February 17, 1993.

James Q. Wilson   "What to Do About Crime," *Commentary*,
September 1994.

World & I   "Special Report: How Violent Is America?"
April 1994. Available from 3600 New York
Ave. NE, Washington, DC 20002.

For Further Discussion

Chapter 1

1. Janine Jackson and Jim Naureckas criticize Ted Gest's viewpoint as a typical example of what they consider to be the mainstream media's distorted coverage of violent crime. Do you agree with their assessment of Gest's viewpoint? Support your answer with examples from the texts. Based on your reading of this chapter, do you believe the news media exaggerate, accurately portray, or underreport the existence of violence in America? Explain your answer.

2. Erik Larson examines statistics in order to argue that violence is not a serious problem in the workplace. Do you think his analysis of these statistics is effective? Why or why not?

3. Barbara Kantrowitz and Mike Males both address the issue of youth violence. Compare and contrast each author's characterization of young people and the violence in their lives. Whose description do you agree with, and why?

Chapter 2

1. Barbara Hattemer argues that a rise in the amount of television and movie violence has taught young people to be increasingly violent. Todd Gitlin maintains that this argument was used against nineteenth-century tabloids and billboards and against moving pictures as early as the 1900s but that little evidence has ever surfaced to link more than a handful of violent incidents to media violence. Which argument do you find more compelling? Why?

2. *Time* associate editor Anastasia Toufexis describes ongoing research that may reveal a genetic cause of violence. What are some of the reasons that this possibility is now being examined more closely? What are some of the arguments against linking violence to genetics? How convincing are these arguments?

3. The two graphs in the viewpoint by Patrick F. Fagan chart the corresponding rise of teenage violent crime and

female-headed, single-parent families. In the text of the viewpoint, what reasoning does Fagan provide to link the two trends? Do you find his reasons convincing? Why or why not?

4. Plea bargains and shorter sentences are putting violent criminals out on the streets where they commit more violence, contends Robert James Bidinotto. Do you find his arguments effective? Why or why not? How might Bidinotto's critics defend plea bargaining and early parole practices?

5. Both Douglas Mattern and Gus Hall argue that the fundamental structure and values of the United States are ultimately responsible for societal violence. What evidence do they use to support their arguments? How effective are these arguments and why? In your opinion, could the solutions that each author suggests succeed in reducing violence? Explain.

6. In this chapter eight of nine authors write about different factors that they say contribute to violence. Consider each of the causes individually, then complete the following steps:

   a. Determine whether each viewpoint is based on facts, values, emotions, or other considerations. Rank the viewpoints in order of the effectiveness of the arguments.

   b. Rank the viewpoints in the order that each corresponds to your own point of view. If this ranking differs from that of effectiveness, explain why.

   c. Examine these causes as different facets of a complete picture of the reasons for societal violence. Do all the viewpoints fit in this picture? Which, if any, do not, and why? Is there any factor that is missing? If so, explain what it is and why you would include it.

Chapter 3

1. In his viewpoint, R. Barri Flowers provides an overview of why domestic violence is a serious problem for women. In hers, Cathy Young contends that advocates for battered women have inflated the seriousness of the problem. Which viewpoint do you find more persuasive? Why? In these viewpoints, a man states what some might expect to be a woman's point of view and a woman presents what

some might expect to be a man's opinion. Does this have any bearing on how you perceive their viewpoints? Why or why not?

2. The first five viewpoints in the chapter debate how serious a problem domestic violence is for women, for men, and for both women and men. How is the reasoning used by Judith Sherven and James Sniechowski similar to or different from that of R. Barri Flowers, Cathy Young, Ellis Cose, and Tish Durkin? Which of the viewpoints do you find most compelling? Why?

3. Battered woman syndrome is used as a legal defense in some cases where abused women have murdered their husbands. Ola W. Barnett and Alyce D. LaViolette argue that battered woman syndrome is a legitimate defense in these cases. Michael Fumento maintains that battered woman syndrome is simply a way for women to avoid going to jail for murder. In your opinion, should women be allowed to use battered woman syndrome as a defense? Why or why not?

Chapter 4

1. Paul J. McNulty argues that the juvenile justice system should harshly punish juveniles who commit violent crimes. George M. Anderson maintains that the system should attempt to rehabilitate violent young offenders. Which author do you agree with, and why? Support your answer with references to the viewpoints.

2. Based on the viewpoints of Suzanne Fields, Joseph Perkins, and Jennifer Vogel, do you think juveniles should be tried in adult courts? Why or why not?

3. Deborah Prothrow-Stith and Michaele Weissman contend that school-based conflict resolution programs can prevent violence among inner-city teenagers. Daniel W. Webster argues that such programs are ineffective because they fail to address the fact that many inner-city youths believe their survival depends on their willingness to engage in violence. Whose argument is more convincing? Explain.

Chapter 5

1. Do you find Nathaniel Hupert's critique of the public health approach to violence persuasive? Why or why not?

2. Joseph R. Biden Jr.'s viewpoint is excerpted from a speech the Delaware senator delivered in his home state. Bruce Shapiro's viewpoint is taken from a magazine article in which he narrates his personal experience as a victim of a violent crime. How do the tone and style of these viewpoints differ? In what ways are they similar? Which viewpoint do you find more convincing? Explain.

3. The U.S. Department of Justice cites statistics to argue that increasing incarceration of criminals during the 1980s resulted in reduced rates of violent crime. James Austin and John Irwin use statistics to support their assertion that increasing incarceration during the 1980s did not result in reduced rates of violent crime. Which use of statistics is more convincing, and why?

Organizations to Contact

The editors have compiled the following list of organizations concerned with the issues debated in this book. The descriptions are derived from materials provided by the organizations. All have publications or information available for interested readers. The list was compiled on the date of publication of the present volume; names, addresses, and phone numbers may change. Be aware that many organizations take several weeks or longer to respond to inquiries, so allow as much time as possible.

Canadians Concerned About Violence in Entertainment (C-CAVE)
167 Glen Rd.
Toronto, ON M4W 2W8
CANADA
(416) 961-0853
fax: (416) 929-2720

C-CAVE conducts research on the harmful effects violence in the media has on society and provides its findings to the Canadian government and public. The organization's committees research issues of violence against women and children, sports violence, and pornography. C-CAVE disseminates educational materials, including periodic news updates.

Cato Institute
1000 Massachusetts Ave. NW
Washington, DC 20001
(202) 842-0200
fax: (202) 842-3490

The Cato Institute is a libertarian public policy research foundation. It evaluates government policies and offers reform proposals in its publication *Policy Analysis*. Topics include "Crime, Police, and Root Causes" and "Prison Blues: How America's Foolish Sentencing Policies Endanger Public Safety." In addition, the institute publishes the bimonthly newsletter *Cato Policy Report* and the triannual *Cato Journal*.

Center for Women Policy Studies (CWPS)
200 P St. NW, Suite 508
Washington, DC 20036
(202) 872-1770

CWPS is a feminist policy research and advocacy organization. It sponsors numerous programs that deal with women's issues, including educational equity, violence against women, and women's health programs. Publications from CWPS on domestic violence include the policy paper *Violence Against Women as Bias-Motivated Hate Crime: Defining the Issues*, the handbook *Legal Help for Battered Women*, and fact sheets concerning girls and violence and violence against women.

Educational Fund to End Handgun Violence (EFEHV)
110 Maryland Ave. NE
Washington, DC 20002
(202) 544-7214

EFEHV is an educational charitable organization dedicated to abolishing firearms violence, particularly as it affects children. The fund acts as a clearinghouse for information and researches the public health issues firearms pose for youth. In addition to its studies *Assault Weapons in America* and *Kids & Guns*, EFEHV publishes the quarterly newsletter *Firearms Litigation Reporter*.

End Violence Against the Next Generation, Inc. (EVANGI)
977 Keeler Ave.
Berkeley, CA 94708
(510) 527-0454

EVANGI views corporal punishment as the primary cause of violence. The organization asserts that youths are taught violence by the actions of their parents and teachers. It further contends that the consequences of spanking and other forms of physical punishment range from mild to rampant aggression. EVANGI publishes articles, booklets, and the books *Corporal Punishment Handbook* and *The Influence of Corporal Punishment on Crime*.

Family Research Laboratory (FRL)
University of New Hampshire
126 Horton Social Science Center
Durham, NH 03824-3586
(603) 862-1888
fax: (603) 862-1122

Since 1975, FRL has devoted itself primarily to understanding the causes and consequences of family violence, and it works to dispel myths about family violence through public education. It publishes numerous books and articles on violence between men and women, the physical abuse of spouses or cohabitants, marital rape, and verbal aggression. Books available from FRL include *When Battered Women Kill* and *Physical Violence in American Families: Risk Factors and Adaptations to Violence in 8,145 Families*.

Family Violence Prevention Fund (FVPF)
383 Rhode Island St., Suite 304
San Francisco, CA 94103
(415) 252-8900
fax: (415) 252-8991

FVPF is a national nonprofit organization concerned with domestic violence education, prevention, and public policy reform. It works to improve health care for battered women and to strengthen the judicial system's capacity to respond appropriately to domestic violence cases. The fund publishes brochures, action kits, and general information packets on domestic violence as well as the books *Domestic Violence: The Law and Criminal Prosecution, Domestic Violence: The Crucial Role of the Judge in Criminal Court Cases: A National Model for Judicial Education,* and *Domestic Violence in Immigrant and Refugee Communities: Asserting the Rights of Battered Women.*

Metro Action Committee on Public Violence Against Women and Children (METRAC)
158 Spadina Rd.
Toronto, ON M5R 2T8
CANADA
(416) 392-3135
fax: (416) 392-3136

METRAC works to prevent all forms of violence against women and children. It educates governments and the public about the harmful effects violence has on women, children, and the whole community. In addition, METRAC promotes research on violence, services for survivors, and legal system reform. Its publications include information packets and the books *Sexual Assault: A Guide to the Criminal System, Violence-Free Schools: Sexual Assault Prevention Manual,* and *Discussion Paper: Developing a Safe Urban Environment for Women.*

Milton S. Eisenhower Foundation (MSEF)
1660 L St. NW, Suite 200
Washington, DC 20036
(202) 429-0440
fax: (202) 452-0169

MSEF works to reduce school dropout rates, delinquency, crime, and drug abuse among inner-city youth. Foundation publications include the newsletter *Challenges from Within* and the reports *Youth Investment and Community Reconstruction: Street Lessons on Drugs and Crime for the Nineties* and *Lord, How Dare We Celebrate? Practical Policy Reform in Delinquency Prevention and Youth Investment.*

National Center for Juvenile Justice (NCJJ)
701 Forbes Ave.
Pittsburgh, PA 15219
(412) 227-6950
fax: (412) 227-6955

NCJJ is a private nonprofit organization that concentrates on research and reform in the area of juvenile justice. It researches juvenile justice court cases, laws, and evaluates justice programs. NCJJ publishes the report *Juvenile Court Statistics,* the annual legal reference index *Kindex,* the monthly *Juvenile and Family Law Digest,* and the report *Juveniles as Criminals.*

National Coalition Against Domestic Violence (NCADV)
PO Box 18749
Denver, CO 80218-0749
(303) 839-1852

NCADV helps empower battered women. It serves as a national information and referral network on domestic violence issues. Its publications include the position paper *A Current Analysis of the Battered Women's Movement*; the *National Directory of Domestic Violence Programs: A Guide to Community Shelter, Safe Home, and Service Programs*; the quarterly newsletter *NCADV Update*; and fact sheets on domestic violence and children and violence.

National Council on Crime and Delinquency (NCCD)
685 Market St., Suite 620
San Francisco, CA 94105
(415) 896-6223
fax: (415) 896-5109

NCCD is a nonprofit organization that works to reduce crime and delinquency. It conducts research on crime control issues and provides reform guidelines for the criminal justice system. NCCD publications include the quarterly *FOCUS Research Briefs*, the journal *Crime and Delinquency*, and semiannual policy-paper booklets.

National Crime Prevention Council (NCPC)
1700 K St. NW, 2nd Fl.
Washington, DC 20006-3817
(202) 466-6272

NCPC helps citizens prevent crime and build safer communities. It manages the McGruff Take a Bite Out of Crime campaign in conjunction with the Advertising Council, Inc., and the U.S. Department of Justice. In addition to its referral services, NCPC publishes brochures, program kits, and the books *Preventing Violence: Program Ideas and Examples* and *Preventing Crime in Urban Communities: Handbook and Program Profiles*.

National Organization of Parents of Murdered Children, Inc. (NOPMC)
100 E. Eighth St., B-41
Cincinnati, OH 45202
(513) 721-5683

NOPMC is a self-help group that provides support and education to the families and friends of homicide victims. It works to prevent the early parole and release of convicted murderers and to stop the entertainment industry's marketing of violence. The organization publishes the booklet *Path Through the Criminal Justice System*.

National Resource Center on Domestic Violence (NRC)
6400 Flank Dr., Suite 1300
Harrisburg, PA 17112-2778
(800) 537-2238
fax: (717) 545-9456

Established by the Pennsylvania Coalition Against Domestic Violence,

NRC focuses on civil and criminal justice issues, child protection and custody issues, and health care access for battered women and their children. The center works to expand the service capacity of community-based domestic violence programs and state coalitions and assists government agencies, policy leaders, and other supporters of victims of domestic violence. NRC publications include brochures, videos, and posters on domestic violence as well as the manuals *Confronting Domestic Violence: Effective Policing Response, Battering and Addiction*, and *Accountability: Program Standards for Batterer Intervention Services*.

NRA CrimeStrike
11250 Waples Mill Rd.
Fairfax, VA 22030
(703) 267-1160
fax: (703) 267-3992

CrimeStrike, a project of the National Rifle Association, organizes grassroots efforts to prevent the early parole or release of convicted felons. In addition, CrimeStrike advocates crime victims' rights and conducts research on violent crimes. Its publications include fact sheets on crime and the reports *Elements for an Effective Criminal Justice System* and *Access to Guns by Minors: A Survey of State Criminal Liability Laws*.

U.S. Department of Justice
Office of Justice Programs
Box 6000
Rockville, MD 20850
(800) 732-3277

The Department of Justice protects citizens by maintaining effective law enforcement, crime prevention, crime detection, and prosecution and rehabilitation of offenders. Through its Office of Justice Programs, the department operates the National Institute of Justice, the Office of Juvenile Justice and Delinquency Prevention, and the Bureau of Justice Statistics. Its publications include fact sheets, research packets, bibliographies, the semiannual journal *Juvenile Justice*, and the books *Questions and Answers in Lethal and Non-Lethal Violence: Proceedings of the Second Annual Workshop of the Homicide Research Working Group* and *Partnerships to Prevent Youth Violence*.

Violence Policy Center (VPC)
2000 P St. NW, Suite 200
Washington, DC 20036
(202) 822-8200
fax: (202) 822-8205

VPC is an educational foundation that works to prevent firearms violence. It asserts that firearms violence is not just an issue of crime but is a widespread public health problem. VPC disseminates its research findings to the public, the media, and to policymakers. Its publications include fact sheets concerning violence prevention, firearms safety, and women and guns; the books *Use the Schools: How Federal Tax Dollars Are Spent to Market Guns to Kids* and *National Rifle Association: Money, Firepower, and Fear*; and the studies *Female Persuasion: A Study of How the Firearms Industry Markets to Women and the Reality of Women and Guns* and *Putting Guns Back into Criminals' Hands: One Hundred Case Studies of Felons Granted Relief from Disability Under Federal Firearms Laws.*

Bibliography of Books

Leonore Loeb Adler and Florence L. Denmark, eds.	*Violence and the Prevention of Violence.* Westport, CT: Praeger, 1995.
Falcon Baker	*Saving Our Kids from Delinquency, Drugs, and Despair.* New York: HarperCollins, 1991.
Constance A. Bean	*Women Murdered by the Men They Loved.* Binghamton, NY: Haworth Press, 1992.
Steven J. Bennett	*Kick the TV Habit: A Simple Program for Changing Your Family's Television Viewing and Video Game Habits.* New York: Penguin, 1994.
David Bianculli	*Teleliteracy: Taking Television Seriously.* New York: Continuum, 1994.
Jerry Brinegar	*Breaking Free from Domestic Violence.* Minneapolis: CompCare Publishers, 1992.
Anne Campbell	*Men, Women, and Aggression: From Rage in Marriage to Violence in the Streets—How Gender Affects the Way We Act.* New York: Basic Books, 1993.
Richard C. Cervantes	*Substance Abuse and Gang Violence.* Newbury Park, CA: Sage Publications, 1992.
Children's Express	*Voices from the Future*, edited by Susan Goodwillie. New York: Crown Publishers, 1993.
Christina Crawford	*No Safe Place: The Legacy of Family Violence.* Barrytown, NY: Station Hill Press, 1994.
Deborah W. Denno	*Biology and Violence from Birth to Adulthood.* New York: Cambridge University Press, 1990.
R. Emerson Dobash and Russell P. Dobash	*Women, Violence, and Social Change.* New York: Routledge, 1992.
Rose M. Duhon-Sells, ed.	*Dealing with Youth Violence: What Schools and Communities Need to Know.* Bloomington, IN: National Educational Service, 1995.
Charles Patrick Ewing	*Kids Who Kill.* Lexington, MA: Lexington Books, 1990.
Jib Fowles	*Why Viewers Watch: A Reappraisal of Television's Effects.* Newbury Park, CA: Sage Publications, 1992.
James Garbarino et al.	*Children in Danger: Coping with the Consequences of Community Violence.* San Francisco: Jossey-Bass, 1992.

| Richard J. Gelles and Donileen R. Loseke, eds. | *Current Controversies on Family Violence.* Newbury Park, CA: Sage Publications, 1993. |

Arnold P. Goldstein — *Delinquent Gangs: A Psychological Perspective.* Champaign, IL: Research Press, 1991.

Ted Robert Gurr, ed. — *Violence in America.* Newbury Park, CA: Sage Publications, 1989.

Robert L. Hampton et al., eds. — *Family Violence: Prevention and Treatment.* Newbury Park, CA: Sage Publications, 1993.

Marsali Hansen and Michele Harway, eds. — *Battering and Family Therapy: A Feminist Perspective.* Newbury Park, CA: Sage Publications, 1993.

Barbara Hattemer and Robert Showers — *Don't Touch That Dial: The Impact of the Media on Children and the Family.* Lafayette, LA: Huntington House, 1993.

Kathleen M. Heide — *Why Kids Kill Parents.* Columbus: Ohio State University Press, 1992.

N. Zoe Hilton — *Legal Responses to Wife Assault: Current Trends and Evaluation.* Newbury Park, CA: Sage Publications, 1993.

Paul C. Holinger et al. — *Suicide and Homicide Among Adolescents.* New York: Guilford Press, 1994.

Aletha Huston et al. — *Big World, Small Screen: The Role of Television in American Society.* Lincoln: University of Nebraska Press, 1992.

Catherine Itzin, ed. — *Pornography: Women, Violence, and Civil Liberties: A Radical View.* New York: Oxford University Press, 1993.

Sara Lee Johann — *Domestic Abusers: Terrorists in Our Homes.* Springfield, IL: Charles C. Thomas, 1994.

Scott Johnson — *When "I Love You" Turns Violent.* Far Hills, NJ: New Horizons, 1993.

Ann Jones — *Next Time, She'll Be Dead.* Boston: Beacon Press, 1994.

Nancy Kilgore — *Every Eighteen Seconds: A Journey Through Domestic Violence.* Volcano, CA: Volcano Press, 1993.

Mary P. Koss et al. — *No Safe Haven: Male Violence Against Women at Home, at Work, and in the Community.* Washington, DC: American Psychological Association, 1994.

Michael R. Mantell with Steve Albrecht — *Ticking Bombs: Defusing Violence in the Workplace.* Burr Ridge, IL: Irwin Professional Publications, 1994.

Michael Medved	*Hollywood vs. America: Popular Culture and the War on Traditional Values.* New York: HarperCollins, 1992.
Paul A. Mones	*When a Child Kills: Abused Children Who Kill Their Parents.* New York: Pocket Books, 1991.
National Research Council	*Understanding and Preventing Violence.* Washington, DC: National Academy Press, 1993.
National Research Council	*Violence in Urban America: Mobilizing a Response.* Washington, DC: National Academy Press, 1994.
Deborah Prothrow-Stith with Michaele Weissman	*Deadly Consequences—How Violence Is Destroying Our Teenage Population and a Plan to Begin Solving the Problem.* New York: HarperCollins, 1991.
Mark Rosenberg and Mary Ann Fenley, eds.	*Violence in America: A Public Health Approach.* New York: Oxford University Press, 1993.
William B. Sanders	*Gangbangs and Drive-bys: Grounded Culture and Juvenile Gang Violence.* New York: Aldine de Gruyter, 1994.
Ira M. Schwartz	*[In]Justice for Juveniles—Rethinking the Best Interests of the Child.* Lexington, MA: Lexington Books, 1989.
Elizabeth Stanko	*Everyday Violence: How Women and Men Experience Sexual and Physical Danger.* London: Pandora Press, 1990.
Michael Steinman, ed.	*Women Battering: Policy Responses.* Cincinnati: Anderson Publishing, 1992.
U.S. Department of Justice, Office of Juvenile Justice and Delinquency Prevention	*Comprehensive Strategy for Serious, Violent, and Chronic Juvenile Offenders.* Washington, DC: 1994. Available from the Juvenile Justice Clearinghouse, PO Box 6000, Rockville, MD 20850.
Ernest van den Haag	*Punishing Criminals: Concerning a Very Old and Painful Question.* Lanham, MD: University Press of America, 1991.
Julia Vernon	*Preventing Juvenile Crime.* Monsey, NY: Criminal Justice Press, 1991.
Neil Alan Weiner, Margaret A. Zahn, and Rita J. Sagi	*Violence: Patterns, Causes, Public Policy.* San Diego, CA: Harcourt Brace Jovanovich, 1990.

Index

is a serious problem, 17-22
see also Federal Bureau of
   Investigation; United States,
   Department of Justice
Crime Bill of 1994
   and community policing, 248
   debate over, 173-74, 258
   and more prisons/boot camps,
      247
   as prevention strategy, 246, 248,
      249, 252
   does not protect citizens, 256
Crime Control Institute, 141
criminal justice system
   based on illusion, 257-58, 259
   contributes to violence, 100-102
      through parole system, 103-105
      through plea bargaining, 106
   and domestic violence, 136
   leniency of, 22
      toward women, 163-64
   relies on arrest and
      incarceration, 229-30
   uses halfway houses/work
      release programs, 105-106
Criminal Violence, Criminal Justice
(Silberman), 174

Danzinger, Jeffrey, 173
Davis, Stanley, case of, 105
Dillingham, Steven D., 280, 281
Doherty, Shannen, 152, 155
domestic violence. *See under*
   violence
Douglas, Susan, 14
Dryfoos, Joy, 206, 207
Durkin, Tish, 151

Edelman, Peter, 19
Eisenman, Russell, 192
Elias, Robert, 26
Ensley, Margaret, 46-47
Erickson, Rosemary, 32, 34

Fagan, Patrick F., 85
family violence. *See* violence,
   domestic
Federal Bureau of Investigation
   (FBI), 122
   statistics, 19, 27, 48
      on battered women, 133, 138,
         140
   Uniform Crime Reports of, 281

and crime rate estimates, 24-25,
   277
   show increased crime, 282,
      283-84
Federal Communications
   Commission, 73
Fields, Suzanne, 184
First Amendment, 76
First Freedom Coalition, 106
Flowers, R. Barri, 130
Frum, David, 164
Fumento, Michael, 162

gangs, 18, 54, 117
   in Chicago, 14, 105
   dangerous rivalry of, 48, 50, 114,
      118
   form in response to family
      environment, 92
   and guns, 47-48, 50, 94, 114
   insignia banned in schools, 216
   in Los Angeles, 48, 53
General Agreement on Tariffs &
   Trade (GATT), 125
Gest, Ted, 17
Gillespie, Marcia Ann, 132
Gilliland, George, 149, 150
Gingrich, Newt, 257
Gitlin, Todd, 70
Goodwin, Frederick, 83
Grossman, Herbert, 215
Groves, Betsy McAlister, 47
Guidry, Ron, 237, 238, 239
guns
   availability of, 76, 232-33, 244
   and drugs, 115-16
   and gangs, 47-48, 50, 94, 114
   increased control would reduce
      violence, 260-66
      con, 267-73
   ownership of is widespread in
      U.S., 261
   restrictions on, 76, 77, 248-49
      should include
         heavy taxes, 263
         limits on sales, 264
         national license, 262, 263
   teen use of, 53, 117-18, 261
      in schools, 47, 94, 218
      for self-protection, 114, 207
   types of
      AK-47s, 50, 54
      assault weapons, 261, 262-63